About This Book

Why is this topic important?

Some experts believe that good management is finding someone with natural ability to manage and placing the person in the position of manager. While that may be partially true, it is widely known that the vast majority of good managers learn how to be one. Some learning takes place by watching other successful managers in action. More important, though, is the need for managers to have a framework for understanding. This includes a small dose of theory that serves as a basis for determining what the most appropriate actions would be for managers. This book is a tool that helps new managers and veteran managers become better at their craft, in turn benefiting their organizations. As a tool, its value is in application and use.

What can you achieve with this book?

By reading the articles in this book, you can revisit some standard approaches to what managers need to be able to do and gain new knowledge about some management skills that have only come up recently. This new knowledge will make you more hands-on when it comes to managing people in ways that bring out optimal performance. I would have welcomed a book like this in my early days of growing people into management. You'll gain greater knowledge and information for now and for the future.

How is the book organized?

This book has three sections. The first contains a set of activities that can be used by management developers as part of a learning event or as stand-alone activities, depending on the need. The second section is an assessment. It is presented as a complete package ready for use. The last section is a collection of articles from a wide variety of perspectives. Each article is an opportunity to gain greater knowledge or develop a deeper perspective on an intervention.

About Pfeiffer

Pfeiffer serves the professional development and hands-on resource needs of training and human resource practitioners and gives them products to do their jobs better. We deliver proven ideas and solutions from experts in HR development and HR management, and we offer effective and customizable tools to improve workplace performance. From novice to seasoned professional, Pfeiffer is the source you can trust to make yourself and your organization more successful.

Essential Knowledge Pfeiffer produces insightful, practical, and comprehensive materials on topics that matter the most to training and HR professionals. Our Essential Knowledge resources translate the expertise of seasoned professionals into practical, how-to guidance on critical workplace issues and problems. These resources are supported by case studies, worksheets, and job aids and are frequently supplemented with CD-ROMs, websites, and other means of making the content easier to read, understand, and use.

Essential Tools Pfeiffer's Essential Tools resources save time and expense by offering proven, ready-to-use materials—including exercises, activities, games, instruments, and assessments—for use during a training or team-learning event. These resources are frequently offered in looseleaf or CD-ROM format to facilitate copying and customization of the material.

Pfeiffer also recognizes the remarkable power of new technologies in expanding the reach and effectiveness of training. While e-hype has often created whizbang solutions in search of a problem, we are dedicated to bringing convenience and enhancements to proven training solutions. All our e-tools comply with rigorous functionality standards. The most appropriate technology wrapped around essential content yields the perfect solution for today's on-the-go trainers and human resource professionals.

Our readers are invited to download customizable materials from this book related to the experiential learning activities and the assessment.
Please see the Website Contents for additional information.
The materials are available FREE with the purchase of this book at www.pfeiffer.com/go/2009ManagementAnnual

Robert C. Preziosi, EDITOR

The 2009 Pfeiffer ANNUAL

MANAGEMENT DEVELOPMENT

Pfeiffer
A Wiley Imprint
www.pfeiffer.com

Published by Pfeiffer
An Imprint of Wiley
989 Market Street, San Francisco, CA 94103-1741 www.pfeiffer.com

For additional copies/bulk purchases of this book in the U.S. please contact 800-274-4434.

Pfeiffer books and products are available through most bookstores. To contact Pfeiffer directly call our Customer Care Department within the U.S. at 800-274-4434, outside the U.S. at 317-572-3985, fax 317-572-4002, or visit www.pfeiffer.com.

Pfeiffer also publishes its books in a variety of electronic formats. Some content that appears in print may not be available in electronic books.

ISBN: 978-0-4703-7146-6
ISSN: 1046-333-X

Acquiring Editor: Marisa Kelley
Director of Development: Kathleen Dolan Davies
Development Editor: Susan Rachmeler

Production Editor: Dawn Kilgore
Editor: Rebecca Taff
Manufacturing Supervisor: Becky Morgan

Printed in the United States of America

Printing 10 9 8 7 6 5 4 3 2 1

Contents

Assessment

Articles

Website Contents

Our readers are invited to download customizable materials from this book related to the experiential learning activities and the assessment. The following materials are available FREE with the purchase of this book at www.pfeiffer.com/go/2009ManagementAnnual.

Activities

Assessment

Preface

The 21st Century is almost a decade old now. How does it compare to your original vision of what it would be like? Did you and your organization make the strides forward that you thought possible and/or probable? What kinds of challenges have managers successfully handled? Are there any opportunities yet to be seized?

I think the answer to the last question offers much food for thought and discussion. The answer to the question is a firm "Yes." As I speak with managers, it is clear to me that the principles and processes of management provide a large buffet to choose from for anyone who wants to become better at managing people, technology, budgets, physical plant, and materials. Many of these people have a personal goal to become the "best," not just a better manager. This seems to be true regardless of the industry they are in. Size of the organization or levels of management don't seem to matter either. But how do you become a "best" manager?

You might begin by indentifying qualities and characteristics that the successful manager possesses. Next, learn what specific behaviors lead to sought-after results, both long term and short term. The third thing is to identify areas of strength and improvement opportunities. Next, craft a learning plan that will power forward the needed improvements. Of course, the final thing is to implement the plan.

It looks easy enough to me. How does it look to you? If all of us who develop managers would use the above approach, then we would have a model to work from. We would find it easier to help managers become the "best" of their species. However, we are so busy "doing" that we can't seem to find time to work on becoming or being a best manager or a best management developer.

That's where *The 2009 Pfeiffer Annual: Management Development* comes in. It is full of information and activities that folks involved in management development can use. Every piece of writing for the *Annual* provides a perspective and practical application of one or more behaviors that can become an element in the crafted learning that was mentioned earlier in this Preface. The most important aspect, practical application, from people working in the field continues to be a strength of the *Annuals*. Perhaps this could be called "reality writing" (until they give me an hour TV show called "reality management development").

I want to thank many people for helping to make this *Annual* a reality. The folks at Pfeiffer are the best, especially Susan Rachmeler. I would also like to thank Pfeiffer champions like Martin Delahoussaye and Dawn Kilgore. I look forward to working with Marisa Kelley in the future.

Many thanks to my family, especially my wife Kitty, who gives up time with me so that I can work on this book. Thanks to my daughters, Lauren and Carly, and son-in-law Dan for keeping my mind fresh. Jonah and Sofia are very energizing.

The ultimate value found in this book is from the contributors. I am very fortunate to have such great people share their writings. They made my job totally wonderful.

Robert C. Preziosi
Davie, Florida
June 2008

Introduction to *The 2009 Pfeiffer Annual: Management Development*

Welcome to *The 2009 Pfeiffer Annual: Management Development*! This is the second time around for this particular *Annual*. As mentioned in last year's volume, this *Annual* addresses the design, delivery, and evaluation of interventions that can be used to improve the performance of managers. This begins, as was noted in the Preface, with those of us whose role it is to develop managers at all levels in the organization. This would include, but is not limited to, (1) people in organizations who are management development specialist or managers of these people, (2) consultants who specialize in management development, and (3) college and university professors who teach management.

All of these different experts share a common need: to raise the performance level of managers. The knowledge, skill, and attitude levels vary among managers in today's workforce—more so than ever before. One reason for this is the broad range of generations. There have never been four generations in the workforce before, which is but one example of why so much variance exists among managers today. The reasons include differences in training and education, work experiences, role models, mentors, organization culture, personal philosophy of life, and so forth. It can make for some lively collaborative learning, but what a massive task to know about and design learning experiences for these managers. Rest assured that it goes way beyond the knowledge of the Americans with Disabilities Act do's and don'ts or the different learning styles of visual, auditory, and kinesthetic. Okay, then, what is involved?

It goes right to the essence of successful managerial performance. If you believe that the primary responsibility for those of us who develop managers is to help managers attain the best results from the best people, then we're on to something.

The best people are brought on board based on an organization's current model of "best" employee. The model is used in employee interviewing. It is up to management developers to make sure that the best people (best for the particular organization) are fully equipped to do the job. People who are successfully equipped owe their abilities to well-developed managers.

This would appear to be quite a responsibility. It is! It is "ginormous," to use one of Webster's newest words. If I weren't totally committed to the task over the last part of my career, I'm not sure what my entry point for helping would be. My radar screen feels fuller than the FAA radar screen during different holiday flying periods. I would certainly be looking for some assistance so that I could develop the best managers.

This was my goal in putting together this edition of the *Management Development Annual:* I wanted something that I could use myself. Thus, you will find things that are familiar to you but have a slightly different twist than you've used when making interventions in the past. You will also find things that are new to you and can be incorporated into your intervention toolkit. Either way, you will find lots of useful information for yourself and others.

The first section of the *Annual* is a variety of activities that have all been used by their contributors in multiple settings. These exercises can be used just as they are or can be customized to your organization's needs, whether you work internally or externally. Remember that the learning design of each exercise has made it work well for others, not just the particular content or subject matter. Whatever you do to bring about the exact learning outcome(s) that you want is the most important consideration.

The second section of the *Annual* is a communication assessment that can be used with any level of management in the organization. It has been used successfully in a variety of settings.

The third and final section of the *Annual* is the articles section. The goal of this section is for each contributor to share a practical point of view with you that you can use in your own work. This is accomplished in a number of different ways by the contributors. As you read through each article in this section, you will be struck by the "performance enhancing intervention" nature of what was written. Not only will you find contemporary takeaways for your own use, but you will also find validations for some of your own work.

Introduction

to the Activities Section

The purpose of the Activities section is to present activities that engage learners actively so that learning is maximized. Each and every exercise has specific goal(s). This makes it easier for a management development expert to determine how useful a particular exercise is for a learning event. All can be used, regardless of the amount of experience that the learning facilitator possesses, because each one is like a recipe (for success) that can be easily followed. A learning facilitator might want to make minor adjustments to fit the learning group.

An important thing to remember, though, is that all of these activities have been used successfully. You are the person who will make it work for you and your learning group.

The 2009 Pfeiffer Annual: Management Development includes eleven exercises in the following categories:

Individual Development: Self-Disclosure

What Shape Are You In? by Yael Schy

Communication: Building Trust

Creating a Community of Learning for Management Development, by F. Barry Barnes

Management ABCs: An Instant Management Tool, by Linda M. Raudenbush and Steve Sugar

Groups: Negotiating/Bargaining

Storm Down in Sales: An Organizational Conflict Management Simulation, by Noam Ebner and Yael Efron

Teams: Problem Solving/Decision Making

Setting Team Performance Objectives: Gaining Maximum Buy-In to Team Performance Measures, by Paul Kearns

Consulting, Training, and Facilitating: Facilitating: Skills

Managers as Change Agents, by Elaine Biech

Navigating the Rivers of Change, by Marilyn J. Corrigan

Turning Over a New Leaf: A Problem-Solving and Team-Building Activity for Managers, by Bevan Gray-Rogel

Leadership: Diversity/Stereotyping

Ageism Awareness for Managers: A Self-Assessment, by Shirley Copeland

Leadership: Styles and Skills

Getting Courage on the Front Burner, by Kitty Preziosi

Organizations: Vision, Mission, Values, Strategy

Crafting Shared Organizational Statements, by George Alexakis

What Shape Are You In?

Activity Summary

This learning experience is a form of visual "check-in," which is good to use at the beginning of any group session. It is a way of allowing participants to nonverbally get in touch with their current moods. By bringing their attention to their bodies, it enables participants to be more present and in the moment. This exercise also allows participants to learn more about each other, by discovering shared moods and common themes among members of the group.

Goals

- To allow participants to understand their own moods and how they are reflected in their bodies.
- To allow participants to learn about the moods of their fellow team members.
- To allow participants to discuss the impact of moods on the group.

Group Size

A group of ten to thirty managers who are either from the same organization or who are from different organizations and are participating in a leadership development program.

Time Required

Approximately 15 to 20 minutes.

Materials

None.

Physical Setting

A large open space, without tables or chairs.

Facilitating Risk Rating

Medium

Process

1. Ask participants to find their own spaces in the room and to stand, making sure that each person has some space around himself or herself.
2. Ask each participant to reflect on what his or her current mood is. After a few moments, ask participants to each take on a body shape or gesture that reflects that mood.
3. Next, ask the participants to add a movement to the shape—one that still reflects their current mood—and to begin to move their body shapes within their own spaces.
4. Now ask the participants to continue the shape and motion and to move around the room, noticing the other people and what shapes and movements they are expressing.
5. Ask participants to each find several other people who have assumed a similar shape and/or movement and to form a small group with those people. (If there are several people left over who cannot find anyone with a similar shape, ask those "unique shapes" to form a separate group. If there are only one or two people who are left over, ask them each to join a group that is the most similar to his or her shape/movement.)
6. Ask the small groups to discuss within their groups what each person's mood was and why they chose the shapes and movements that they did.
7. Have each group, in turn, demonstrate their shapes and movements to the larger group, and ask a spokesperson from each group to summarize their group discussion.
8. Ask the following questions of participants to debrief the activity:
   - How did you feel during the exercise?
   - Did it make a difference in your mood to find other people with similar moods and shapes?

- How do you feel now?
- Did your mood change during the course of the exercise? If so, why?
- What did you learn about how your body reflects your mood?
- How might your moods and emotions impact your work?
- How can getting in touch with what you are feeling help you to better manage your moods and emotions in the workplace?

Variations

This exercise could be used for a variety of training objectives, including the following:

- *Emotional Intelligence:* To help participants get in touch with their moods and emotions
- *Presentation Skills:* To help participants become more aware of their body language
- *Cultural Diversity:* To help participants explore cultural differences in the meaning of body language
- *Communication Skills:* To help participants understand the impact of their moods and body language in communication
- *Team Building:* To explore differences in body language among various personality types (use in conjunction with a personality type assessment tool)

Submitted by Yael Schy.

Yael Schy, MSW, *is a leader in using expressive arts in organizational learning and development. She is principal of Dramatic Strides® Consulting, specializing in leadership development, communication skills, team building, and creative decision-making techniques that help people and organizations move forward together. Ms. Schy also serves as a faculty member at the American Management Association and at City College of San Francisco. She brings a unique perspective by combining twenty years of management experience with her background in improvisational theater and dance to create dynamic interpersonal skills training and coaching in the workplace. Ms. Schy's unique* Teamwork Tango® *workshop, which teaches leadership and team-building skills through the metaphor of partner dancing, has been presented at numerous professional conferences and organizations in the United States and abroad. She is co-author of the book,* Teamwork Tools: A Revolutionary Approach for Managers and Trainers *(2008).*

Creating a Community of Learning for Management Development

Activity Summary

This is a remarkably powerful yet simple way to create a working bond in the guise of an icebreaker at the beginning of a single or multiple-day management development program involving those who do not already know one another. While the need for managers to be highly skilled at being able to refer to every employee by name is emphasized in this activity, so also is there emphasis on memory skills that are important during presentations that managers make and at other times.

Goals

- To build trust.
- To improve name memory skills.
- To create a foundation for a community of learning.

Group Size

Fifteen to twenty people who do not know one another.

Time Required

20 minutes for interviews and debriefing, plus 3 minutes per participant for introductions.

Materials

None required.

Physical Setting

A training or meeting room with chairs.

Facilitating Risk Rating

Low

Process

1. Begin the session by asking participants to form pairs.
2. Ask participants to take 5 minutes to "interview" each other and learn some basics about one another (family/personal, managerial experience, current work challenges, etc.)
3. After the 5-minute "interview" period, ask the first participant to introduce his or her new colleague, giving the person's name and other basic information.
4. After the first four participants have been introduced, ask for a volunteer to recall all their names.
5. Continue the paired introductions.
6. After eight participants have been introduced, ask for a volunteer to recall all their names.
7. Discuss the value of using names including such points as:
    - How do you feel when someone calls you by name?
    - How do you feel when you don't remember someone's name?
    - Is it more comfortable to work with someone new when you know each other's names?
    - What do managers gain by strengthening memory skills?
8. Discuss the typical belief that "I have a terrible memory for names."
9. Explain that remembering names requires some simple efforts:
    - Be sure to get the name correctly when introduced. Ask again if you didn't hear it or are uncertain about pronunciation or spelling.
    - Use the name during the introduction to reinforce short-term memory.

- Use the name again on parting to reinforce short-term memory.
- Recall the name again in twenty-four hours to move the name to long-term memory.

10. Continue the paired introductions with volunteers recalling all those introduced after every additional four have been introduced.
11. Remind participants that it's not necessary to have 100 percent recall, but that simply making the effort to remember and use participants' names improves recall significantly.
12. Conclude this activity and move on to other activities.
13. Ask for volunteers to recall all names after two hours, again after four hours, again after six hours, and at the end of the day.
14. If participants meet on a second day, begin it with a recall of all names.
15. One additional recall of names at mid-day of the second day should provide nearly 100 percent recall for all participants.
16. Discuss the general importance of managers needing and using memory skills.

Submitted by F. Barry Barnes.

F. Barry Barnes *is professor and chair of leadership at the H. Wayne Huizenga School of Business and Entrepreneurship, where he has taught since 1997. He teaches a variety of courses in both the MBA and doctoral programs, including Strategic Decision Making, Leading Change, and Organizational Behavior. In addition, he works with clients in south Florida and around the United States in a variety of roles. His recent research and writing focus on the innovative and improvisational business practices of the legendary rock band, the Grateful Dead.*

Management ABCs

An Instant Management Tool

Activity Summary

Facilitator polls manager participants for feedback on any topic.

Goals

- To assess manager input, opinions, or concerns.
- To obtain a poll of manager attitudes on specific issues.
- (Variation) To experience cooperation, negotiation, and competition.

Group Size

A group of five or more managers who have a stake in the concept or issue being presented to the group.

Time Required

From 3 minutes for simple assessments requiring no follow-up discussion to 30 or more minutes for assessments involving group dialogue or discussion.

Materials

- One set of prepared Management A, B, C cards for each manager (see Preparation).
- Flip chart and felt-tipped markers.

Physical Setting

No special set-up is required, but small tables are best for more complex discussions and for the Variation.

The 2009 Pfeiffer Annual: Management Development.

Facilitating Risk Rating

Moderate.

Preparation

1. Prepare the card sets on three different colors of index cards. Select one color for "A," another color for "B," and a third color for "C." On each card, write the letter A, B, or C. Prepare a three-card set (one A, one B, and one C) for each participant.
2. For the Variation, prepare a large version of the Payoff Matrix.

Process

1. Distribute one set of A, B, C cards to each participant.
2. For a simpler version of this activity, ask or display a position or issue with two or three choices on an overhead projector. For example:

   "My favorite management style is:

   A. authoritarian

   B. participative

   C. laissez faire"

   "The term that managers use when helping subordinates to perform better is . . .

   A. mentoring

   B. coaching

   C. influencing"
3. Invite participants to respond by displaying the card that represents their most appropriate response.
4. Note or count the responses; comment as necessary.
5. Invite participants to comment or use the following questions:
   - What prompted you to make your choice?
   - What did you feel when you observed everyone's selection?
   - Did you want to change your card?

6. To review the material, ask someone with the correct response to explain his or her reasoning.
7. After one full game, rearrange the dyad partners and repeat the process.
8. Next, restrict dyad communications to non-verbal only.
9. Debrief with the previous questions, but add the following questions:
   - For this game, how was your choice of strategy impacted by your experience of already playing the game?
   - Changing partners?
   - Any communication restriction?
   - How does this experience reflect managerial interactions?
   - What lessons can you apply to your work or personal situations?

Variation

This is a one-on-one activity in which managers experience the dynamics of negotiation, cooperation, and competition using the card sets you created above.

1. Divide participants into pairs and have them sit across from each other. Have each pair designate one person as Player 1 and the other as Player 2.
2. Inform participants that the object of this activity is "to collect as many points as you can" over five rounds of play. Tell participants that there is no restriction on communication during the game.
3. Each round consists of a "showdown" in which each player displays one of his or her cards to receive a score prescribed by the "Payoff Matrix."
4. Post the Payoff Matrix and begin the activity.

Payoff Matrix

Points	Player 1 Shows	Player 2 Shows	Points
5	Card A	Card B	0
0	Card B	Card A	5
3	Card B	Card B	3
0	Card A	Card A	0

5. For Round 1, announce: "Players ready? One, two, three . . . show your cards!"

6. Have players take a moment and record their scores on the Payoff Matrix.
7. Play four more rounds played in the same fashion.
8. Have each person total his or her scores.
9. Use the following questions to debrief:
   - What prompted you to make your choice?
   - What did you feel when you observed your partner's selection?
   - Did you change your card on the next round?
   - What made you choose cooperation or competition?
   - Which strategy—cooperation or competition—was more successful?
   - Which strategy did you use?
   - Thinking about your work as a manager, how often do you choose cooperation? Competition?
   - What might you do differently as a result of this activity?

Submitted by Linda M. Raudenbush and Steve Sugar.

Linda M. Raudenbush, Ed.D., *is a certified leadership coach with twenty-five years' experience in training and organization development. At present she provides internal HRD/OD consulting and leadership coaching at the U.S. Department of Agriculture. Raudenbush has taught a mix of undergraduate management and graduate education courses for eighteen years at University of Maryland, Baltimore County (UMBC). Her writings are featured in a variety of books and journals, including* The Adjunct Faculty Handbook, Creative Employee Orientation Programs, *the* Pfeiffer Annuals, *and* The Training and Performance Sourcebooks.

Steve Sugar, MBA, *is the author/co-author of five books:* Games That Teach, Games That Teach Teams, Primary Games, Games That Boost Performance, *and* Training Games. *His games and activities have been featured in over two dozen* Pfeiffer Annuals, *professional journals, and ASTD* Info-Lines. *Sugar has been a featured presenter of national conference workshops since 1982, including ASTD, ASCD, ISPI, Lilly-East (college/university teaching), NASAGA, and TRAINING. He currently teaches in the management and education curriculums at the University of Maryland, Baltimore County (UMBC).*

Storm Down in Sales
An Organizational Conflict Management Simulation

Activity Summary

Storm Down in Sales is a role-play simulation designed to help managers improve and increase their skills in managing intra-organizational conflict.

Goals

- To allow participants to practice their negotiation and communication skills.
- To give participants an opportunity to explore conflict management.
- To allow participants to explore a variety of topics related to conflict management, such as the effects of an organizational setting on conflict management, the challenges inherent in eliciting information sharing, and the role of the mediator in in-house conflict management settings.

Group Size

Best conducted with a group of nine to fifteen participants.

Time Required

1½ to 2½ hours.

Materials

- Set of instruction sheets for each triad:
    - Storm Down in Sales Instructions for Party A

    - Storm Down in Sales Instructions for Party B
    - Storm Down in Sales Instructions for the Human Resources Department Mediator

- Flip chart and felt-tipped markers.

Physical Setting

Training or meeting room with small tables, one for each group of three participants. Alternatively, several small rooms adjacent one to another.

Facilitating Risk Rating

Medium.

Process

1. Explain to participants that they will use a simulation to learn conflict-management skills. In the scenario, there are two employees working together who suffer intense clashes of style and personality. Their constant bickering is affecting not only their own productivity, but that of the entire department. Their manager refers them to a new mediation program administered by the human resources department. They will form groups of three and play the following roles: the two disputing employees and the human resources representative (mediator/conflict manager).
2. Divide the participants into groups of three. Extras can be assigned to be a co-mediator in an existing group. Assign one participant in each group to each role, and hand out the role instructions.
3. Instruct participants to read their instructions carefully and to try and flesh out the scene based on their own knowledge, emotions, and experience. Explain that through their "owning" their roles in this manner, the simulation will become more lifelike, enabling them to understand what parties to a conflict managed by a third party truly experience.
4. Instruct the mediators to consider the type of process they wish to use, establish ground rules, note the stages the mediation will go through, and think about the atmosphere they wish to create. Remind them that they are not being tested. Rather, they are being given a chance to improve their conflict-management skills. If mediators are working together in pairs (co-mediation), suggest they take some time to coordinate their efforts. (15 to 20 minutes.)

5. Tell participants that each triad may begin as soon all the members are ready.

6. Because participants are usually quite comfortable in their roles and capable of managing this simulation with very little external tweaking, let them play it out in whatever way they see fit, intervening only with process tips when needed (e.g., reminding the HR representatives they might like to call for a break, or initiate private sessions with each party).

7. End the simulation when most triads have either reached an agreement or an insurmountable impasse. If time constraints demand it, the simulation can be cut off at any arbitrary moment. This sometimes helps to focus the debriefing on the mediation process itself, rather than on any outcomes achieved.
   (45 to 75 minutes.)

8. Begin the debriefing by asking which of the groups reached agreement and then asking a couple of them for the main points of their agreements. Next, ask a group who did *not* reach agreement whether there had been a last refused offer on the table, or what their impasse looked like (to allow participants still engrossed in the game to join the group, others to vent a bit, and, in general, to stress the joint-but-separate experience of the groups, transforming them back into one large learning-group). Next, focus the discussion on specific themes, according to training goals, and the dynamics that unfolded in each group's process. Following are some themes and related questions for managing the debriefing session, but these are not intended to limit the scope of questions or discussion themes:

Negotiation Strategy

- How would you define the overall mediation strategy in your group? (Help participants frame a short strategic definition, such as "working cooperatively" or "trying to beat the other guy.")
- Why did you choose this strategy? Did it prove to be effective?
- Have you observed similar strategic choices in real-life situations?
- What can you learn from your own simulation about the ways in which people approach disputes in organizational settings?

Communication Skills realign as above

- What communication tools did your group members use throughout their discussion?
- What communication techniques did the mediator(s) in your group employ for the purposes of trust-building and information gathering?
- Did any communication problem arise over the course of the negotiation? What was its source? How did your group address it?
- What did you learn about the way communication affects the conflict's development and management stages? How will you bring this to bear in real-life situations?

Information Sharing

- Was there an atmosphere of trust built between the parties?
- Did the parties share information openly, or were they more restrained?
- What actions or circumstances proved conducive to information sharing, and what actions or circumstances inhibited it?
- What did the mediator(s) do in order to allow or promote information sharing?

Exploring Options

- How did the processes of problem solving and searching for options begin?
- Did the search for options (or the final agreement) focus on elements that were very much on the table, or were attempts made to expand the pie?
- Did the mediator(s) take an active role in generating or evaluating options for agreement?
- What effect did this have on the process? What might have been done differently?
- Was any attempt made by the mediator(s) to *impose* a solution on the parties? If so, what effect did this have on the process?
- What have you learned from this experience about creativity? About giving disputing parties an active role in tailoring solutions to their issues? How will you bring this to bear in real-life situations?

Mediation Process Management

- Did the mediators set/discuss process management rules, such as ground rules, time frame, permitted language, or communication rules?
- What effect did these rules have on the process? Was there any need to remind parties of these rules, or to enforce them during the discussion?
- How did the mediators manage the process? If you were a mediator, do you feel you managed the process "by the book"—moving from one stage of the model to the next in a conscious and controlled manner? Do you feel that the structured process you tried to manage got away from you every so often?
- What effect did the process have on the disputing parties? If you were one of the disputants, do you feel that your relationship shifted at different stages of the mediation? What was the mediator(s)' role in bringing this about (if any)? What did the mediator(s) do in order to help you face your problems constructively?
- What effect did the process have on the problem at hand? Do you feel that the process was a suitable one for working out your differences?
- If you were a mediator, do you feel that the process was a suitable one for assisting the parties?
- Can you identify any particular elements or characteristics of typical workplace disputes that might make them suitable for a similar dispute resolution process?
- Do you feel that, as managers, your previous approach to managing disputes might be enriched as a result of what you learned during this simulation? Might you consider employing tools and approaches different than those you tended to use in the past?

(30 to 45 minutes.)

Variation

The simulation can be conducted as a negotiation scenario, by cutting out the mediator role and by instructing parties that the head of the department has told them they have to work things out on their own, and on their own time. In this case, the process and debriefing would focus on participants' negotiation and communication skills.

Submitted by Noam Ebner and Yael Efron.

Noam Ebner *is a visiting professor at Sabanci University in Turkey and at the UN's University for Peace in Costa Rica. His teaching focuses on negotiation and conflict management in international disputes as well as in business and legal settings. He also specializes in negotiation and mediation processes conducted online.*

Yael Efron, *an attorney-mediator, teaches negotiation at several colleges in Israel, in programs on management and economics. She is at the forefront of dispute resolution in Israel, complementing her own mediation practice with acting as a consultant to the Ministry of Justice, private mediation initiatives, and community mediation centers. Her writing and research focus on negotiation pedagogy.*

Together, Noam and Yael direct Tachlit Mediation and Negotiation Training, located in Jerusalem, Israel, which provides mediation services as well as negotiation and conflict management training in Israel and abroad.

Storm Down in Sales Instructions for Party A

You completed your MBA last year and began working in the sales department of a large import company. You know that the job is beneath you. With your abilities and education, you could be running the department better than its current head does. However, you'd long ago decided you wanted to start at the bottom, gaining as much experience as possible by the time you reached the top.

One of the workers in the department, a junior client manager like yourself, has been giving you a hard time since your first day on the job. You feel he is constantly measuring the length of your breaks and listening in on your phone calls. Besides making comments about how you waste company time, he has also repeatedly laughed at you for your "fancy education" and for wearing a tie to work every day.

This guy has worked for the company for a long time and is a good example of everything wrong that's wrong with it. He has no business education at all, but he's responsible for a large budget and makes all kinds of decisions affecting employees' lives. He's always raising his voice at people, his desk is a mess, and his presence really makes the office an unpleasant place to be. When you tried to make friends with him and help him out with some advice to make his job easier, he shouted at you to mind our own business. At a staff meeting last week, when you mentioned that in most leading companies upper management positions are reserved for MBAs, he screamed at you to shut up—in front of the whole department.

Your department head recently spoke to you and requested that you make a real effort to work things out with the guy because the friction is taking its toll on the whole department. He's turned the whole issue over to the human resources department, which is operating a pilot program for settling in-house conflict. You don't know much about the process, but you knows that the parties participate in talks, on their own free time, assisted by an expert from the HR department. You are about to meet with this expert, along with your annoying co-worker. While the department head wants to let you work this out in whatever way you see fit, he expects you to give this process your best shot. Good luck!

Storm Down in Sales Instructions for Party B

You have worked in the sales department of a large import firm for the past ten years. Having proven yourself as a salesman, you worked your way up to the position of junior client manager. You lack university education—you've been supporting yourself since you were sixteen—and you know that this position may be as high as you will go. Still, you aspire higher, and work hard in order to earn it, just as you always have.

About six months ago the company hired a new junior client manager. This kid really annoys you. He's straight out of business school and is starting off at the position it took you seven years to move into! He is always talking about his school and offering you and everyone else the wisdom of his professors—as if that has anything to do with the real world! And he keeps making annoying comments about the way you work and your personal habits—as if he were your boss—while he himself takes long lunch breaks and is always on the phone. You feel he is stuck-up and disrespectful, and his rich-kid university manners are making the office an unpleasant place to be.

When you complained to the department head, he suggested you teach the kid how things are done around here. You've tried to do so, but he always starts lecturing you about the changes *he* thinks should be made until you lose patience and walk off. At last week's staff meeting, he proposed that only managers with MBAs should be assigned mid-level positions in the department. With your own job on the line, you lost your temper and shouted at him.

Your department head recently spoke to you and requested that you make a real effort to work things out with the kid because the friction is taking its toll on the whole department. He has turned the whole issue over to someone from the human resources department, which is operating a pilot program for settling in-house conflict. You don't know much about the process, but you know that the parties participate in talks, on their own free time, assisted by an expert from the HR department. You are about meet with this expert, along with your annoying co-worker. While the department head wants to let you work this out in whatever way you see fit, he expects you to give this process your best shot. Good luck!

Storm Down in Sales Instructions for the Human Resources Department Mediator

You have been working at a large import company for two years, specializing in organizing in-house training and handling individual personnel problems. After taking a mediation course, you advocated implementing an in-house conflict resolution program in the firm to settle internal conflicts at all levels. You convinced your department head to let you run a pilot program for conducting in-house mediation, in which parties participate on their own free time. You are now working at writing a description of the process, as well as mapping out how it would work.

Sooner than you expected, you've received your first case. The head of the sales department called you with a problem he has with two employees, both of whom he values, who suffer from personality clashes and work-style differences. Their constant bickering is driving the whole department nuts and is lowering productivity. While he could certainly impose a solution from above (such as firing one or both of them, or transferring one or both to another department), he feels that the firm would be better off if they were able to work it out between them. He thinks a third party might be able to help in this case, as the two parties seem to be unable to work it out on their own, and they are rarely in the same room together without fighting! He has told them that he expects them to partake in the process, and that you would explain the purpose and rules to them.

You have set up a meeting with the two employees, and it is about to start. Consider how you want to run the process, form your initial introductory opening, and get to work. Good luck!

Setting Team Performance Objectives

Gaining Maximum Buy-In to Team Performance Measures

Activity Summary

An exercise for team leaders to determine a clear set of principles for involving their teams in identifying the most appropriate measures for individual and team performance. The group can either be all team leaders or one team leader and his or her own team.

Goals

- To fully appreciate the importance of following sound principles when choosing the most appropriate performance measures.
- To enable team leaders to guide team members in choosing performance measures to which they will be totally committed.
- To use a performance measurement and objective-setting process as the basis for a constructive dialogue.

Group Size

A group of six to twelve is ideal, but the activity can work with smaller or larger groups.

Time Required

Approximately 60 to 90 minutes.

Materials

- Flip chart or large whiteboard with markers.
- Pens or pencils and writing pads for participants.
- (Optional) A calculator.

Physical Setting

A training or meeting room with chairs arranged in a circle.

Facilitating Risk Rating

Moderate.

Process

1. Explain the activity to the participants. You can use the following script or adapt the wording as you see fit.

   "We are going to look at the whole subject of how to set measurable performance objectives by working through a structured exercise during which we have to decide, together, what we all think is the best performance measure for us to focus on. The complete exercise has three parts.

   "Part 1 asks us to think in advance how best to set up a performance objective team meeting.

   "Part 2 is about exploring what specific questions we might expect to be raised at such a meeting.

   "Part 3 involves establishing some clear principles applicable to all performance discussions.

   "I will be leading the exercise in as realistic a fashion as I can. Therefore, I want you to react as naturally as you would if we were having a real team meeting at work."

2. Answer any questions participants have before beginning. Explaining to the team that management has dictated that all company car drivers must improve their gasoline consumption in an effort to reduce overall car fleet costs. This is the starting point for the discussion of performance objectives.

3. Ask the participants how they want to address this performance question with their teams, using the following questions:

   - How would you announce the meeting to staff members?
   - How would you structure the meeting? For example, would you state the objective in advance of the meeting or would you break the news gently?
   - How will you introduce the subject of the meeting?
   - What information would you have to have available before beginning?
   - What objections might you anticipate from your team?

4. Once these issues have been discussed and a method for calling the meeting and announcing the topic are resolved, the group can move on to Part 2.

5. Tell participants that they now will determine what questions must be asked to resolve the performance issue (use of gasoline) satisfactorily. List the following questions on the flip chart that may help them prepare for their meeting. You can use it as a template, but feel free to amend or change as you see fit. Make sure you take them through each of these questions to check their understanding and elicit any other suggestions they might have.

   - What is our specific objective and what is the timescale involved?
   - Did management set a clear objective originally? Is a reduction in gasoline consumption really required, or is the real objective a reduction in fuel costs? These look very similar, but in fact are very different performance objectives. The start of performance measurement is having a crystal-clear objective with a specific measure.
   - What is the baseline? What units should we use? Before you can move forward, you must establish the baseline measure. Depending on the actual objective you choose, the units of measure will be different. So if it is consumption, it could be miles per gallon. On the other hand, fuel costs could be cost per mile (cents per mile).
   - Once you have established the units or metrics to be used, ask what everyone is achieving currently.
   - What is the improvement target? What units should we use? Let us assume at this stage that the real objective is fuel cost and that the average fuel cost is 10 cents per mile. The improvement target could be

set at a 10 percent improvement, which would make the performance measure a one cent per mile reduction. Again, this is a very different objective from setting a miles per gallon increase, which could be moving from 30 mpg to 33 mpg.

- What cost constraints are there? You must consider cost constraints in advance of performance discussions. What if one of the team members suggests that a fuel saving could be achieved by tuning all the engines more frequently? The cost of this extra maintenance and servicing could outweigh a 10 percent saving on the cost per mile.
- What other constraints are there? Deciding on the boundaries or limits of the team's decision making is very important and should keep the discussion on the right track. Is one of the givens that there will be no change in the company car policy, for example? That is, no one can change cars to achieve a higher miles per gallon rating or move to diesel fuel.
- What can each individual do to help achieve this objective? Having set a group performance measure, have you already asked each individual about his or her own personal gasoline consumption? The ways in which each individual can achieve his or her own performance objective will vary according to the person's existing personal performance. The drivers who speed could perhaps just slow down. The best drivers now may have to make sure they buy their gasoline at the lowest price available. Interestingly, if the objective agreed on was to improve miles per gallon, then buying cheaper gasoline has no effect on this measure, and yet it would save the company money. Build this into the discussions.
- Who else needs to be involved? Would you ask the fleet manager to attend the meeting? How about someone from accounting to agree how the information is to be collated and reported back?
- What other ideas do you have that are currently outside of the constraints?
- Would everyone agree to use diesel? Could the car policy change to allow smaller, faster cars but with better mileage?

6. Only when you are satisfied that there has been an open, honest, and very thorough discussion of all the issues, should you move on to Part 3. During Part 3, ask the team to consider what principles have been

established during Part 2. A principle can be defined as a fundamental truth that guides an individual's behavior (e.g., "Honesty is the best policy"). In other words, what have you learned from Part 2 that you will be able to use again and again in any future performance discussions? What should guide the way you control the meeting and the discussion? For example, do you follow a principle that any idea is a good idea? How do you then deal with ideas that are plainly not going to work?

7. As learnings are drawn out, capture the principles from Part 3 on a flip chart/whiteboard to see whether there is common agreement. It should be emphasized that, in practice, a point will be reached where there is common agreement, regardless of how difficult this might be.

8. List any objections from those who are still not happy with the measure to be used. These can be used at a future meeting when reviewing how the performance measure has worked. It can be the starting point for further issues for discussion around the subject of performance management.

Trainer's Note

When managers have actually tried this exercise out, they will realize that even something as straightforward as improving gasoline consumption can become very complicated if they do not have well-defined objectives and measures at the beginning. So point out that a principle of simplicity may be required. Also, point out the importance of everyone on the team knowing how he or she is currently performing and having some type of yardstick to gauge their performance.

Some other types of issues that can be handled using this format include:

- What is the company's declared policy on performance (e.g., "Underperformance will not be tolerated") and does everybody understand it fully?
- How well are strategic, business, performance objectives and key performance indicators being communicated?
- How well are operational performance measures cascaded from the strategic objectives?
- To what extent is performance top down, as opposed to inviting staff to offer their own improvement ideas bottom up?
- To what extent is performance managed across departments?

Variations

- Once the group has worked through Parts 1 through 3, you can run the exercise again, but this time use a real performance objective (e.g., sales, costs, output, productivity, customer satisfaction, complaints, etc.).
- Award a prize for the best suggestion, as even hypothetical "gold stars" can motivate people and add to the sense of fun.
- Present an additional scenario to the team: If, after this exercise, they wanted to go back to management to challenge some existing company objectives, how might they present their case and the views of the team?
- You might ask your team to run one of these scenarios themselves while you observe.

Submitted by Paul Kearns.

Paul Kearns *is the founder and managing director of PWL, an HR and learning consultancy that he established in 1991. His work focuses on how to use measurement as a very powerful learning, development, and behavioral tool. He has written several seminal works on HR strategy, human capital reporting, and training evaluation as well as measuring and managing employee performance. In addition to his consultancy practice, he teaches HR strategy on MBA programs and is a trainer and facilitator in demand around the world. His latest book,* The Value Motive, *shows how to connect human values to the search for maximum organizational and societal value.*

Managers as Change Agents*

Activity Summary

A quick activity that helps managers identify their strengths and weaknesses in their role as a change agent.

Goals

- To explore the role of a manager as change agent.
- To identify a manager and or change/agent's strengths and weaknesses in addressing change.
- To identify specific characteristics required of a change agent in one's own organization.

Group Size

Ten to twenty managers and/or change agents of a single organization that is experiencing a change.

Time Required

50 to 90 minutes, depending on the size of the group.

Materials

- A flip chart prepared with the list of characteristics from the Change Agent Characteristics handout.
- One Change Agent Characteristics handout for each participant.
- One green and one orange highlighter for each participant.

*This activity is adapted from the book *Thriving Through Change: A Leader's Practical Guide to Change Mastery* published by ASTD.

Physical Setting

Tables and chairs with room to move around and to form teams of two for discussion purposes.

Facilitating Risk Rating

Low.

Process

1. Gather the managers together who will serve as change agents, either full time or as an assigned collateral duty.
2. Provide each of them with a copy of the Change Agent Characteristics handout and a green and an orange highlighter.
3. Review the instructions on the handout, emphasizing that they should mark their top five strengths with the green highlighter and the five areas in which they may need additional support with the orange highlighter. Allow about 5 minutes.
4. When time is up or when everyone has finished, tell them to stand and locate someone who has selected a strength (green) that matches one area in which they need support (orange) or vice versa, and to discuss the questions listed on the handout. Give them 10 to 15 minutes for the discussion.
5. While participants are working in pairs, circulate among them offering support and ensuring that they are addressing the four questions:
   - Why is the selected characteristic a strength for one of you?
   - Why is it not a strength for the other?
   - How important do you believe this particular characteristic is for the task of being a change agent?
   - How can you help each other?
6. Call time and bring the group back together. Ask for a few volunteers to provide several highlights that occurred during their discussions.
7. Ask participants to return to the lists of characteristics and to each circle the five that they believe are the most important in the organization for success as a change agent.

8. Using the prepared flip chart, go through each characteristic and ask participants to raise their hands if they think it is a required characteristic for success. Post the number of votes on the left side of each characteristic on the chart. Next, go through the list asking them to raise their hands if they marked it as one of their strengths. Post the numbers on the right side of the flip chart.

9. Lead a discussion using the following questions:

   - What do these numbers tell us?
   - How can we leverage the strengths in the group?
   - Which areas do we need to improve the most?
   - What will the impact be if we do not improve?
   - How can we improve the areas that need to be improved?
   - What are the next steps for this group?

Variations

- This activity works best with at least ten people. If you have fewer than ten, you may want to work through Step 4 as a large group instead of in pairs.
- You may wish to compile the comments in Step 9 and forward them to the managers after the session or to use as input to your next meeting with them.

Submitted by Elaine Biech.

Elaine Biech *is president and managing principal of ebb associates inc, an organization development firm that helps organizations work through large-scale change. Biech has been in the training and consulting field for twenty-six years and is the author or editor of dozens of books and articles, including* Business of Consulting *(2nd ed.),* Training for Dummies, *and* Thriving through Change. *A long-time volunteer for ASTD, she has served on ASTD's National Board of Directors and was the recipient of the 1992 ASTD Torch Award, the 2004 ASTD Volunteer Staff Partnership Award, and the 2006 ASTD Gordon Bliss Memorial Award.*

Change Agent Characteristics

Below is a list of effective change agent characteristics.

Ability to influence	Achievement-oriented
Attentive listener	Big picture vision
Collaborator	Creative idea person
Credible	Customer-focused
Deals well with negativity	Detail orientation
Eager for improvement	Excellent communicator
Interest in change	Logical thinker
Organizational knowledge	People person
Persistent	Process oriented
Realistic	Restless
Self-confident	Sense of timing
Tolerance for ambiguity	Trusted and respected

Instructions: First, identify the five characteristics from the list above that you think are your strongest and highlight them with a green marker.

Next, identify the five characteristics for which you think you may need support and highlight them with an orange marker.

When instructed to do so, find someone who has selected a strength for which you need support or vice versa (you marked it as a strength and someone else needs support in that area).

In your pair, discuss the following questions:

- Why is the selected characteristic a strength for one of you?
- Why is it not a strength for the other?
- How important do you believe this particular characteristic is for the task of being a change agent?
- How can you help each other?

Navigating the Rivers of Change

Activity Summary

This activity is designed for leaders/managers to simulate their current challenges with organizational change initiatives.

Goals

- To problem solve identified obstacles to change.
- To increase the effectiveness of team communication.
- To focus the team on common goals and interdependence.

Group Size

Teams of five or six leaders from the same organization who are leading any change initiative (change sponsors, advocates and/or key leaders).

Time Required

3 to 4 hours, depending on the number of teams.

Materials

- One copy of Navigating the Rivers of Change Exercise Parameters for each team.
- One copy of Navigating the Rivers of Change Obstacles List for each team.
- Two flip charts and markers for use in Steps 3 and 4 (one for each team).
- Paper and pens or pencils for participants.
- A photo of snow on mountains melting into rivers (see Step 7) and an overhead or computer projector on which to show the image.
- (Optional) Prizes (see Step 13).

Physical Setting

A training or meeting room with small tables and additional chairs. You'll also need breakout rooms or sufficient space for teams to work independently.

Facilitating Risk Rating

Moderate.

Process

1. Whether this activity is conducted during a leadership module or as a stand-alone, introduce it by making a few key points about the impact of change on leaders and employees. These points should reflect the present change initiatives and a summary of recent change models that have been used. If one specific model has not been applied in the past, share your preferred model.
2. Separate the participants into two groups of approximately equal size, give each group a flip chart and markers, and be sure they are far enough apart in the room that they will not disturb one another.
3. Give Group 1 the following assignment: Conduct a four- to five-minute brainstorming session around the question, "What pressure points have the current change initiatives created for leaders?" Ask Group 1 to record their responses on the flip chart.
4. Give Group 2 the following assignment: Conduct a four- or five-minute brainstorming session around the question, "What impacts have the current change initiatives had on employees?" Ask Group 2 to record responses on the flip chart.
5. Have each group report out its brainstorming results and briefly compare the lists. This information will be good background for the exercise that follows. (20 minutes.)
6. Divide the participants into two new teams of five or six. The diverse departments present should be represented on each team.
7. Set the stage of change for the Navigating the Rivers of Change exercise by projecting the image of rivers and saying, "What appears to be the end may really be a new beginning. As you project the picture, explain that, in Alaska, this image is described as the ribbons of rivers. Say that,

to navigate these rivers, travelers have to avoid all the obstacles (rocks) to reach their goals. Explain that each team will simulate a journey across this type of terrain in the form of a skit.

8. Distribute copies of the Navigating the Rivers of Change Exercise Parameters and the Navigating the Rivers of Change Obstacles List to all participants. Provide paper and pens or pencils for all participants. Explain to the teams that they will be creating a 15- to 20-minute skit about the current change journey the organization is undertaking. Using the image of the river (leave it on the projector), the teams are to describe the speed and impact of the change on leaders and employees alike. Tell them to use the information collected in the earlier brainstorming exercises as a source for their descriptions. The participants may want to describe the change in terms of rapids, fast currents, or waterfalls. Explain that, during the skits, the teams must demonstrate how they plan to navigate around the obstacles (rocks) they encounter on their change journey. Say that some of the "rocks" may be large and visible, and some may be half-hidden in the water. Each team must first decide on and be able to describe the strategies they plan to use. Discuss the specific resources that could be used, if teams seem to be stuck.

9. Assign each team to its breakout area and tell the teams to begin working on their skits.
(60 minutes, including a short break.)

10. Move among the groups to clarify any questions about the obstacles or the skit requirements. Remind participants to build in a short break.

11. When time is up, bring the teams back together and ask for a volunteer team to begin. Each team will present its skit in turn, explaining the obstacles and their methods of overcoming them as they act out their skit.
(15 to 20 minutes per skit.)

12. After the teams have presented, discuss the common themes and approaches. Capture the answers to the following questions on a flip chart:

    - What new obstacles did you include in your skits?
    - What patterns or similarities did you see in the strategies that were described by the different teams?
    - How do strategies you are going to need for the current change initiative compare with the strategies demonstrated in the skits?

- Which new strategies do you think could have the greatest impact on employees? (Refer back to the brainstorming flip-chart pages.)
- What organizational and individual resources will be needed to implement these strategies?
- How do the insights gained from creating the skits relate back to the pressure points for leaders? (Refer back to the brainstorming flip-chart pages.)

13. (Optional) Prizes can be given for the skits in categories such as most creative journey, most humorous journey, or most organized journey.
14. Conclude the session by summarizing the observation and insights shared during the exercise and ask the group to identify action steps to move the organization's current change initiatives forward.

Submitted by Marilyn J. Corrigan.

Marilyn J. Corrigan *is a management consultant specializing in leadership, executive coaching, change communications, conflict resolution, and career development. For over twenty years, she worked as a leader in the management and employee development and public affairs functions of major corporations. She implemented programs in leadership for supervisors and middle managers as well as succession planning. In addition to her work as a consultant and as an adjunct faculty member in the MBA programs of several Twin Cities universities, Corrigan has held leadership positions in the American Society of Training and Development (ASTD)at both the local and national levels. She holds a B.A. in psychology from Whitman College and an M.A. in education from the University of Denver.*

Navigating the Rivers of Change Exercise Parameters

Guidelines for Planning Your Change Journey

- Review the Navigating the Rivers of Change Obstacle List, choose your "other" obstacles, and identify your additional two obstacles.
- Plan how to navigate the river with the rocks (obstacles) that are blocking your progress.
- Describe any conditions or change you visualize that may occur on your trip.
- Describe the resources you will need for this journey.
- Create a fifteen- to twenty-minute skit to present to the large group that demonstrates how you will deal with obstacles in your way as you face change.

Parameters Connected to the Organization

- Meeting the financial goals of the organization.
- Meeting the requirements of the change initiative itself.
- Operating as one team.
- Focusing on "where we are"
- Continuing to describe the goal (destiny) as is appropriate.
- Respecting the change model that was described in the session (if applicable).

Navigating the Rivers of Change Obstacle List

Instructions: Choose a total of seven obstacles (rocks) from the lists below that are true at the present time for your organization as it faces change, three from the Common Obstacles category (all items on that list), two from the Other Obstacles list, and two other obstacles identified by the team (write in your two additional obstacles below).

Common Obstacles

- Cynicism
- Fear
- Time pressure

Other Obstacles

- Changing customer expectations
- Perception of overstepping boundaries of position responsibility
- Limited resources
- Complexity of the customer population
- Duplication of efforts
- Trying to be more than we can be
- Regulation requirement
- Budget constraints

Additional Obstacles Identified by the Team

Turn Over a New Leaf
A Problem-Solving and Team-Building Activity for Managers

Activity Summary

This is an activity that can stand alone or be integrated with a team-building, communications, or problem-solving workshop for managers.

Goals

- To help managers create awareness of how a team solves problems together.
- To understand how a team of managers communicates and works together in a challenging situation.
- To learn strengths of the team and ways to improve team effectiveness so that managers can assist teams they work with.

Group Size

This is an activity for at least 6 managers who are interested in learning how they and their teams work together as a group-and how they can improve team effectiveness

Time Required

60 to 90 minutes, depending on size of group.

Materials

- An appropriate size bed sheet (use a single sheet for up to twelve people; use a double sheet for more than twelve people or break participants into two groups and use two single sheets) .
- Flip chart pad and markers.
- Watch or timer.

Physical Setting

Make sure you have enough open space in a training room or outside to spread the bed sheet out.

Facilitating Risk Rating

Medium.

Process

1. Introduce the activity by explaining that the way teams work together to solve problems determines how long it will take to solve the problem and how effective the solution will be. Say that this activity will help the managers experience how a team works to solve a problem together. (You do not want to spend too much time talking about how team members should solve problems, communicate with each other, or think creatively about making decisions. Participants will learn about this through participating in and debriefing the activity.)
2. Lay the sheet out on the floor.
3. Ask everyone to stand on the sheet. Say, "The objective is to turn over the sheet without anyone stepping off the sheet at any time. No one can ever touch the ground (hands or feet) or get off the sheet."
4. Explain to participants that the activity is timed; effective teams should take no more than 20 minutes. If someone falls off the sheet or touches the ground, you will call foul and start over. (You can be stringent with fouls to start, but as time goes by, let up on fouls a little if the group is getting frustrated. You want to stretch them a little and get them into an uncomfortable place.)

5. As you observe the group trying to turn the sheet, take notes on particular situations or conversations among team members. Look for leadership, dominance, communication styles, creativity, diversity in styles, and so forth. (You can bring out these observations in the debriefing.)
6. If the team still does not figure out how to turn the sheet within 25 minutes, call time and continue with a debriefing.
7. Begin the debriefing with the following questions:
   - How well did the procedures you used get you to the final result?
   - What were some of the key factors that helped the team solve this problem?
   - What were some of the issues or challenges that got in the way of turning the sheet?
8. Ask each participant to complete the sentence: "I feel like this group is effective when . . ." (Have people answer as they are ready.) As a facilitator, look for themes from all participants' answers. Capture key points on a flip chart.
9. Continue the debriefing with additional questions:
   - How does the diversity of the team enhance or retard accomplishing the task?
   - Did you support each other? What did that look like?
   - How do you support your teams at work? (Look for ties between the activity and work.)
   - If you were to do this activity again, what would you do differently?
   - What are the lessons to be learned from this activity that you can take back to the job? (Encourage answers around communication, diversity, and team processes such as decision making and problem solving.)

Variations

- If you have a group of sixteen to twenty-five, you could have two groups with two sheets and have them compete against each other.
- If time permits and it seems appropriate, after the debriefing, participants can do this activity again, applying lessons learned and trying to improve their time and process.

Submitted by Bevan Gray-Rogel.

Bevan Gray-Rogel *is the president of Graylan Consulting, LLC, an organization development consulting firm. Her consulting services help in assisting individuals, teams, and organizations maximize their effectiveness and performance. She has over twenty-five years of experience in the fields of human resource development and organization development. She has worked for profit and non-profit organizations in staff positions and as an external consultant. Her specialties are process consultations, facilitating groups, change management, strategic planning, team building, and leadership development. She partners with clients/client project teams to achieve desired outcomes and also helps to transfer capabilities to the client and their organization. Her clients have included organizations such as Tampa Electric Company, City of Fort Lauderdale,* The Tampa Tribune, *Diebold, University of Florida, The Zenith, GTE-Verizon, and Capital One. Gray-Rogel received her BA in psychology at Lake Forest College and her MBA in organizational behavior and development at George Washington University. She has served on the national, regional, and local levels for ASTD.*

Ageism Awareness for Managers
A Self-Assessment

Activity Summary

This learning activity focuses on assessing and discussing the attitudes toward older workers that influence the behavior of managers.

Goals

- To increase awareness of ageist attitudes that can influence decisions about hiring, firing, training, promoting, and retaining workers.
- To introduce a discussion about valuing intergenerational diversity in the workplace.

Group Size

Fifteen to twenty managers.

Time Required

About 40 to 45 minutes.

Materials

- A copy of the Ageism Awareness Assessment for each participant.
- A pen or pencil for each participant.
- Flip-chart pad on easel.
- Markers.

Physical Setting

A standard training room with chairs and a writing surface.

Facilitating Risk Rating

Low to moderate.

Process

1. Introduce the topic to the training group, making the following key points:
   - People from as many as four generations are found in today's workplace.
   - Successful managers understand and appropriately deal with this type of workforce.
   - Awareness of personal beliefs and attitudes play a key role in manager's successful performance.
   - Awareness is increased through self-assessment and discussion.
2. Tell participants that they are about to participate in an activity that has two parts: self-assessment and discussion.
3. Distribute copies of the Ageism Awareness Assessment and pens or pencils to each participant.
4. Tell participants that they will have about 10 minutes to fill out and score the assessment.
5. Ask participants to share their total scores with the rest of the training group.
6. Lead a discussion using the following questions and record the responses on a flip chart:
   - Which attitudes/beliefs revealed in the self-assessment do you feel strongest about?
   - Which attitudes/beliefs does the organization feel strongest about?
   - What organization policies and practices support the appropriate attitudes/beliefs?
   - Which attitudes/beliefs do you need to be more personally committed to?
   - Which attitudes/beliefs does the organization need to be more committed to?

- What actions will you take to increase personal and organizational commitment to the values/beliefs?

7. Discuss how increased commitment will make people better managers.
8. Summarize information shared during the entire activity.
9. End the activity by encouraging the participants to conduct this self-assessment on an annual basis within their organizations.

Submitted by Shirley Copeland.

Shirley Copeland, Ed.D., *is president of the Learning Resource Group, LLC, a management consulting firm she founded in 1993. Her company specializes in evaluation, performance improvement, workforce shaping in the federal sector, and leadership development. She has designed and developed award-winning materials and is a frequent contributor to training and development publications.*

Ageism Awareness Assessment

Instructions: For each statement below, circle the response that most closely aligns with your personal opinion.

1. Older workers are a valuable asset to my organization.
   Disagree Neutral Agree
2. When considering two equally qualified candidates for a promotion, I would probably select a younger worker over an older worker.
   Disagree Neutral Agree
3. Older workers experience a decline in their ability to learn new things.
   Disagree Neutral Agree
4. Older workers are less productive than younger workers.
   Disagree Neutral Agree
5. I would rather work in teams with people who are closer to my own age or younger.
   Disagree Neutral Agree
6. Older workers are dependable and reliable.
   Disagree Neutral Agree
7. Older senior-level executives hinder my ability to move up to a higher position.
   Disagree Neutral Agree
8. Older workers are as open to change as others in the organization.
   Disagree Neutral Agree
9. If I had to downsize my department, I would make my decisions based on previous productivity and performance rather than age.
   Disagree Neutral Agree
10. I would rather give training opportunities to younger workers than to older workers.
    Disagree Neutral Agree
11. I would consider flexible work arrangements to accommodate older workers who want to continue working with fewer hours.
    Disagree Neutral Agree

12. I would prefer to offer older workers early retirement, rather than offer training opportunities for new skills.
    Disagree Neutral Agree
13. Older workers have more problems when new technology is introduced in the company.
    Disagree Neutral Agree
14. Older workers cannot cope with the physical demands of the job.
    Disagree Neutral Agree
15. I treat all workers equally, regardless of age.
    Disagree Neutral Agree

Determining Your Score

For each "agree" answer to questions 1, 6, 8, 9, 11, and 15, give yourself 1 point.

For each "disagree" answer to questions 2, 3, 4, 5, 7, 10, 12, 13, and 14, give yourself 1 point.

If your total score is 12 or higher, your attitudes and beliefs are appropriate for encouraging a diverse workplace. If your total score is below 12, you may have adopted unfounded myths and stereotypes about aging and should examine your potential for age bias in interacting with older workers.

Getting Courage on the Front Burner

Activity Summary

This learning activity is used as an introduction to a management workshop or seminar that deals with a management task that requires taking a firm position and acting on it.

Goals

- To discuss the components of courage.
- To increase awareness of various courageous actions.

Group Size

Twelve to sixteen managers.

Time Required

1 hour to 1 hour, 15 minutes.

Materials

- One copy of the Leadership Courage Worksheet for each participant.
- A pen or pencil for each participant.
- Flip chart pad on easel.
- Markers.

Physical Setting

Training room with tables for three to five participants each.

Facilitating Risk Rating

Low to Moderate.

Process

1. Introduce this activity by relating a personal story in which courage was evident.

2. Write the question, "Why is courage important?" on a flip chart. Record participant responses on the flip chart.

3. Ask participants to discuss in their table groups what is meant by the statement, "A key to managing your own destiny is personal courage." (15 minutes.)

4. Ask each group to report out key points of its discussion; record the points on a flip chart.

5. Introduce the four components of courage: (1) self-confidence, (2) self-mastery, (3) wisdom, and (4) strength of resolve. Provide a personal example of each component or an example everyone would recognize. For example:

   - Self-confidence is displayed when a person has full personal knowledge and awareness of his or her values, such as Jack Welch at General Electric.

   - Self-mastery is apparent when a person handles any fears he or she has, such as Carly Fiorina at Hewlett-Packard.

   - Wisdom is observed when a person does what is right, such as the whistle blower at Enron.

   - Strength of resolve occurs when a person musters the will to do the right thing and follow through, such as Rick Wagoner's tenacity in moving General Motors through a new strategy.

6. Distribute a copy of the Leadership Courage Worksheet and a pen or pencil to each participant. Tell participants they have 15 minutes to record their individual responses on the worksheet.

7. While participants are completing their worksheets, write each question from the worksheet at the top of a sheet of flip-chart paper.

8. For each question, ask participants for their responses and record them on the appropriate sheet, focusing on one question at a time.

9. Open the floor for participants to make any other points or to ask questions.
10. Summarize by reviewing all of the flip charts.
11. Then segue into the major content of the workshop or seminar.

Variations

- This could be a stand-alone activity as part of a lunch-and-learn seminar or in a similar format.
- After summarizing, you could ask each participant what he or she thinks the most important thing is to remember about personal courage.

Submitted by Kitty Preziosi.

Kitty Preziosi's *expertise comes from twenty-five years of "rolling up her sleeves and getting it done" everywhere she works. Preziosi excels in designing and implementing new management and leadership practices, employee management systems, consultative and strategic selling practices, succession planning, employee opinion surveys, and redesigning processes for customer service, manufacturing, and financial management.*

Her consulting clients have included Miller Brewing Company, Combined, JM Family Enterprises, Perry Ellis International, VISA International, and New South, Inc., ABB Combustion Engineering, and United Technologies.

She has held senior executive positions in training, HRD, and OD for Coca Cola, John Alden Financial, and Liberty National Life insurance.

Leadership Courage Worksheet

1. Provide examples of other people's courage—people you have observed or work with. Explain the example and why it was courageous:

   What were the results?

2. Provide examples of your own courage:

   What were the results of your actions?

   How were those results known/observed? Reported?

   How did you feel?

   How did your peers, boss, and direct reports act?

   How were you rewarded?

   Did you reward yourself?

3. How have you used previous acts of courage to lead to other acts of courage?

4. Are there barriers to acts of courage? Is so, name them.

   How have you overcome them?

   Have you experienced barriers to acts of courage? What are they?

   How did you overcome them?

5. Have you seen a courageous act backfire or not work successfully? How? Why?

   Could the situation have been prevented?

6. Can courage be driven down to lower levels of an organization?

   If so, how?

What is your role as a leader in nurturing courageous acts?

What can you do to stimulate courage by others?

7. What courageous acts may be on the horizon for you?

How do you think you will respond?

8. What did you learn from this discussion about leadership courage?

Crafting Shared Organizational Statements

Activity Summary

A brainstorming and analysis activity intended to aid teams in creating formal organizational statements, including a vision statement, a mission statement, goals, objectives, and an organizational philosophy.

Goals

- To understand the importance of shared organizational statements and organizational alignment.
- To consider divergent points of view and to exchange information and ideas.

Group Size

Five to twenty managers from different levels of the same organization (preferably) who generally represent its values.

Time Required

4 to 5 hours.

Materials

- A few sheets of blank paper for each participant.
- One pen and one pencil (with eraser) for each participant.
- A whiteboard and markers or flip charts with markers or overhead projector with transparencies and markers.

Physical Setting

A training or meeting room with tables, chairs, and enough space for participants to move around freely.

Facilitating Risk Rating

Moderate.

Process

1. Introduce this activity by describing *shared* visions, missions, and other formal organizational declarations. Take some time to discuss the benefits of having different people in the organization contribute to such statements. Caution participants that the process of orchestrating collective thoughts is more challenging than it might originally seem.

2. Define an organizational vision, explain its purpose, and give examples of excellent ones. Say that a vision statement is a declarative statement that articulates the organization's main long-term ambition. It is a clear view of where the organization wants to arrive in the future. The statement should ideally orient all stakeholders in the same direction. All such declarative statements are supposed to be for employees and not customers (as is erroneously assumed by many companies). A good vision is strategic but easy to remember. The organization's *mission* and, in turn, its long-term goals, should emanate from the vision statement. Depending on the industry, an organization's vision can be modified in a few years or in a few decades. Some examples of simple, powerful, and excellent vision statements are:

   There will be a personal computer on every desk running Microsoft software. (Bill Gates)

   To be the world's best in chemicals and electronic imaging. (Eastman Kodak)

   To build the premiere financial services company in the U.S. (Nations Bank)

   To build the largest and most complete Amateur Radio community site on the Internet. (eHam.net)

> To be widely recognized as the premiere provider of innovative financial products and services. (Option One Mortgage)

Ensure that participants recognize what makes for an outstanding vision statement.
(10 minutes.)

3. Conduct a ten- to twenty-minute individual brainstorming session around the question, "What is your view of where this organization should ideally be in the future? A vision statement is a lofty long-term goal, so re-imagine the organization as much as possible while simultaneously envisioning a realistic, credible, and attractive future. Keep in mind the organization's character and culture. Also think about factors that are very likely to significantly affect our industry ten to twenty years from now."
4. Distribute the paper, pens, and pencils and ask participants to record their responses. Tell them not to take too much time before responding. Say that, in brainstorming exercises, people should feel free to suggest wild ideas, focus on quantity instead of quality, and not evaluate ideas (their own or those of others).
5. After the allotted time, collect and post the responses (with the assistance of one or more of the participants).
6. Use your preferred voting method to have the participants rank the responses.
7. Based on the voting outcome, assist the group in shaping a vision statement that expresses where the organization wants to go in the long term (e.g., ten, fifteen, twenty, fifty, one hundred years). In other words, where should their organization be in the distant future? If possible, the statement should be no longer than fifteen words.
   (20 minutes.)
8. Tell the group that you'll now be going through a similar process to create a mission statement. Ensure that the group understands that a mission statement emphasizes the here and now. The questions that may be asked are, "What is your view of our organization's purpose? Why should the organization exist? and What should every person who works here be doing? A mission statement orients employees to what they have to do every day at work. For instance, the Ritz Carlton's mission statement is 'We are ladies and gentlemen serving ladies and gentlemen,' and Disney's

mission statement is 'To make people happy.'" Remind them again that declarative statements, such as the mission statement, are for employees and not for customers. It is important that a mission statement be very easy for every employee to memorize.

9. As with the vision statement, go through Steps 3 through 7 to create a mission statement.
(30 minutes.)

10. The next process is for each participant to come up with several goals that would help the company (each employee in the company) to achieve the mission. The goals should be general and brief (less than a sentence each), for example, "To provide excellent employee health insurance."

11. Repeat Steps 3 through 6 to create the goals. Rather than creating a single statement at the end, the group should select three goals from all those suggested. The participants should take a few minutes, once the goals have been selected, to confirm that the goals support/align with the vision and mission statements.
(30 minutes.)

12. Next, the participants will come up with three *objectives* for each of the three goals. Objectives, for the purpose of this exercise, are more specific and slightly longer than goals. For example, if the goal is "To lead our industry in customer service excellence," then an objective might be "Fully utilizing guest history software to anticipate the needs of our repeat customers." Use a process similar to that used for creating the objectives. Once they've been selected, check that each of the final nine objectives support the vision and mission statements and the goals.
(30 minutes.)

13. Next, have participants work individually to create a central philosophy for the organization, an unshakeable uncompromising credo and unwavering commitment to something besides making money.
(15 minutes.)

14. Once this is done, break the participants into small groups of three to four members each.

15. Ask them to share and discuss within their groups their ideas about organizational philosophy. Tell them that they will have thirty minutes to discuss and then to summarize their discussions and prepare to present them to the entire group.
(30 minutes.)

16. Move around the room to be sure that all groups are making progress. Let groups know when there are ten minutes left to ensure that they make time to prepare to present their ideas.

17. After thirty minutes, call time and ask one of the small groups to post their respective collective philosophy on the board and to present it to the whole group. Continue this rotation of quick presentations until every group has presented.
    (20 to 50 minutes, depending on number of groups.)

18. Point out similarities and differences among their answers throughout the presentations. Note them on the flip chart or whiteboard. Work with the groups to synthesize all the organizational philosophies.
    (20 minutes.)

19. When finished, pose the following questions for group discussion:

    - What have you learned today about the practice and process of articulating organizational statements?
    - If you were the consultant charged with helping an organization come up with the declarative statements that you created today, how would you go about it? What would you recommend?
    - What have you learned from this activity that has broader applications to your role as a manager?

    (15 minutes.)

20. Conclude the session by reiterating the importance of *shared* visions, missions, and decision making.
    (5 minutes.)

Variations

- Breakout groups could be formed earlier, instead of waiting until the philosophy segment.
- If you have limited time, stop after the organizational objectives portion is completed and debrief.
- If you have more than the allotted time, have all the participants start by writing their own personal vision/mission statements.
- You can add iterations for *statement of core values, guiding principles, code of ethics*, and so forth.

Submitted by George Alexakis and dedicated to the memory of Dr. Gerry Work ("The Rev").

George Alexakis, Ed.D., *has been a full-time business and hospitality management professor for universities in the state of Florida since 1995. He has taught for public and private institutions, published articles on pedagogical methods, received a teaching award, and coined the term "anthrogogy" (to replace the outdated gender-specific term "andragogy"). He also conducts professional training seminars in the areas of training and development, interpersonal communication, HRD, and executive education for leaders from a host of organizations throughout the world.*

Introduction

to the Assessment Section

Management development professionals use many different assessments in their work. It is commonly known that it is difficult to know yourself unless you have appropriate tools.

Assessments are exactly that—appropriate tools. They help managers better understand themselves. This gives management developers an opportunity not just to determine strengths, but also to identify areas for improvement. While use with an individual manager one-on-one is one way to use an assessment in learning, an assessment could also be used with a group of managers in a learning event.

The 2009 Pfeiffer Annual: Management Development includes one inventory from the following category:

Communication

Communication Style: An Important Factor for Successful Communication, by Ronald C. Fetzer

Communication Style

An Important Factor for Successful Communication

Ronald C. Fetzer

Summary

A leader's communication style choices have a direct impact on outcomes, whether explaining work procedures, performance coaching, providing on-the-job skill development, clarifying or questioning procedures, or offering or asking for constructive feedback. With the recent emphasis on development and retention of human talent in organizations, workplace communication has become more important than ever. Thus, this inventory is intended to help leaders identify their communication style (COM Style) preferences, whether with peers, superiors, or subordinates.

Attention to communication style (COM Style) on the job can make the difference between success and failure and contributes to a positive environment. Robert Norton (1983) defines COM Style as the way in which one verbally, nonverbally, and paraverbally interacts to signal how literal meaning should be taken, interpreted, filtered, or understood. He argued that the way a person communicates indicates how he or she thinks about him- or herself and also affects how others perceive him or her. Norton believed that certain patterns recur with individuals who have regular exchanges, as people learn to associate these patterns with one another. In short, because leaders use communication patterns in the workplace, their employees consciously or unconsciously react and respond to those patterns—COM Styles.

Gayle and Preiss (2002) describe these patterns as impression leaving, being contentious or challenging during a disagreement, being revealing, or opening up to share feelings. Either party displays behaviors that reflect being dominate by taking charge, being dramatic by telling stories, or being very precise with documented evidence. They can appear to be relaxed, friendly, encouraging, attentive, or

The 2009 Pfeiffer Annual: Management Development.

animated. Supervisors also use positive and expressive humor when engaging with employees. Cardello, Ray, and Pettey (1995) describe how patient satisfaction correlates positively with physicians' COM Style.

COM Style varies depending on the context. However, over a period of time, we notice that certain behaviors and personality traits are present. These frequently repeated traits and behaviors constitute our COM Style profile. We come to rely on the traits and behaviors that we have observed in others, giving little thought to *how* they say *what* they communicate. With better results, leaders can understand *how* to control their styles and be more flexible when interacting with employees.

There is no one best style for leaders to use in the workplace, although any of the four COM Styles could be ineffective at a given moment. Each style has its strengths and its weaknesses in the workplace, where there is constant interaction among individuals. The challenge to communicate effectively in the 21st Century workplace is very real. Because of all the technology advances, the need for effective and efficient communication has sharply increased, not decreased.

Leaders must understand and recognize their current style preferences and adapt them for use in various workplace situations. No COM style is a rigid structure, but rather each represents a continuum of assertiveness and responsiveness factors.

When Training staff consider COM Style, the CEO's preferred communication style is often most obviously linked to the organization's climate or culture and may be the focus of an intervention. But training all employees about COM Styles can reduce the stress level in the workplace and improve relationships among employees. Leaders who are conscientious about their own COM Styles will be able to lead their employees more effectively and efficiently. Leaders must serve as role models, supporting and coaching others to pay attention to the COM Styles of those with whom they work.

Communication style is often examined from two perspectives: (1) an interpersonal perspective, to explain how open or closed one is when speaking with others and (2) an assertiveness perspective, to show how one reacts to an immediate situation. In an effect to identify COM Style, Paul Mok (1991), Robert Norton (1983), and James McCroskey (1984) found that:

1. Individual differences exist, and these differences are important to each individual.
2. Individual COM Style differences tend to be stable when observed over time.
3. A single style tends to be preferred by each person, which over time is also observable to others.
4. People make judgments about others' COM Style preferences based on their own COM Style preferences.

The ability to understand, observe, and manage COM Style is a powerful way to positively influence others. Leaders can quickly benefit from using these techniques. Using the appropriate communication style is critical.

Much of the COM Style literature is based on the work of psychologist Carl Jung, who said there are four basic personality styles: Thinkers, Feelers, Sensers, and Intuitors. His MBTI Profiler was developed to assess personality style. Numerous profile instruments have been developed to identify style preferences for listening, learning, leading, managing conflict, teaching, training, socializing, working in teams, and managing change.

This article presents a Communication Style Identifier for use in a general leadership development program. This instrument, generated from many different instruments and based on the research mentioned earlier, is yet another effort to develop leaders for today's workplace.

The instrument is designed for use in a leadership development program. Table 1 provides a suggested training design plan, including training objectives, enrollment guidelines, and a description of the module, which can be used for either a half-day or full-day training session.

Administration of the COM Style Identifier

It is best to begin the workshop by reviewing the training objectives and then immediately, without any discussion of communication style, to administer the instrument. Give everyone a copy of the instrument and a pen or pencil. Read the directions as a

Table 1. Leadership Training Module

Time Frame	4 hours
Training Objectives	By the end of this session, participants will be able to (1) tabulate their COM Style scores, (2) identify their COM Style preferences, (3) interpret their score results; (4) improve their workplace communication skills when engaging with other employees; and (5) coach their direct reports on specific techniques for modifying their communication styles
Participants	8 to 12 for half a day; 16 to 20 for a full 8-hour day
Description	This module uses the **Communication Style Identifier**, a one-page instrument to help leaders recognize their preferred learning style: **Supportive, Reflective, Directive,** or **Emotive.** Using a four-quadrant grid to identify their style preference, participants determine the frequency of use of their preferred styles and learn how to recognize the preferred communication styles of others. Participants discover how to select a complementary COM Style as a technique to engage in more meaningful communication with others and how to use the communication style flexing technique.

group and check for any questions. Allow fifteen to twenty minutes for completing the instrument. While participants are working, be available to answer questions.

When everyone has finished, hand out the Scoring Sheet and have participants follow the instructions for plotting their scores on the Assertive axis (horizontal) and the Responsiveness axis (vertical). Then have them transfer their numbers to the Scoring Grid, which shows each individual's COM Style preference. Remind participants to check their math and plotting procedure carefully to ensure there are no errors.

At this point, the group is ready to learn about the specifics of COM Style, so hand out the Defining Communication Styles sheet and give everyone fifteen or twenty minutes to read it. Ask for questions and clarify as necessary. Then have participants break into small groups to discuss the implications of their own scores, based on what they have read. After discussion has slowed, bring the group together and lead a general discussion of the implications of COM Style in their organization. Post major points on a flip chart.

If, during the discussion, any leader clearly believes that his or her results do not present an accurate depiction of his or her COM Style, have the person review his or her rating responses, the sum calculations, and the mean score reached for the Assertiveness and Responsiveness columns. When individuals truly believe the style reflected on the gird is *totally unlike them,* it is prudent to take the time to recalculate and check the placement of the plot points for both Assertiveness and Responsiveness data.

When the Communication Style Identifier appears to describe the person accurately and the plot point is in the *Excessive* Zone for any of the four styles, then it is also beneficial to discuss how that leader might deliberately modify his or her current style and shift from the *Excessive* Zone into the *Flexive* Zone of that style. Such flexing can appear extremely difficult. Flexing is not the same as completely changing to a different COM Style, but it does start the process. Flexing does not take immense effort, nor call undue attention to what the leader is attempting to do. The results the leader gets tend to be better, and workplace stress tends to be reduced. Communication in the workplace becomes more efficient, and less time is taken to obtain desired results. Point out to the participants that a change in style can result in less work for them in the long run.

Leaders often find employees who have COM Styles in the Excessive Zone. Point out that they can use what they are learning to help their employees transition into their respective *Flexive* Zones. Table 2 shows some typical excessive behaviors and traits found in the COM Styles. Post these and discuss with the leaders simple tactics they can use if an employee is exhibiting excessive behaviors. Explain that the suggestions do not involve disciplinary actions, but are simply descriptive statements they can make or questions they can ask that naturally encourage shifting

Table 2. Excessive Behaviors and Traits Found in COM Styles

Preferred COM Style	Common Behaviors and Traits	Leader's Complementary Style
1. Excess Supportive	**1a.** Attempt to gain approval by agreeing with everyone; **1b.** Constantly seek reassurance; **1c.** Refuse to take a strong stand; **1d.** Tend to apologize a great deal	Leaders can assume a more ***Directive Style*** by saying things like: **1a.** "Your take on the issue of real interest to me." **1b.** "You are making a very good point." **1c.** "I would be interested in your take on this issue." **1d.** "No apology is called for. You are entitled to your opinion."
2. Excess Reflective	**2a.** Tend to avoid making decisions; **2b.** Seem overly interested in details; **2c.** Are very stiff and formal in dealing with others; **2d.** Avoid displaying emotion	Leaders can assume a more ***Emotive Style*** by saying things like: **2a.**"We have reached a point at which it is time to decide." **2b.**"These details are distracting us from our objective." **2c.** "We can speak candidly since we share a common need." **2d.** "We need to put our feeling about this issue on the table."
3. Excess Directive	**3a.** Are determined to come out on top; **3b.** Will not admit to being wrong; **3c.** Tend to be cold and unfeeling with others; **3d.** Use phrases such as "always," "never," or "we can't'	Leaders can assume a more ***Supportive Style*** by saying things like: **3a.** "Are we more determined to win or to find the best solution?" **3b.** "Is there some middle-of-the-road approach to consider?" **3c.** "Would it help to put us in this situation?" **3d.** "What might be the outcome if we could do it?"
4. Excess Emotive	**4a.** Tend to express highly emotional opinions; **4b.** Are outspoken to the point of being offensive; **4c.** Seem unwilling to listen to views of others; **4d.** Use exaggerated gestures and facial expressions	Leaders can assume a more ***Reflective Style*** by saying things like: **4a.** "What might cause any of us to feel like that?" **4b.** "What good does it do to point fingers?" **4c.** "Should we listen to all views before deciding?" **4d.** "What good can come from over-dramatizing this situation?"

from the *Excessive* to the *Flexive* Zone. Brainstorm for other ideas for handling excessive behaviors back on the job.

Tell participants that if they want to check on their own progress at COM Style flexing, it may be worthwhile for them to take a few minutes to re-take the Communication Style Identifier in the future. It is interesting to note when a preferred COM Style has moved from the *Excessive* to the *Flexive* Zone, or the *Flexive* to the *Routine* Zone. Explain that using this system not only will make them aware of their own COM Style preferences, but will also help them to become sensitive to the style preferences of peers. Routine flexing is a great way to communicate with peers as well as subordinates in the workplace.

Say that, over time, co-workers, customers, supervisors, suppliers, and others with whom they have frequent work-related communication may also notice some changes. They may also find the ideas helpful in their interpersonal relationships. Other job-related stressors may start to diminish as they feel more confident with their routine communication.

Suggest that they seek out peer mentors to coach them in changing their styles. A good source for such a mentor is another participant, so urge them to make arrangements to mentor one another before the training session ends. In time, it becomes routine to observe how other employees communicate in the workplace. It is especially a good practice for leaders to observe the COM Style tactics of other employees whom they respect for their communication ability.

Style Flexing also involves specific tactics to use when communicating with others with each specific COM Style. Some of these tactics are shown in Table 3. Lead a discussion around these and brainstorm some more ideas.

Style flexing can support a positive communication climate within an organization. When there is a positive communication climate, employees are more trusting and supportive of one another. This can result in better performance output, and promotes an environment for new learning and the ability to deal with change that is so prevalent in the workplace today.

Leaders who have been trained in COM Style flexing may discover that it is worthwhile to train and coach their employees—and even long-time customers and suppliers—about COM Style and style flexing.

Recommend that participants use the Communication Style Identifier with their subordinates as jumping off point for discussion. They will be able to use the information to improve the overall communication climate within their work units or in project groups. Plotting the COM Styles of all employees in a department onto a single grid will provide them with valuable insight. Over time, employees' awareness of one another's preferred communication styles will result in more effective and efficient work groups.

Table 3. Flexive Strategies for Use When Complementing a Specific COM Style

Employee COM Style Displayed	Leader Flexing Strategy or Behavior
Supportive	Show sincere interest in the person by taking the time to identify the areas of common interest.
	Patiently draw out the person's values and goals by listening and being responsive to his or her needs.
	Present your own view in a quiet, non-threatening manner by not being pushy verbally or non-verbally.
Reflective	Appeal to the other's orderly systematic approach by being organized when speaking and in presenting the content.
	Approach the other person in a direct manner by beginning with the purpose for the dialogue.
	Be as accurate and realistic as possible when presenting information.
Directive	Be specific, brief, and to the point for efficient use of time.
	Present facts logically and be prepared to respond to specific questions.
	If you must disagree, focus on the facts, and not on personality issues or traits.
Emotive	Take time to build social as well as business relationships by allowing time for relating and socializing.
	Display interest in the other person's ideas, interests, and experiences.
	Do not place too much emphasis on details. Keep things fast-paced, with inspirational, motivational comments.

Remind participants that they have the ability, in their leadership roles, to coach, train, and support their employees. The simple ability to use COM Style flexing to communicate can have great benefits for everyone.

When leaders use their *preferred* COM Styles in the *Excessive Zone*, it is often an unconscious habit. They may have an immediate defensive reaction if the COM Style Identifier results suggest that they use their preferred styles in the *Excessive* Zone. However, you can help them engage in some peer group dialogue about typical communication exchanges on the job, unnoticed habits, hidden routines, and unexplainable patterns that become apparent. In most cases, leaders will begin to recognize some of their own excess behaviors and share them within the small groups, where they will hear suggestions for change.

At this point, it may be beneficial for you to lead a discussion about the communication climate of their workplace. Frequently, a workplace climate has some sort of effect on preferred COM Styles. The level of openness and trust among employees may be somewhat negative. Some or possibly many of the employees may feel reticence to speak too openly or use too much candor with their bosses, or possibly have these same feelings when talking about work with their own peers.

Be sure to wrap up the session with some suggestions for change back on the job, creating action plans and assigning "buddies" to help them change their workplace behavior. As we said earlier, it is a good idea to administer the Communication Style Identifier at a later time to check on progress in learning to flex style.

References

Cardello, L.L., Ray, E.B., & Pettey, G.E. (1995). The relationship of perceived physician communicator style to patient satisfaction. *Communication Reports, 8*, 27–37.

Gayle, B., & Preiss, R. (2002). An overview of individual processes. In M. Allen, R. Preiss, B. Gayle, & N. Burrell (Eds.), *Interpersonal communication: Interpersonal communication research*. Mahwah, NJ: Lawrence Erlbaum Associates.

Jensen, D. (2000). *Communication styles*. Sedona, AZ: Search Masters International.

Jung, C. (1974). *Psychological types*. San Diego, CA: Harcourt, Brace.

Margerison, C. (1978). *If only I had said: Conversational controls for managers*. Rochester, NY: Mercury Book Division.

McCroskey, J.C. (1984). Communication competence: The elusive construct. In R.N. Bostrom (Ed.), *Competence in communication* (pp. 259–268. Thousand Oaks, CA: Sage.

Mok, P. (1991). *Communication style basics* (pp. 1–8.) Richardson, TX: Training Associates Press.

Norton, R. (1983). *Communicator style: Theory, applications, and measures*. Thousand Oaks, CA: Sage.

Norton, R.W. (1978). Foundation of communicator style construct. *Human Communication Research, 4*, 99–112.

Parks, M.R. (1994). Communicative competence and interpersonal control. In M.L. Knapp & G.R. Miller (Eds.), *Handbook of interpersonal communication*(2nd ed.) (pp. 589–620. Thousand Oaks, CA: Sage.

Sullivan, M. (2008). *How your communication style speaks to remote colleagues*. www.careers.wsj.com/columnists/perspective/20001021 2fmp.html.

Ronald C. Fetzer, Ph.D., *is retired emeritus faculty in the communication department at Wright State University in Dayton, Ohio. He is currently a visiting professor, department of communication, at Miami University in Oxford, Ohio. Additionally, he has operated his own HRD consulting practice for over thirty-five years, working with clients throughout the United States and internationally.*

Communication Style Identifier

Ronald C. Fetzer

Instructions: Consider each of the paired terms in Column 1, Assertive Scales, and Column 2, Social Responsiveness Scales. Think about how you speak, listen, write, and react to others in your workplace interactions. Based on what you know about your own verbal and nonverbal communication behavior, circle the number nearest the word in each pair that best describes you when talking with others at work. Separately total Columns 1 and 2. Then divide each by 14 to get your mean score for each column.

Column 1: Assertive "Take Charge" Description Scales

Cooperative	1 2 3 4 5	Competitive
Submissive	1 2 3 4 5	Authoritative
Accommodating	1 2 3 4 5	Domineering
Hesitant	1 2 3 4 5	Decisive
Reserved	1 2 3 4 5	Outgoing
Compromising	1 2 3 4 5	Insistent
Cautious	1 2 3 4 5	Risk Taking
Patient	1 2 3 4 5	Hurried
Complacent	1 2 3 4 5	Influential
Quiet	1 2 3 4 5	Talkative
Shy	1 2 3 4 5	Bold
Supportive	1 2 3 4 5	Demanding
Relaxed	1 2 3 4 5	Tense
Non-assertive	1 2 3 4 5	Assertive

Total ASSERTIVE Score

MEAN Score [Divide by 14]

Column 1 Final Score

Column 2: Social Responsiveness Description Scales

Precise	1 2 3 4 5	Flexible
Controlled	1 2 3 4 5	Expressive
Serious	1 2 3 4 5	Lighthearted
Methodical	1 2 3 4 5	Unstructured
Guarded	1 2 3 4 5	Open
Calculating	1 2 3 4 5	Spontaneous
Introverted	1 2 3 4 5	Extroverted
Aloof	1 2 3 4 5	Friendly
Formal	1 2 3 4 5	Casual
Reserved	1 2 3 4 5	Attention Seeking
Cautious	1 2 3 4 5	Carefree
Conforming	1 2 3 4 5	Unconventional
Reticent	1 2 3 4 5	Dramatic
Restrained	1 2 3 4 5	Impulsive

Total RESPONSIVE Score

MEAN Score [Divide by 14]

Column 2 Final Score

Communication Style Identifier: Scoring Sheet

Instructions: Based on your mean score from the bottom of the Assertive column of your Communication Style Identifier, locate a point on the horizontal axis and mark it. Do the same with your mean score for Social Responsiveness and mark a point on the vertical axis. To determine your preferred style, draw a straight line along the axis (a horizontal line for assertive and vertical for responsiveness) from each point. The intersection of these two lines is your **plot-point** and should be within a quadrant within one of the four communication styles: **Supportive, Reflective, Directive,** or **Emotive.**

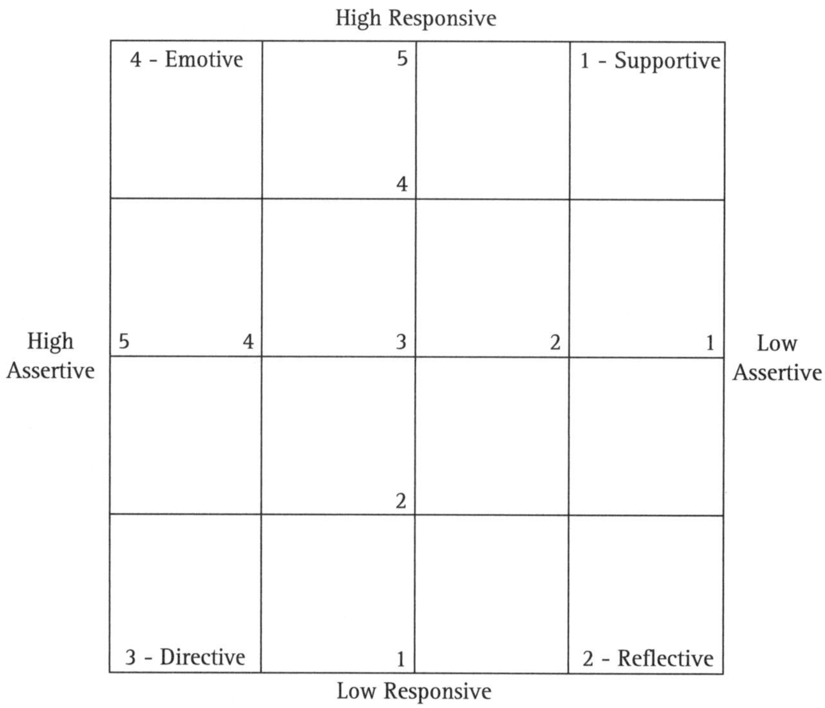

Communication Style Identifier: Scoring Grid

Instructions: Place your third plot point on the Zone Grid below, which indicates the intensity of your style preference. Pinpointing a specific location within a preferred quadrant shows just how strong our COM Style preference is. This zone location may also indicate our comfort level with using a style and may indicate our frequency for employing a style when interacting with others.

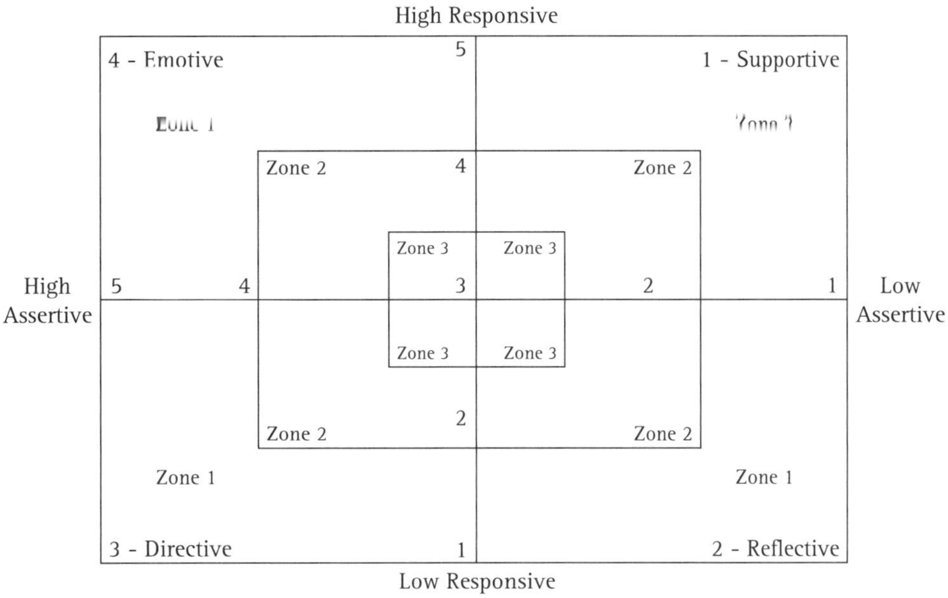

My preferred COM Style is

- ☐ Supportive ☐ Reflective
- ☐ Directive ☐ Emotive

My preferred Zone Location is

- ☐ Routine (1) ☐ Excessive (3)
- ☐ Flexive (2)

Personal notes related to my preferred COM Style:

Communication Style Identifier: Defining Communication Style

Communication (COM) Style is defined as the patterns of behaviors that others can observe about us as we communicate with them. Each person has a preferred style. COM Style is viewed on two continua: assertiveness and responsiveness. These two dimensions of communication style are depicted in Figure 1.

When each factor is viewed on a continuum of low to high, four distinct COM Styles are generated, as shown in Figure 2.

Each style is defined by a unique combination of high or low preference for both Assertiveness and Responsiveness factors. A combination of these two factors generates four very different and unique styles, titled Supportive, Reflective, Directive, and Emotive. In order to understand what make each style unique, it is important to more closely examine the two factors of Assertiveness and Responsiveness.

Assertiveness

Simply put, assertiveness is a take-charge attitude individuals may choose to use when communicating with others in the workplace. Some people speak out easily, not holding back. Others, by contrast, are less verbal, holding back to hear what the other person has to say first. This tendency is based on habit as much as on personality.

Assertiveness can be viewed on a continuum, with the *low end* characterized by people who tend to be cooperative and eager to listen to others. These people may

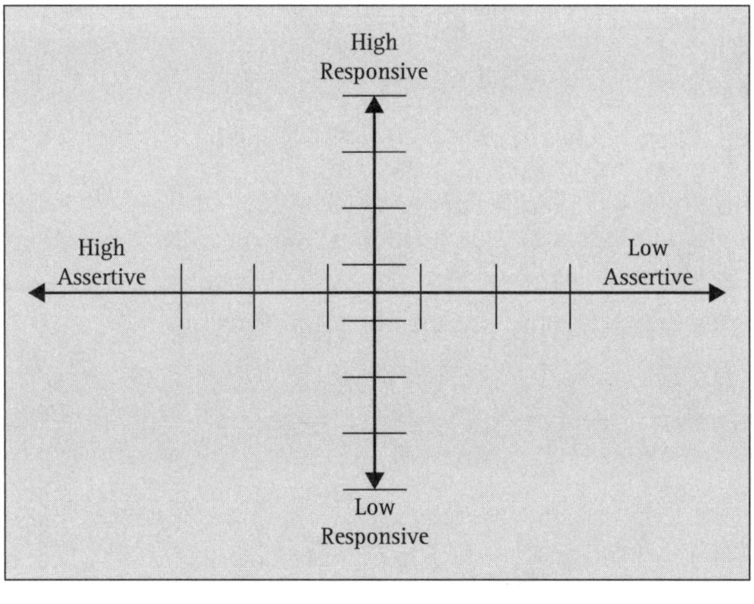

Figure 1. Component Factors of COM Style

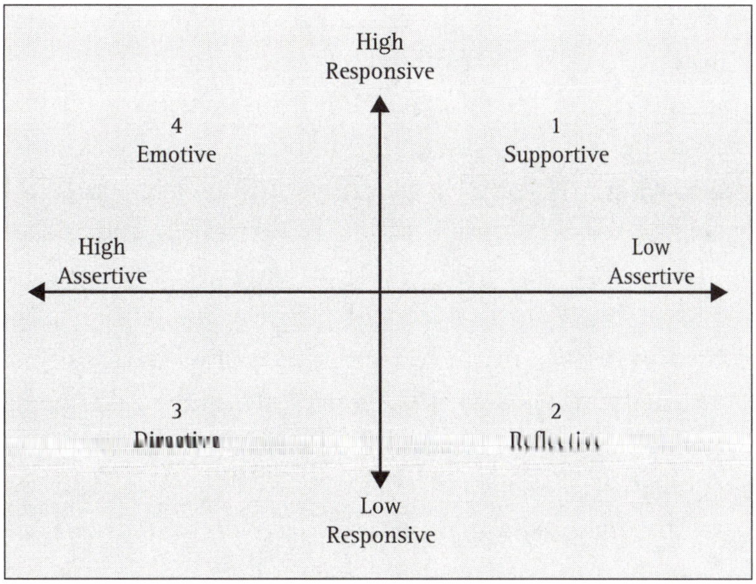

Figure 2. The Four COM Styles

be more easily controlled or more willing to be influenced by other people when involved in a communication exchange.

On the *high end* of the Assertiveness scale, people give opinions more freely and frequently initiate demands. They take more control of the communication interaction and may have greater influence on the outcome or intended objective of the exchange.

According to Norton (1983), males are more *status assertive,* meaning that they use greater effort to enhance their social standing through their relationships. On the other hand, women are more *status neutralizing,* meaning that they use assertiveness to reduce the difference of social rank when interacting with others.

Responsiveness

Responsiveness is defined as the tendency to seek out and enjoy social interaction with others. It is a measure of how people control or freely express their feelings and thoughts as they reach out to others. Norton (1983) defines this responsiveness as knowing when not to say too much, or possibly not to say anything. At times, the *response of silence* may be as important as knowing just *what* to say in a given situation. Responsiveness can also be observed on a measured continuum scale of low to high. Gayle and Preiss (2002) found that the responsiveness dimension of communication style relates to the attractiveness of a task, the importance of non-confrontation, or the perceived need for resolution. Charles Magerison (1978) defines responsiveness as knowing when to speak and when to listen when engaged in dialogue with another person.

At the *low end,* people are characterized as being reserved and more formal in social interaction exchanges. According to Margerison (1978), the lower end is considered an indicator of an individual's desire to respond to criticism, to get information quickly, to be convincing whether handling objectives or making proposals, to quickly assess where the other person is coming from, and to use communication exchanges as a way of solving problems and developing social relationships.

At the *high end* of the responsive scale, people are more talkative, exhibit more sociability traits, and seek more personal associations, which allow them to interact more freely with others. Again Margerison (1978) defines this as the ability to manage conflict, negotiate well, listen reflectively, and actively encourage the other person to plan and implement ideas and suggestions.

As people begin to examine themselves on both the Assertiveness and Responsiveness dimensions, they quickly discover that they have preferences on both scales when communicating in the workplace. These sets of preferences form the basis of an individual's preferred COM Style, as shown in Figure 2.

Each of the four COM Styles represent a combination of either a high or low position on each of the Assertiveness and Responsiveness scales. The unique combination of high or low position on each scale defines each learning style. The styles can be described briefly as shown below.

Assertiveness and Responsiveness Factors Define Style

Style Type	Factor Combination Mix
1. Supportive	HIGH Responsive and LOW Assertive
2. Reflective	LOW Assertive and LOW Responsive
3. Directive	LOW Responsive and HIGH Assertive
4. Emotive	HIGH Assertive and HIGH Responsive

Figure 3 presents each style, listing some of the verbal, nonverbal, and paraverbal traits that communication style researchers describe (Gayle & Preiss, 2002; Mok & Paul, 1991; Norton, 1983).

Even though individuals have preferred COM Styles, they have to be willing to adapt to and communicate with those using the other three styles. For workplace leaders, the ability to recognize the styles of other workers is very beneficial.

For example, an emotive leader and an equally emotive employee would have a serious challenge in the context of a performance review if neither was willing to modify his or her COM Style. Since both would be asserting their right to speak, rather than making a conscious effort to be responsive to the other, the outcome

High Responsiveness

High Assertiveness		Low Assertiveness
4. EMOTIVE Style *(Cheerleader)* • High energy display and movement • Informal, personal, first-name basis • Naturally persuasive, dramatic, forceful • Fast speaking rate, gestures; few pauses	**1. SUPPORTIVE Style** *(Therapist)* • Animated listener with head nodding • Displays feelings in voice, face, posture • Deliberate, thoughtful pauses with direct eye contact to encourage and focus	
3. DIRECTIVE Style *(Supervisor)* • Projects no-nonsense, business attitude • Shares distinct opinions; dominant posturing • Powerful volume, gestures, facial expression • Limited displays of feelings and emotions	**2. REFLECTIVE Style** *(Philosopher)* • Passive listener with few mannerisms • Appears in deep thought; may seem sullen, limits speaking • Orderly, attentive to cognitive details • Limited gestures, facial expression, eye contact	

Low Responsiveness

Figure 3. Descriptions of the Four COM Styles

might be less than desirable. If at least one person is more attuned to the dynamics of COM Style and willing to do some style flexing, the outcomes are usually better.

Leaders should know their own preferred styles and also become savvy at identifying the styles of others. By doing so, leaders will have more effective (mutually satisfying) and more efficient (better use of time) communication. For example, in a job coaching situation, an effective leader, by switching from an emotive (highly charged speaking) style to a reflective (passive listening behavior) style, can encourage the employee to ask questions. Then the leader can give specific and immediate support. Furthermore, the communication exchange will save both leader and employee time and be more effective.

After such an exchange, the leader can alter his or her COM Styles, reverting back to directive style.

It might be helpful to view a situation from each of the four style perspectives. For example, a supervisor walking through his department stops by the office cubicle of a worker, remembering that he has some questions to ask this employee concerning an upcoming work project. However, at the moment, the employee is busy working on a project that is due the next day. The supervisor stops at the employee's desk and says that he would like to talk for a few minutes about the upcoming project. The employee, depending on his COM Style preference, may respond as follows:

- As a *Directive,* the employee might respond by stating that this is not a good time to talk because of his work on his current project.
- As an *Emotive,* the employee might stop work on the current project and launch into a dramatic question, "I am reeealy working in a crisis mode trying to finish this current project that is due TOMORROW morning!"
- As a *Reflective,* the employee might pause and then suggest there might be a better time the two could talk about the new project, adding quietly, "I am sure you already know my deadline is tomorrow morning on this job."
- And finally, as a *Supportive,* the employee might stop working, use direct eye contact, and say, "I know you are busy with a lot of work on your plate, and as you know, I need to wrap up this project today because it is due first thing in the morning. However, I would be more than happy to stop by your office to talk about our new project as soon as I turn in this one."

It is sometimes helpful to see the COM Styles in the context of specific people, which can make it easier to understand the differences among the four styles. Another method to remember them is to apply them to well-known public figures. Table 2 shows how some famous personalities align with the four COM Styles.

Comedic couples such as George Burns and Gracie Allen, Lucille Ball and Desi Arnaz, Bud Abbot and Lou Costello, or the Smothers Brothers are examples of actors who assume specific COM Styles with their partners to create humorous situations while communicating neither effectively nor efficiently. The Abbot and Costello scenario of "Who's on First!" is a classic use of COM Styles gone berserk.

The preference for a specific COM Style also operates within what is referred to as a Style Zone. Each style can be placed in one of three different zones, described as follows.

Table 2. COM Style Preferences of Public Personalities

Style 4. Emotive	**Style 1. Supportive**
Bill Cosby, Carol Burnett, Dinah Shore, Oprah Winfrey	Perry Como, Paul Simon, John Denver, Joyce Brothers
Style 3. Directive	**Style 2. Reflective**
Barbara Walters, Lee Iacocca, Sam Donaldson, Mike Wallace	Albert Einstein, Eric Sevareid, Jimmy Carter, Ghandi

Zone Patterns Within the COM Style Grid

Figure 4 displays the three zones for each of the four COM Styles: the Routine, Flexive, and Excessive. Note that each COM Style has its own area in each of the three zones.

The *Excessive Zone* (3) for each style borders the outer edge of the grid, hence the term "excessive." Anyone, regardless of individual style preference, who falls in the *Excessive Zone*, is considered to be using a very habitual, readily observable, and predictable style. Such people show little style flexibility when working with other employees.

If a person's style appears in the *Flexive Zone* (2), it suggests a person's willingness to adjust or experiment with his or her COM Style when engaging in communication with others. This zone represents those who have an awareness and willingness to flex their styles in response to others. This is where evolutionary change can occur.

And finally, if a person's preference is within the *Routine Zone* (1), it suggests that he or she routinely and deliberately adjusts his or her COM Style when engaging in communication based on the other person's preference. Because unique features and behaviors are characteristic of each zone, it is important to examine them in more detail.

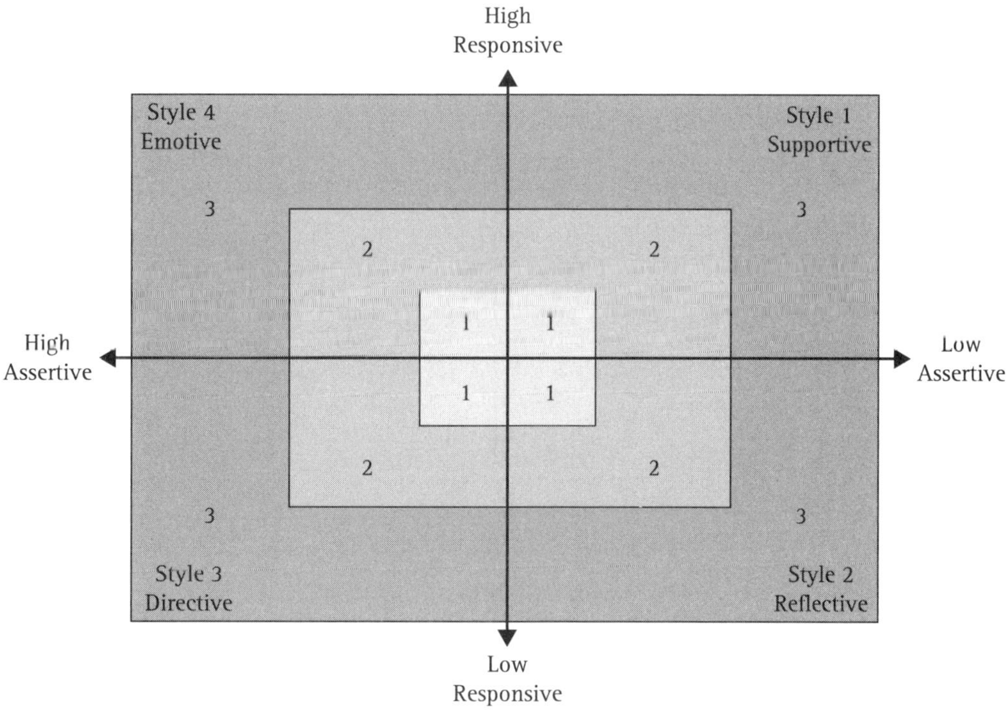

Figure 4. COM Style Zones

Routine Zone

Figure 5 shows the *ideal* zone for a leader's communication style to be in, because leaders are in a position to communicate with others often, and they should focus on their employees, using the employees' preferred COM Styles, if at all possible. By routinely flexing their styles appropriately for employees, leaders establish an open communication climate in their departments.

COM Style *Flexing* is the deliberate effort of one of the two parties engaging in a communication to, after recognizing the other individual's preferred COM Style, make a conscious effort to adjust his or her preferred COM Style in a complementary way.

Figure 6 is an example of when an employee displayed a *Directive Routine Style* (meaning he has high assertive traits paired with low responsive traits). The leader is in the complementary style zone as a *Supportive*. In short, the employee has something specific to tell his boss, and the boss, recognizing the employee's *Directive style*, assumes the *Supportive style* so that he listens without interrupting.

In short, when two styles are complementary, they foster efficient and effective communication. This type of diagonal posturing on the COM style grid is referred to as "flexing to assume a complementary position." By the leader adjusting his own assertiveness and responsiveness to the employee's, open communication is possible, trust is built, and a supportive climate is maintained.

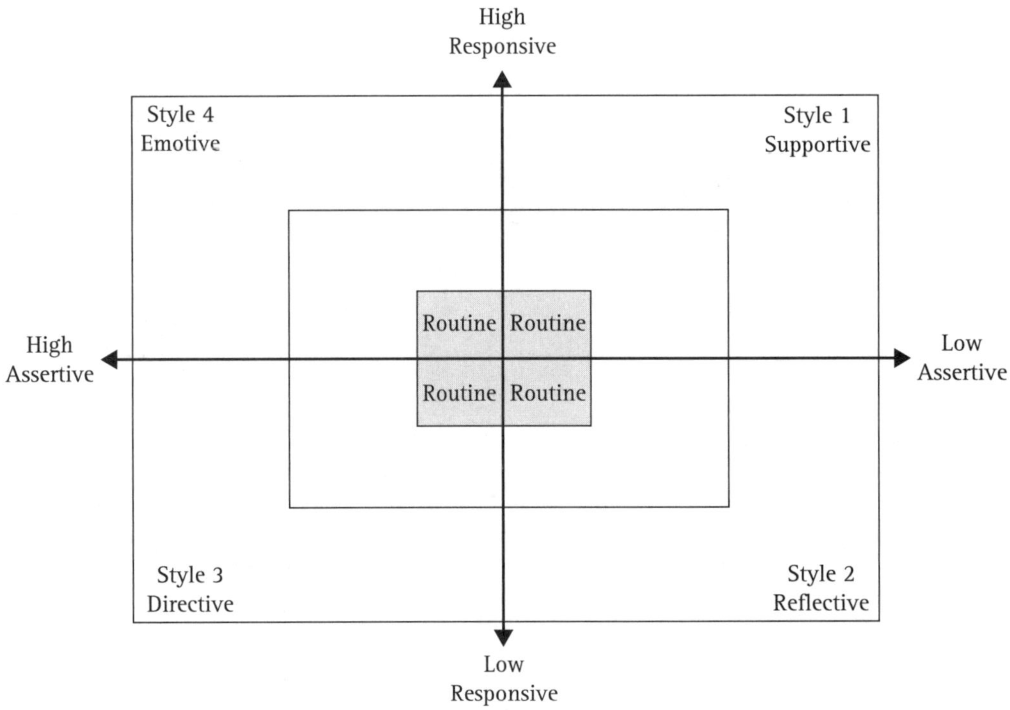

Figure 5. Routine Zone

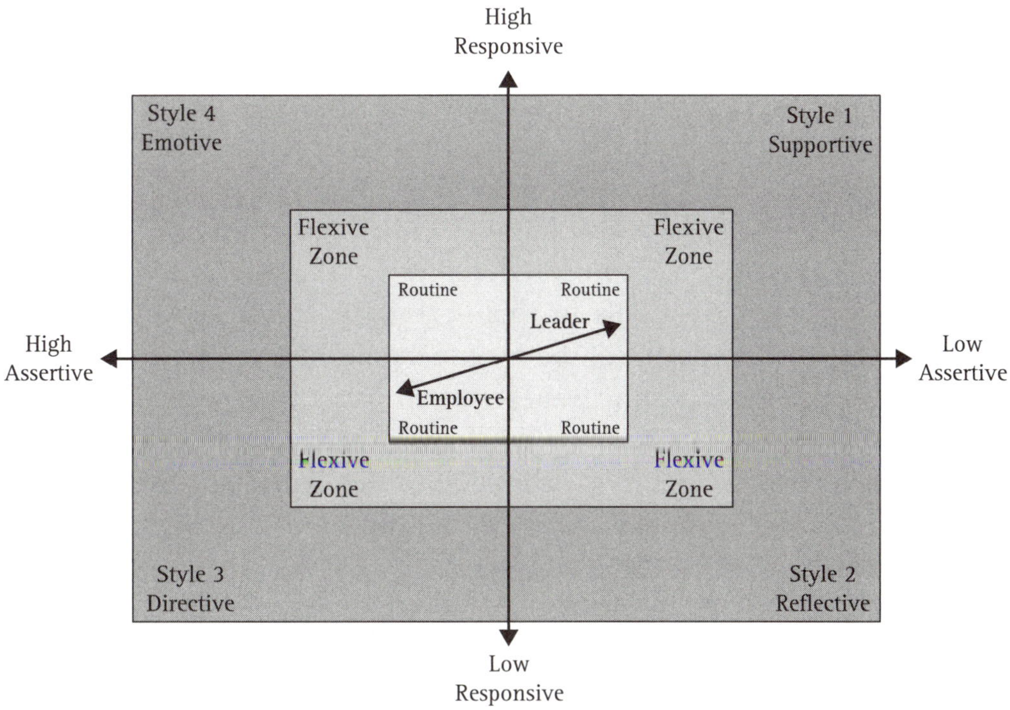

Figure 6. Flexive Posturing to Assume a Complementary Position

Over time, with open communication and deliberate style flexing, leaders can also help employees to adapt their personal style preferences. With practice, style flexing can be a very powerful strategy.

For example, if an employee is involved in a serious accident at work, the situation may call for a supervisor to transition quickly into an Emotive style in the Excess Zone as the supervisor talks the employee through a specific action.

Flexing to the *Emotive* style could also be useful when explaining a simple but important job task, or when explaining crucial information for an employee's safety when operating equipment. A dramatic and frequent example is the situation of a fireman talking a terrified victim into leaping from a second-story window of a burning building into the safety net because the victim is not able to think clearly in the situation.

When leaders can communicate easily in any of the four COM Styles, they can adjust to any situation and any other person's style. For example, if a supervisor's COM Style is Emotive and he uses it within the *Routine* Zone, an effort to flex to Directive, Reflective, or Supportive is not difficult. With awareness and practice, flexing becomes a habit, a routine way of communicating. The immediate benefits for both the leader and the employee are obvious: a better interpersonal relationship, less job stress, and both feeling better about their work performance. The long-term benefits, less obvious but equally important, are an open and trusting workplace climate in which employees enjoy their work, interact more effectively and efficiently with their peers, and develop a loyalty to their supervisors and to the organization.

Flexive Zone

Figure 7 shows the mid-range zone on the style grid that the four COM Styles share. When one's preferred style falls in this mid-range, he or she does not respond as seamlessly to the COM style of the other person. Leaders whose style preferences fall in this Flexive Zone instinctively resort to using their preferred COM Styles. However, with training and practice, they can learn how to flex their own styles to those of others. Sometimes this is referred to as the "learning curve phase" because leaders have to make a conscious effort to modify their COM Styles based on what they perceive to be the COM Styles of others.

However, either the leader or the employee can adapt his or her COM Style to ensure effective and efficient communication. Consider the COM Style grid's four distinct styles. If one person is communicating in the Emotive style, the other would contribute to the quality of the exchange by adjusting his or her communication to the Reflective style. From looking at Figure 7, it is clear that the Emotive and Reflective styles are complementary, being on a diagonal from one another on the grid.

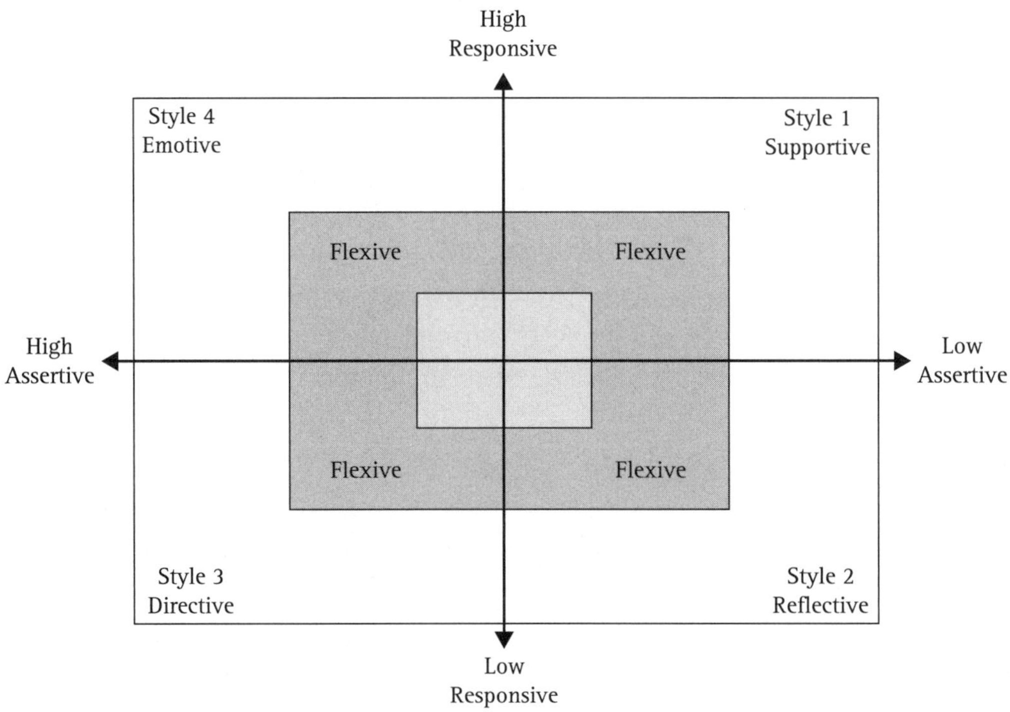

Figure 7. Flexive Zone Area

Being sensitive to the communication dynamics taking place, the leader, more often than not, can move within this flexive zone to assume a complementary positive more easily than the employee can. If neither the leader nor employee is aware of the COM Style preference of the other, communication will not stop or necessarily be totally a waste of time. But the leader may discover that it is necessary to repeat or restate what was shared. Communication results may take longer to come about under such circumstances.

However, if either the leader or the employee deliberately flexes to the complementary grid position, this has an effect on the communication behavior of the other. Such flexing can encourage turn-taking with speaking and better listening behaviors. Flexing also enhances openness and trust between leader and employee. Style flexing may not dramatically improve the communication climate, but it certainly will not contribute to a negative communication climate.

Leaders communicating in the *Flexive* Zone must work harder to communicate with employees than leaders accustomed to communicating in the *Routine* Zone. It takes more energy, attentiveness, and willingness to engage within the *Flexive* Zone. However, over time, it becomes routine, requiring less energy. The payoff is more effective and efficient communication in the workplace.

Excessive Zone

The Excessive Zone is the external area that borders the entire grid. This zone reflects the highest degree of intensity and rigidity for any of the four COM Styles. See Figure 8, which shows this zone as the peripheral edge. When a leader's COM Style preference plots in this area, it suggests that the style is more than preferred, it is rigid and the "routine" style. With this level of rigidity, flexing may be very challenging. A person whose style falls in the Excessive Zone not only feels very comfortable using his or her preferred style, but depends on it to the extent that, if forced to flex to another style, he or she may feel a loss of self-confidence. It takes a deliberate effort to shift from the *Excess* Zone, regardless of which style one prefers.

Leaders who routinely communicate in this Excessive Zone rarely go out of their way to compromise due to the strong bias they have for their own styles. They rely on the sense of self-confidence they feel when interacting with others.

Unlike leaders communicating in the *Routine* Zones, and also much more exaggerated than leaders engaging in the *Flexive* Zones, leaders communicating in the *Excess* Zones use extreme traits, such as long periods of silence or speaking nonstop with minimal active listening. If both the leader and the employee display COM Styles in this *Excessive* Zone, there will be awkward silence or much chaos with both talking at the same time—and neither one willing to listen to the other. Neither of these scenarios is effective or efficient in any workplace!

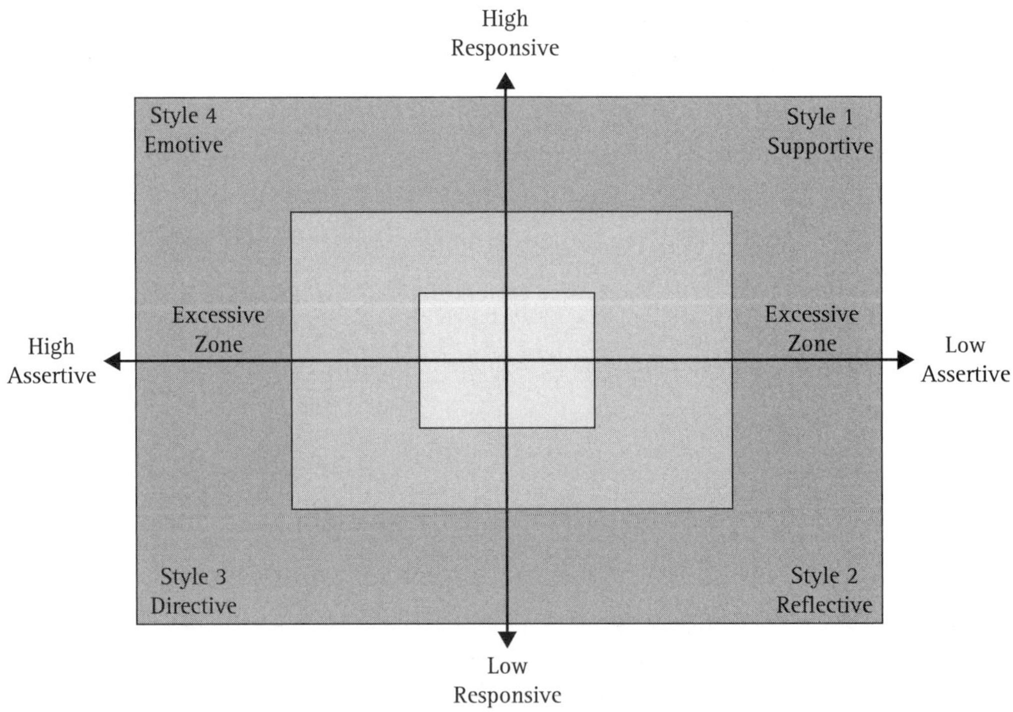

Figure 8. Excessive Zone

Communication between leaders and employees in the Excessive Zone is usually ineffective, highly time-consuming, and rarely produces positive outcomes. If both persons prefer *low* Responsiveness, superficial listening (*courtesy-based*) will take place, but not active listening. It is highly unlikely that useful feedback will be generated. Beyond the lack of communication, *low* responsiveness that is preferred by both individuals also results in poor productivity and reduced quality.

Some may argue that two individuals who are in complementary Excess Zone styles should still be able to achieve some productive communication exchanges. But even an *Emotive* leader and *Supportive* employee, if one is *Low* Assertive while the other is *High* Assertive, both could prefer *High* Responsive, with the intent to express strong personal opinions, while neither one is actively listening to the other. Such situations offer minimal satisfaction to either party because communication objectives are not achieved.

The Excess Zone, by its very nature, does not encourage any constructive exchange. Because they talk "at" one another, minimal positive outcomes result for either party. Because there is little or no productive exchange, such encounters are judged a waste of time and employee talent, not to mention the additional cost of poorly executed communication.

The open-ended comments written by employees who have taken employee surveys give a sense of the impact of poor use of COM Style. Comments such as "My boss never hears me" "We talked, but didn't get anything done today" "We just rehashed the same old ideas we talked about last week". "Talking with my boss was a waste of my time that I could have used to work at my desk" are common.

The cost of Excess Zone COM Style preferences is not always apparent or easy to calculate. Ignoring COM Style can be very detrimental to businesses, and the impact on job dissatisfaction and workplace-related stress is a real concern in the 21st Century.

References

Gayle, B., & Preiss, R. (2002). An overview of individual processes. In M. Allen, R. Preiss, B. Gayle, & N. Burrell (Eds.), *Interpersonal communication: Interpersonal communication research*. Mahwah, NJ: Lawrence Erlbaum Associates.

Margerison, C. (1978). *If only I had said: Conversational controls for managers*. Rochester, NY: Mercury Book Division.

Mok, P. (1991). *Communication style basics* (pp. 1–8.) Richardson, TX: Training Associates Press.

Norton, R. (1983). *Communicator style: Theory, applications, and measures*. Thousand Oaks, CA: Sage.

Introduction

to the Articles Section

The Articles section of this *Annual* offers the experience and expertise of numerous experts in the field of management development. All articles address considerations to make and/or actions to take when making an intervention to improve the individual, team, or organization. The information in each article can be used in many different ways, including serving as a basis for comparative analysis, as a stand-alone tool for application, as an opportunity for personal learning, or for sharing with senior executives to increase the credibility of proposed interventions.

In this section, we have brought together a diverse set of articles. Some address an intervention that is an aspect of things we may have thought about doing or have done. Others may be less familiar, that is aspects of management that the vast majority of us have not thought about or done anything about. However, it may be the opportunity to change our thinking.

This *Annual* has twelve articles arranged in the following categories:

Individual Development

Behavioral Based Interviewing: Avoiding Bias in the Employment Interview, by Sandra Torres

Becoming an Effective Networker, by Michaeline Skiba

Communication

A Six-Step Process for Implementing Mentoring Programs in Learning Organizations, by Arthur L. Jue

Leadership Coaching: The Developmental Power of the One-on-One, by Maggie W. Dunn

Problem Solving

What Happened to the Other 20 Percent? How Addressing the 20 Percent of Effects Left Aside by the Pareto Principle Can Increase Management Performance, by Alejandro Palacios

Why People with Disabilities Might Really Be Leaving Work: An Exemplar Case with Lessons for Managers, by Margaret H. Vickers

Provision of Outplacement Services During Redundancy: Lessons from Australian Executives, by Melissa A. Parris and Margaret H. Vickers

Affirmative Action: Tool for Diversity or Favoritism, by Sean T. Foley and Kristie J. Loescher

Consulting/Training

Leveraging Your Human Resources Partner: Leaders at All Levels Must Become Effective Talent Managers, by John E. DiBenedetto

Leadership

The Strategic Manager: Success Competencies for Managing Organizations in the New Economy, by Peter Vultaggio

Developing Leaders in the Federal Courts: The Federal Judicial Center's Leadership Development Program, by Michael Eric Siegel, with Anthony Teke Quickel

Expatriation and Repatriation: Different Directions, Similar HR Concerns, by Lincoln H. Marshall

Behavioral-Based Interviewing

Avoiding Bias in the Employment Interview

Sandra Torres

Summary

Hiring the best candidate can be a difficult task for managers. Many of us have spent countless hours poring through resumes, scheduling interviews, and meeting potential team members. These days you can receive hundreds of resumes in response to one ad for a single job opening. Just determining which candidates you want to interview out of the pool of resumes you receive is a time-consuming and difficult process.

To further complicate matters, we all have subconscious triggers that may influence our judgment and, ultimately, our final selection decision. As a result of bias we can over- or under-estimate a candidate's ability to perform based on non-job-related information. The good news is that learning and practicing a process that focuses on past experience and job-related factors can eliminate these deceptive influences and help every manager to make better hiring decisions.

This article will provide some examples of the kind of common bias that gets in the way during the selection process, thus helping readers to take the first step toward eliminating the potential for bias from the interview. It also discusses how you can be sure that you are measuring someone's ability to meet job competencies and getting to the valuable information you need so you can make great employment choices.

Dream Sequence

Manager Jane Doe (in her dream) is starting off her weekly staff meeting. Everyone is in attendance, on time, and has all the information that they need for the meeting neatly compiled in front of them. One by one, they report out and all of their work is done, perfectly and on time! Next, Jane raises an issue from the agenda that she suspects may create some conflict among the team. Amazingly, everyone agrees with her point of view and the meeting is promptly adjourned, five minutes ahead of schedule. It's been another day in Manager Paradise. Then the morning alarm sounds and Jane Doe wakes up to face another real-life workday.

And Now, Back to Reality

While Jane Doe's dream may seem like the perfect situation from a manager's perspective, it is not really reflective of how the world works and it is not the most effective scenario for a work team. No doubt, it is easy to manage a team consisting of like-minded individuals who always agree and never deal with internal conflict. But a homogenous work team is deficient. When everyone thinks alike, there are many perspectives that are never considered during project work, decision making, and strategic planning. It is much more challenging to manage a work team of individuals with diverse styles, ideas, and work processes. A well-rounded team makes better decisions and brings a wealth of resources to the table that may well be lacking in the homogenous team.

Like Me = Good; Not Like Me = Bad

As much as we all would like to believe that we don't make judgments about others and that we are open and accepting of differences, human nature causes us to be most comfortable around others who are similar to us. We often think of differences as being confined to the obvious categories of race and gender. But difference extends far beyond these areas into education, physical characteristics and ability, economic status, ethnicity and family culture, hobbies and interests, communication and personal style, and the list goes on. Some differences are physically obvious, while others are revealed through conversation, and still others become known to us only after we have developed a relationship with an individual. But one thing is for sure: the information we gather about others causes us to view them either positively or negatively. We measure others using our own yardsticks—against ourselves and our way of doing things. Because much of this "evaluation" of others occurs on a subconscious level, our judgments manifest themselves as "feelings" or intuitive assessments (also known as gut feelings). While these gut feelings are subjective, we experience them as objective judgments about a person's competency level. Often we judge others based on our own comfort level (or lack thereof) with an individual. This is how our hiring decisions are skewed by difference.

To illustrate how this works, let's assume that you are a hard-core New York Yankees fan. You are interviewing a candidate for a network consultant position on your information technology team and, to break the ice, you ask the candidate how he or she is doing. The candidate responds by saying, "I'm just great! I was at the ballgame last night and I truly enjoyed watching the Boston Red Sox pulverize the New York Yankees!"

I think we can all agree that this response might not be the wisest choice on the part of the candidate, but for discussion's sake, you now know that this candidate supports a ball club that is a notorious rival to your own personal favorite. Do you know a Yankees fan who would be tempted to end the interview right there and then? I do know someone like that.

Does this candidate's support of the Red Sox impact his or her ability to perform as a network consultant on an information technology team? The answer is no, it does not have an impact. We learn nothing about someone's skills or abilities as a network consultant by knowing which baseball team he or she likes. But this non-job-related information can conjure up an emotional response. This response might be negative or positive, depending on whether the candidate's preference supports or contradicts our own preference. While this may sound like an extreme example, hiring decisions are made every day based on information equally irrelevant to job skills and qualifications.

Here is another real-life interviewing example that someone once shared with me. A panel of male interviewers were interviewing a female candidate whom they considered to be very attractive ("hot" is the term they actually used). Throughout the course of the interview this candidate said, "I don't really have any experience in this area, since I haven't done this type of job in the past." After interviewing several more experienced candidates, the interview panel convened to make their final choice. Four out of the five people on the panel voted the "hot" candidate as their top pick for filling the position. The fifth interviewer didn't agree. He pulled out his extensive interview notes and was able to use solid, job-based data to convince the others that not only was she not the best candidate, but she was, in fact, the least qualified candidate. After hearing the evidence, the panel agreed and selected a different candidate. While the interview panel members may have enjoyed being around this particular female candidate, her appearance was not relevant to getting the job done. In fact, she admittedly had no experience to qualify her to do the job, yet four out of the five panel members were ready and willing to hire her over other, more qualified candidates.

These illustrations demonstrate how we are inadvertently influenced by emotional reactions. Subconscious judgments are more dangerous than the ones we make consciously because they cause us to make mistakes without realizing what we are doing.

Think back now to your own hiring experiences. Can you recall thinking that someone was absolutely great during the interview process, only to find out afterward that the candidate lacked the skills, discipline, or behaviors required to succeed in the job? If so, perhaps bias played a role in that decision.

How Much Does a Bad Hire Cost?

The U.S. Department of Labor estimates that a bad hire costs a company anywhere from 50 to 100 percent of the hire's annual salary, provided that the error is found and corrected within the first six months of employment. If the bad hire is not terminated within the first six months, the costs continue to escalate throughout the term of employment of the bad hire. Many elements contribute to the cost of making a bad hiring choice, such as recruitment costs; training costs; down time while the new hire is learning the job; costs in terms of lowered morale for existing staff; salary costs for recruiters, managers, and supervisors who do the interviewing and training; loss of customer satisfaction while the bad hire is in place; the cost of mistakes made by the bad hire; and so forth. Multiply these costs by the number of bad hires made per year in the average organization and you will see that bad hires are indeed very costly. Therefore, time spent learning how to make better hiring decisions will result in measurable bottom-line improvements.

Behavioral-Based Interviewing

One tried-and-true interview method that leads to better selection decisions is called Behavioral-Based Interviewing. This process involves asking predetermined, competency-based questions and evaluating candidates on their real-life, past experience, as opposed to using hypothetical questions or just having general conversation with a candidate to determine his or her fit for the job.

Determine Appropriate Job Competencies

The first step in making better selection decisions is to start with the job description for the open position. Decide which competencies are critical to successful performance in the job and prioritize them. While some competencies can be learned or developed on the job, others are required at the time of hire for success. Go into the interview with an awareness of which skills you need right now and which can be developed on the job. In most cases several people will interview candidates, so everyone who will be involved in the interview should have an understanding of the desired competencies and their priorities. Have all of this information clearly defined and communicated to all interviewers before starting the interview process.

Once you have selected and prioritized competencies, the next step will be to develop a few interview questions for each competency in order to learn whether and how the candidate has demonstrated the competency in the past.

Developing Experience-Based Questions

Very early in my career, I interviewed for a claims processing job with an insurance company. The interviewer asked, "If you could be anyone in history, who would you be and why?" What exactly was this interviewer looking for? I don't recall knowledge of history as a job requirement for that particular position.

Hiring managers have used a wide variety of ineffective methods for "getting into the psyche" of a job candidate. The question above is one such method, and another is to pose hypothetical questions. But the best way to determine how a candidate will respond to a given situation is to ask for an example of a time when he or she was faced with that situation. This is the underlying philosophy behind experience- (or behavioral-) based interviewing.

Assume that one of the competencies you've identified as a requirement for success in a given position is the ability to effectively handle stress. A traditional question to ask might be, "This job can be quite stressful. Do you think you can be effective in a stressful environment?" This question will get you a yes or a no response, based on the opinion of the candidate. But you need to have factual information in order to make the best decisions and many traditional interview questions are designed to check for opinions, feelings, and hypothetical responses. Behavioral-interview questions, on the other hand, are designed to obtain historical, fact-based information from the candidate regarding past performance. Assuming you are interested in finding out about someone's ability to manage stress, a behavioral question you can ask is, "Tell me about a time when you've found yourself in a very high-stress situation. How did you handle that?" This question is worded in a way that will encourage the candidate to respond with an actual story versus an opinion or feeling. Because you're asking for an actual experience, and not what the person thinks he or she would do, the response will give you information about how this person has responded to stress in the past. The information you gather about how the candidate worked under stress in the past will help you determine whether he or she has the skills needed to be successful as your employee in the future. A helpful tip to keep in mind when developing behavioral-based interview questions is to start off with phrases such as "Tell me about a time when . . ." or "Think about a situation when. . . ." This introduction will help to ensure that your question elicits an experienced-based response and not an opinion or hypothetical answer.

Getting the Complete Picture

When using questions that require a story in response, such as behavioral-interview questions, it is important to be sure that you are getting the complete picture. Look for three elements to the answer: background/situation, action, and result.

Background/Situation

The background/situation is a description of what was going on at the time—the circumstances of the story. For example, when describing the background or situation, one might say: "It was a really busy day and we had a few staff members who were out, so we were really short-handed during the afternoon rush. The lines were long and customers were getting really angry."

Action

The action is the part of the story that describes what the candidate did—how he or she handled the situation described in the background section. In keeping with the previous example, when describing the action the candidate might say: "I remembered that we had received a large shipment of samples just a few days before. I quickly put some on a tray and offered them to the customers in line while I apologized for the unusually long wait."

Result

The result is the outcome of the story, or the impact of the actions taken by the candidate. For example, the candidate described above might say, "Even though I couldn't do anything to get people through the line more quickly, they were happy to have free samples and a personal apology so they didn't mind waiting so much and left satisfied with their experience."

This example shows that the candidate was able to identify an emerging problem, take action, and use creativity to diffuse the situation, ending in a positive result. Keep in mind that *it is important to obtain all three elements* of the story. Often, candidates will tell part of the story, but one or more elements may be missing. Without all three elements, you may be mislead. Here is an example of an incomplete response: "A customer of mine wanted the same sales presentation six times in a period of a month, so I kept going back and giving it."

On reading this response, what impression do you have about the candidate? Some might feel that this person wasted a lot of time going back to give the same presentation over and over again, while others might read this as a sign of persistence, and view it as a positive response. But there is really no way of knowing for sure whether this action had a positive or negative impact, because the statement contains the background and action elements, but it is missing the result. Without the result, we don't know how things turned out so we can't really tell whether the candidate made the right choice and took the best action. By asking this applicant something like "How did it all turn out?" you can acquire the result and hear the whole story. Let's add a result to the statement and see how the response will change: "A customer of mine wanted the same sales presentation six times in a period of a month so I kept going back and giving it. Finally, I was able to get the client to sign and we now have a $3 million contract with him."

This statement provides a lot more information on which to base a decision. It tells us the impact of the candidate's action, so we are not left to draw our own conclusions. Clearly, this sales candidate made the right decision and her persistence resulted in a large sale for the organization. This is why it is very important to get the whole story when using behavioral-based questions.

Opinion Versus Data

Behavioral interviewing is designed to gather specific, fact-based data about past performance. Often candidates will provide us with responses that represent thoughts, opinions, or feelings. While these answers may make for interesting conversation, they do not tell us much about the candidate's qualifications. Here is an example of a response that represents opinion: "I was really great at handling employee complaints, whether they were pay problems or about working conditions or overtime assignments. I really nipped these problems in the bud."

What we learn through this response is that the candidate believes he or she is a good problem solver. In order to turn this response into behavioral, fact-based information, the interviewer might follow up by saying, "Can you tell me about a specific complaint or problem that you handled successfully? Give me some background and then tell me what you did and how it turned out."

This kind of interview uses probing questions and requires specific responses. Some candidates may find the behavioral-based interview to be a difficult experience. However, a candidate who has the appropriate experience will be able to provide examples as requested, and because you are making your decisions based on facts and not conjecture, you will have the information you need to make solid hiring decisions.

Note-Taking

One more important aspect of the behavioral-based interview is the process used for taking notes. Statistics show that when interviewers fail to take notes or don't take good notes, they tend to overestimate the abilities of all candidates, and they see less distinction between candidates. Because of this, they may struggle to select the ideal person for the job. By taking good notes, you can simplify the decision-making process and make better choices. Here are some tips on note-taking:

- Devote your time to recording facts rather than editorializing on your personal reactions to the candidate. There will be an opportunity to record your reactions and evaluations later.
- Use the actual words of the candidate, rather than your interpretations, whenever possible. When you use the candidate's actual words, you will see more differences in responses among candidates because the notes will reflect the candidate's words rather than your interpretation of the candidate's answers.
- Do not write down any comments about a person's physical appearance. In the event your hiring decision is challenged in a court of law, your notes can be called into evidence. Keep your notes focused on job-related responses from the candidate to avoid any possible implications of discrimination.
- After the interview is over, take some time to summarize your thoughts about the candidate's qualifications as they relate to the competencies required for job performance.

Summary

By using the behavioral-based interview process, you can avoid bias and make hiring decisions based on past performance and experience that is specifically related to the opening you are trying to fill.

Be sure to develop your questions in a manner that will obtain the responses you need, avoiding hypothetical and yes/no (closed-ended) questions. By starting your questions off with phrases like "Tell me about a time . . ." or "Give me of an example of a time when . . .," you can be sure that you are asking behavioral-based questions. This will help you to avoid making judgments about a candidate based on opinions, thoughts, or feelings.

Be sure to get the whole story—background/situation, action, and result. If one of these elements is missing from the candidate's response, you can be easily be mislead.

Note-taking is a critical part of evaluating candidates. Without good notes, it will be harder to distinguish between interviewees and you may tend to overestimate everyone you interview.

Final Comments

Our manager from the opening paragraph, Jane Doe, may have a perfectly homogenous team in her dreams, but when she wakes and goes into the real work world, she knows that having a diverse team with different viewpoints and perspectives will help her to be more effective. Behavioral interviewing helps all managers avoid personal bias in the employment interview, and it results in better hiring decisions for the team and the organization. Ultimately, a good interviewing process helps avoid lost revenue spent on "bad hires" and helps avoid the limitations of a homogenous workgroup.

Sandra Torres *has more than twenty-five years of experience in the training and organization development field. Her credits include five years as the president of TrainingBuz.com and five years as director at Comcast University. Her career focus has been on leadership and management development, culture change, and team effectiveness. Ms. Torres is currently working in organization development with ARAMARK Healthcare, advancing the organization's efforts to integrate OD into the clinical support services industry.*

Becoming an Effective Networker

Michaeline Skiba

Summary

To meet and engage prospective employers inside your organization, you must cultivate a network of business and personal contacts who are available and willing to help *if and when needed*. Decision-makers prefer to hire people who have been recommended by someone they trust. The tips in this article are designed to help you create a network that will serve you well within your current place of employment as well as in the future.

What Is Networking?

Networking can be defined as a powerful marketing strategy for smart professionals who create, sustain, share, and support their career development goals.

Why Networking Has Grown

- Most companies cannot promise a life long career, and the "social contract" between employees and employers has disappeared.
- Corporate loyalty has disappeared. Everyone is responsible for creating and sustaining his or her own career path.
- Establishing professional contacts is considered good business, and now it's an unspoken requirement.
- The "hidden job market" (unposted jobs) is where the best career opportunities lie.

- Companies reorganize and often lose sight of what they need. Networking into the right "circles" can help them realize what they are missing.
- People are helping one another more and more.

"Mediated" Networks

Mediated networks are contacts heard about or originated through print and electronic media. They include Internet research websites and job search networking groups that meet online to share/provide information. These include the following:

- Employer-sponsored ads intended to reach the passive job candidate who may not actively seek employment but is receptive to making a change.
- Evite.com suggests locations for professional meetings and parties, issues your invitations, tallies up the RSVPs, and shows you who has accepted or declined.
- MeetUp.com links you to people who share similar interests. If you belong to a professional association, you can use the site to schedule private meetings, notify members, gather RSVPs, and show who is attending.
- Job search aggregators such as Indeed.com, Jobster.com, and SimplyHired.com scan job boards for appropriate openings in your location and then notify you every day with all of the links.
- Referral job sites offer financial rewards for referrals through sites such as LinkedIn.com and Jobster.com. H3.com offers cash rewards from employers to employees and their contacts who refer new hires.
- LinkedIn.com is a social networking website that allows professionals to expand their online rolodexes by linking to those of friends and colleagues.

Print Media

Print media include community announcement boards, brochures, newspaper business columns, invitations to community-sponsored job fairs and trade association meetings, invitations to social events (class reunions, alumni associations, volunteer group meetings), business card collections, and books of sources and contacts related to your job search.

"Live" Networks

Networking requires the cultivation of relationships with *all* types of people, not just key decision-makers. Prepare yourself with the following:

- View networking as a life-long process versus the end result of a job search.
- Concentrate on working *with* and helping others versus working on others (how they can help you).
- Move away from your computer and go out and get in front of others who can help! Even though you may need to use your computer to learn about the groups with which you want to network, meet and become acquainted with those groups.

Different types of networks can be tapped. Whether they are used to relax and socialize, to find assistance with projects, or to gain career advice (such as company-specific information), they will help you move forward with your career and your life:

- An in-person, "exploratory" business discussion is usually conducted in an office setting. *This is probably the most effective tool that you can use* because it is personal and interactive. In this situation, you meet with the contact in his or her own environment and on his or her schedule, and you have a relaxed, professional conversation about your mutual business interests.
- Client-centered networking involves clients, vendors, or distributors with whom you have developed strong relationships over months or years. These contacts have first-hand knowledge of an employee's work habits and the inner workings and culture of a prospective new employer. Proceed with caution, since this technique may jeopardize your current job or offend potential contacts.
- Alumni association meetings (high school, college, and graduate school local and regional gatherings). You meet these people less often than social acquaintances, but you never know when they are in a position to give good advice or open a door.
- Courses, seminars, adult education programs. Any type of educational setting will engage dozens of new people—and new networking colleagues—who share common interests. Take the time before or after class to chat with classmates and professors, and keep in touch by email.

- Community-based, church-based, and industry-specific career planning and networking groups. These groups have sprung up everywhere. Go to a few meetings. They usually meet in the evenings or on Saturday mornings, so that your business hours are free for in-person networking and interviewing.
- Professional associations. If you are not a member of a professional group, consider joining one because you will have a great deal in common with the people who attend meetings and keep in touch with one another. The visibility will draw others to you and improve your career development efforts.
- Career fairs. If you view these events negatively, think about the other job seekers who are there, whom you can meet in passing and who may happen to have a lead for you.
- Executive recruiters. Most recruiters conduct their job placement work by phone and very rarely meet with candidates. While they may not be able to place you in another job, they could give you valuable business information that will help you in other ways.
- Volunteerism. If you don't do volunteer work in your community, seriously consider it. Not only will you make new and interesting contacts, but you will also boost your self-esteem by helping others while you are in transition.
- Social settings. Don't overlook the invitations you receive for holiday parties, fund-raisers, or other types of celebrations. Many of these functions are great networking opportunities because the people who attend them usually are relaxed and in good moods.
- Hobbies/other interest groups and clubs. You never know whether your next job will focus on something that you've considered as a hobby or personal interest. For example, a military officer who retired at a young age and who needed to continue working found his niche in conducting tours of Civil War battlegrounds. Because he collected antique firearms and books, he was already an "expert" in this field.
- Holiday networking. During major holidays, employers continue to hire because pressures such as competition, growth, and strategic considerations simply never stop. In addition, competition for positions might decrease, which gives you a distinct advantage. If your functional area has experienced a slow-down, reconnect with old contacts, sharpen your presentation skills, and use the holiday invitations to let people know you are there.

The Do's and Don't's of Networking

There are no hard and fast rules of networking. However, there are some do's and don'ts.

The Don'ts

- *Don't procrastinate*. Let's say that your company is planning to open a new facility in your area, but you learned that they aren't going to open their doors for three months. Should you wait for three months before contacting anyone? As the saying goes, "Strike before the iron gets hot" when businesses are in the "plan for launch phase" and long before they advertise for employees.
- *Don't underestimate anyone*. Here are two examples of how job seekers sabotaged themselves and their job prospects:
    - A business executive couldn't reach another executive because his phone calls were being screened by an executive assistant. Instead of treating the assistant in a professional and friendly manner, the job seeker sounded frustrated and short-tempered—neither of which helped him befriend the person who could help him reach his contact. The lesson: Be considerate, respectful, and complimentary toward those who open the door.
    - A job seeker who works in advertising ran into a high school friend who works in the pharmaceuticals industry and who gave him a lead about a job opening in the marketing department of his company. The job seeker ignored his referral, thinking that there was no possible connection between this job and his background. What a mistake! The job required the successful candidate to possess advertising contacts.
- *Don't be nervous*. Professionals understand why you are networking. People change jobs and careers for a number of reasons, and if you take the right approach, most people will be willing to help you. After all, one day they may need *you*.
- *Don't leave a contact without obtaining at least one or two job leads or other contacts*. Although one of the end results of networking is landing the right job, what you do to *get there* is more important. Your next position may not last forever, but the networking contacts that were cultivated should last a lifetime.

- *Don't meet with anyone unless you are in a positive, self-confident state of mind.* If you find yourself in a really low or negative mood, reschedule your meeting. Why waste a good lead when you don't have the emotional energy to manage it?
- *Don't think "What can you do for me?"* Approach all networking contacts with this thought: "How can I help you?" Prospective decision-makers would rather see proof of your talents and ability to produce profit and results, versus hearing your career history.
- *Don't give up.* Even though some of your contacts may prove fruitless, you never know when one of them may need you. Everything changes—companies, businesses, employees—and some of these changes may work in your favor at some point in time.
- *Never, ever, ever ask for a job.* Your purpose is to make a connection—preferably one that will last for many years. By asking for a job, you put the other person on the defensive, especially if the person doesn't have any jobs to offer to you.

The Do's

- *Believe that networking is the most effective job search tool.* Today, most hiring is done through networking, and it appears to surpass other tools such as newspaper and Internet-based job postings.
- *Realize that your network can become a lifelong "safety net."* You may need to find a job now, but if you must conduct another search in the future and you have a good network of contacts and colleagues, the process will be easier. Think about networking as an investment in your future.
- *Know that your network will grow.* With attention and persistence, you will eventually possess a network that is a life-long resource for everything from finding a job through gathering information. Another added bonus: You will meet some wonderful people along the journey.
- *Use your contacts to create a "snowball" effect.* If you obtain two or three meaningful contacts from one person and you continue to double or triple that number from those contacts, the leads continue to grow and grow to potentially hundreds (or even thousands) of people!
- *Be persistent with the generation of leads.* If a networking contact cannot think of anyone to whom you should be referred, suggest that you will call

or email within a few days to follow up. Sometimes, business people have such large networks of their own that they have to refer to their own files.

- *Pay attention.* Don't feel as though you have to do all the talking. Be curious and listen to others.
- *Follow up with your contacts.* After you've mastered the listening part of networking, keep track of names and reconnect with these people periodically.
- *Treat everyone in the same (professional) way.* Respect everyone. It's the Golden Rule: "Do unto others as you would have done unto you."
- *Find a role model.* Try to find and cultivate a relationship with someone within your organization who is great at making connections. It's contagious!
- *Say "thank you" to everyone who helps you.* This is common courtesy, but especially so if it means a terrific opportunity.
- *Create mutually beneficial relationships.* Instead of viewing the process as "What can you do for me?" think about how you can focus on a set of connections based on mutual benefit.
- *Know the skills and talents you have to offer.* Prepare yourself in advance of in-person meetings, and get organized with your self-presentation. This will boost your confidence and help you market yourself effectively. Know what you do best so others can convey that information.
- *Polish your communication-specific presentation.* In written, spoken, and presentation forms, you are your own message. Make it a great one.
- *Polish your attitudinal presentation.* People aren't interested in or impressed by anyone who is too arrogant, too pushy, too meek, too confused, or too *anything*.
- *Polish your personal presentation.* Look good when you meet networking contacts in person. This means paying attention to grooming, personal hygiene, and well-tailored clothing.
- *Remember the saying: You never get a second chance to make a first impression.* Experts say that a first impression is made within the first few seconds of the encounter. If that's all you have, look and sound impeccable!
- *Realize that most people understand your situation and want to help you if they can.* Most people will try to help you because they realize that one day,

they may need *you*. Furthermore, people love to give advice, to be asked for their opinions, and to offer helpful counsel.

- *Maintain your network*. What tells you that all of these efforts are productive? The answer is simple: When your contacts call you without being prompted. That is why building relationships is the main purpose of this activity.

To sustain what you developed:

- Stay in touch with your contacts and show interest in their lives as well.
- Find ways to connect outside of your job search, especially if you belong to an interest group or association.
- After you start a new position, send the news to your contacts.
- Meet with at least one of your contacts for lunch or coffee every month.
- Remember your contacts at the holidays. Send cards with thanks and good wishes for the New Year.

Helpful Resources

The following are some other tools that may assist you in networking your expertise:

- "Enterprise zones." These are areas the state government has earmarked to attract businesses, especially in terms of urban development. This is where a great deal of state money is focused.
- Areas where business activity is being attracted are known as "business incubators." Review the following website for more information: www.nbia.org.
- Small business development centers are worth reviewing for potential opportunities. The website to search is www.sba.gov.
- A library resource worth investigating: *Weddle's Guide to Employment Sites*.
- Read the business section of newspapers to get a sense of current business activity and who is in "ramp-up" phase.
- *Reference USA* (a library tool) is a good source for all information and personnel within various companies.

Michaeline Skiba, Ed.D., *is an assistant professor in the Management and Marketing Department of the School of Business Administration at Monmouth University in West Long Branch, New Jersey. In business, she designed, developed and delivered both line and staff management marketing and management materials. Dr. Skiba earned a B.S. in education and biological sciences at Loyola University in Chicago; a MSIR in human resources at Loyola University Chicago; an M.Ed. in instructional technology at Boston College; and an Ed.D. in communication at Columbia University.*

A Six-Step Process for Implementing Mentoring Programs in Learning Organizations*

Arthur L. Jue

Summary

This article discusses the nature and value of formal mentoring programs in corporate environments and provides a case study in which a Fortune 100 technology company implemented a mentoring initiative for emerging leaders in one of its major divisions. A theoretical and practical exploration of concepts related to mentoring informs the development of a six-step implementation framework that may apply to a variety of organizational settings. The case study highlights the role of mediating factors such as technology, culture, organizational structure, business strategy, company lifecycle, human interaction systems, and diversity in the introduction and integration of corporate mentoring programs. The resulting ideas and concepts presented are aimed at assisting managers and leaders of high-growth and/or rapidly transforming organizations to either innovate and/or improve mentoring practices within their own companies and workplaces.

*This article is derived from a presentation originally delivered during a professional development workshop sponsored by the Academy of Management Mentoring Committee at the 2005 Academy of Management Annual Conference held in Honolulu, Hawaii.

The 2009 Pfeiffer Annual: Management Development.

An Overview of Mentoring in the Corporate Milieu

Those who seek mentoring will rule the great expanse under heaven.

Those who boast that they are greater than others will fall short.

Those who are willing to learn from others, become greater.

Those who are ego-involved will be humbled and made small.

—Shu Ching, circa 6th Century B.C., *Chinese Book of History*

An estimated 70 percent of Fortune 1000 firms provide formal mentoring programs (Smith, Howard, & Harrington, 2005). Mentoring is commonly employed in public and private enterprises today as a method of developing expertise, retaining key talent, grooming leaders, improving morale, integrating employees, fostering diversity, and increasing organizational capability. Empirical experience has suggested that a correlation exists between mentoring and enhanced organizational effectiveness, competitive advantage, and improved employee performance (Anonymous, 2003; Friday, Friday, & Green, 2004; King, 2005; Reingold, 2001). In addition, according to the Corporate Leadership Council (2003), mentoring is one of the top five developmental strategies preferred by senior executives. As such, mentoring represents a strategic tool for managing and engaging high-performing talent.

Mentoring may also help facilitate the socialization of knowledge and learning in organizations (Muscatello, 2003). Nonaka and Takeuchi (1995) created a popular framework for the development of learning organizations whereby knowledge managed transforms into knowledge effectively applied. In Nonaka and Takeuchi's model, the communication of knowledge occurs through both tacit transfer (interaction/example) and explicit transfer (formal language and systems). Moreover, the act of socialization (one-to-one interaction) can become a prelude to greater externalization (one-to-many dialogue), which may lead to combination (many-to-many exchange) and finally internalization (many-to-one assimilation). These authors argued that this circular knowledge spiral within organizations reflects a key to sustaining and enhancing innovation in perpetuating the organizational lifecycle.

To advance organizational learning, mentoring may occur through numerous modalities. For example, group mentoring has become an increasingly prevalent practice in some firms as well as in academia (Herrera, Vang, & Gale, 2002; Tahmincioglu, 2004a). In addition, e-mentoring has become popularized through the advent of Internet technologies (Davis, 2004; MentorNet, 2005). Notwithstanding the mentoring methods utilized, a fundamental characteristic of the process of mentoring is that it involves the transfer of knowledge, experience, and/or skills from a mentor to a protégé (Ambrose, 2000; Shea, 1997). In other words, mentoring involves at least a dyadic relationship in which interaction between individuals results in mutually beneficial interpersonal rapport. Ideally, these relationships stimulate growth for participants, either through an informal imparting of tacit knowledge or a more formal explicit process of identifying goals, responsibilities, and/or desired outcomes.

According to Starcevich and Friend (1999), differences exist between the roles of mentors, coaches, and supervisors. A *mentor* usually serves as a sounding board, focusing on issues related to personal and professional career-related growth or role-modeling. A *coach* generally focuses on business-oriented and/or job-related feedback. Coaches tend to remain impartial and skills-oriented. A *supervisor*, on the other hand, tends to provide performance- and/or assessment-related guidance, often reflecting more directive versus nurturing behaviors. Whereas mentoring involves penalty-free exchanges between mentors and protégés (unencumbered by evaluations tied to performance incentives and/or other assessments), decision making about an individual's efficiency and/or effectiveness generally remains within a supervisor's purview.

In some corporations, the roles of mentor, coach, and supervisor/manager may successfully overlap (Starcevich & Friend, 1999). Although frequently discouraged in applied practice, supervisors may serve as positive coaches or mentors, and vice-versa. In addition, serving as a mentor sometimes becomes associated with formal job descriptions and/or specific career development objectives. Rather than an entitlement or mandatory practice, mentoring in corporations typically first appears as a voluntary, unstructured, and/or spontaneous informal vehicle for personal and professional growth (Friday, Friday, & Green, 2004; Smith, Howard, & Harrington, 2005). As mentoring becomes institutionalized, the organization may begin to sanction, sponsor, manage, and/or mandate formal programs. Notwithstanding the popularity of formal mentoring programs, the efficacy of formal versus informal methods is still under intense debate, requiring additional study and applied research (Blake-Beard, 2001; Garfinkel, 2004; Mujtaba, 2006; Raabe & Beehr, 2003).

Reemergence of the Mentoring Meme: An Historical Overview

One approach to understanding the evolution of mentoring in organizations may involve examining changes in the socio-economic ethos of various historical epochs. For example, one of the earliest forms of mentoring occurred in Greek mythology. Mentor served as a teacher entrusted to educate Odysseus' son, Telemachus. As such, Mentor became a role model, example, teacher, and protector to Telemachus, nurturing his growth and development (Huang & Lynch, 1995). According to Huang and Lynch, an even earlier use of mentorship occurred in grooming potential leaders as part of the royal succession process among Chinese emperors between 2333 and 2177 B.C. In addition, apprenticeship and guilds were a prominent part of early Federalism in the West, which fostered high collaboration and cooperation in ensuring community survival and socio-economic prosperity (Cook & Yanow, 2001; Jacques, 1996). Fenelon, an 18th Century French educator, used the term in his writing, and mentoring behavior was common in ancient African communities (www.mentors.ca/mentorrationale.html).

However, with the advent of bureaucratic management and scientific rationality (Taylor, 2001; Weber, 2001), new employee-employer relationships arose based on power differentials, self-interest, and paternalistic organizational structures. Jacques (1996) called this epoch the Industrial Disciplinary Era. The prevailing ethos of this age was defined largely through the mechanics of mass production. That is, industrialization in Western nations seemed to demand a mindset attuned to top-down autocratic management and bureaucratic control. Ensuring efficiency and effectiveness became the locus of focus, rather than individual growth and development.

As the post-industrial era commenced during the 1960s with increasing technological complexity and globalization, a new breed of knowledge workers began to emerge. Competence, rather than command and control, became the keyword within many organizations. Old notions of productivity changed as the meritocracy of skills began to supplant hierarchical pyramidal relationships. The effective management of human rather than financial capital became a critical success factor in the marketplace and workplace (Anderson, 1992; Fitz-enz, 2000; Jacques, 1996; Morgan, 1998).

Consequently, many practitioners grew increasingly attuned to organizational learning that involved a renewed emphasis on mentoring and facilitative approaches for workforce development. The human relations movement and person-centered learning theories derived from humanistic philosophers such as Carl Rogers (1969) influenced the revival of mentorship as a learning strategy, particularly within Western enterprise. Mutual accountability created equanimity between co-workers and gradually formed the basis for a more free flow of shared experiences over time (Katzenbach & Smith, 1999; Perrow, 1986).

Understanding learning in organizations has increased in tandem with the expansion of the mentoring meme, an evolving culturally transmitted idea. For example, hitherto an individual's age was assumed to reflect the hallmark of knowledge in the workplace. Subsequent workplace andragogies presupposed that adult workers operate in fully developed stages of prolonged adolescence or self-actualized/self-directed autonomy. Conversely, Clark (1981) argued that facilitative learning remains critical in creating shared meaning and in fostering peak performance. Findings such as these tend to support the need for increased mentoring within institutions and organizations.

Today, organizational learning is commonly regarded as more organic and collaborative, versus ritualistic and individualistic. In this environment, interactivity becomes as important as the work itself for creating healthy corporate cultures (Katzenbach, 1998). Mentors within organizations serve to emphasize process and form among protégés as well as traditional content and competence. Mentors thereby yield transformational leadership and long-term facilitative learning in organizations (Klagge, 2001; Lashway, 1995). The revitalization of mentoring in postmodern organizations certainly seems to prepare knowledge workers for greater agility and future success amid intensifying uncertainty and complexity in the emerging global economy.

A Process for Creating Corporate Mentoring Programs

Since organizations reflect different industries, employee populations, geographic locations, organizational structures, and stages in their lifecycles, perhaps no single approach or best practice exists for implementing and maintaining a successful mentoring program. The corporation's strategic principles and purposes behind formal mentoring should generally serve as the key guiding variables in governing the evolution of mentoring practices and programs (Friday & Friday, 2002). However, the following case study of a Fortune 100 high-technology company may illustrate one approach to formulating mentoring frameworks within large organizations. For purposes of maintaining anonymity, the company's name has been changed as well as some demographic and statistical information.

A Traditional Mentoring Mindset

During the early 1990s, XYZ Corporation had more than 250,000 employees worldwide and was a premiere global provider of information technology. Its mission was to create shareholder value through technology solutions for customers across the world. The company created products in computers, software, networking, storage, and microelectronics.

In order to sustain a competitive advantage in its markets, XYZ had invested heavily in creating a culture that emphasized employee development and education. Around this time, the company's human resource management strategy began to reflect a move toward greater employee career self-management. The employee, rather than the manager, became owner of his or her own career direction. XYZ's corporate mentoring processes also embraced an employee self-service strategy whereby a broad set of tools was offered to employees for initiating mentor relationships, such as web-enabled training, online forms, checklists, and intranet articles.

Potential mentors and protégés could learn about and form mentoring relationships spontaneously or as part of an employee's development plan as coordinated with the employee's manager. The program was self-initiated and allowed for regional variances according to local practices and business needs. General guidelines were provided to mentors and protégés, including communication techniques, selection guidelines, formal agreements, and criteria for assessing the effectiveness of the mentoring relationship.

Thinking Global, Acting Local

During the 1990s, the XYZ Corporation also embarked on an innovative initiative to aggressively pursue new business in the services sector. The initiative quickly became a major cash cow for the company. XYZ's services business was initially tasked to provide customers with technology consulting, systems integration, solution development, and other technical support such as telephony, disaster recovery, and data center outsourcing services.

The new strategy required an intensified investment in human capital management, and the workforce's intellectual skills became the organization's primary marketable asset. The XYZ Services Group quickly discovered that it was necessary to develop entirely new employee career paths. As customers outsourced their technology operations to the company, they frequently transferred their employees to the XYZ Services Group as well. Within the XYZ Services Group, operations were organized into functionally specialized divisions. One of the functional divisions that provided managed technology operations was divided further into four geographic regions, each of which experienced phenomenal growth rates during the late 1990s. In less than three years, for example, the Western region (XYZ Western Services) grew from a few culturally disconnected locations with fewer than five hundred employees to more than five thousand employees distributed across almost one hundred locations in more than twenty-five states.

With such a geographically diverse employee population, mix of company heritages, rapid growth rate, and high concentration of new employees and managers, the organization became increasingly concerned with (1) the integration and retention of its workforce, (2) employee development, and (3) cultural cohesion. The need for a more proactive mentoring program than currently existed via the corporate self-service offering became readily apparent. Senior managers of XYZ Western Services decided to take the lead in embarking on an effort to establish a more formal mentoring program as part of a strategic local and divisional resource management initiative.

A Six-Step Implementation Framework

In designing and implementing a more robust mentoring program, XYZ Western Services decided to focus first on mentoring emerging leaders. To pursue this strategy, the organization intuitively followed what could be characterized as a six-step implementation framework, which became an iterative—albeit tacit—process. Once the six steps were completed, for example, the cycle was informally repeated for other subgroups requiring formal mentoring such as new employees and managers. The six steps of the framework, shown in Figure 1 and described below, include (1) assessing organizational readiness; (2) securing executive sponsorship; (3) establishing appropriate expectations; (4) cultivating cultural acceptance; (5) leveraging technology effectively; and (6) measuring program effectiveness (see Figure 1).

1. Assessing Organizational Readiness

Evaluating organizational readiness has been characterized as an essential step in identifying potential barriers to successful implementation of formal mentoring programs and in ensuring strategic organizational fit (Anonymous, 2002; Friday & Friday, 2002). To assess XYZ Western Service's readiness for cultural transformation, focus groups were conducted throughout the organization with managers and employees. Unstructured, open-ended questions regarding the organization's culture, need for change, and specific areas of improvement were solicited from all

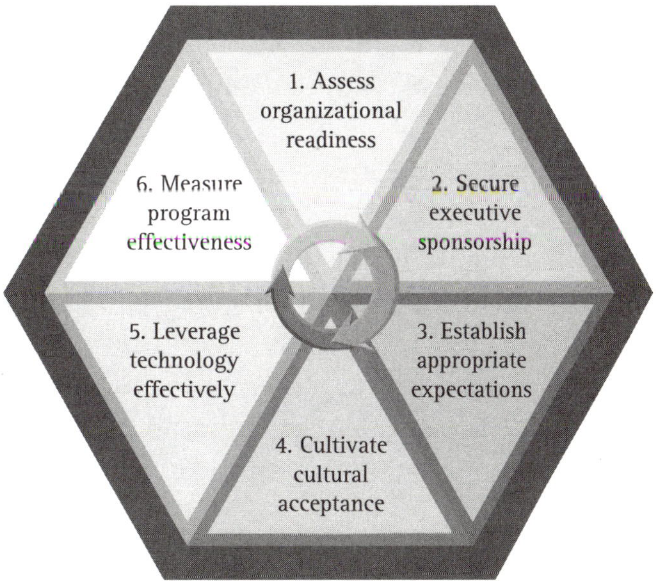

Figure 1. Scalable Six-Step Framework for Creating Formal Corporate Mentoring Programs

participants. Participant responses were qualitatively analyzed against (1) XYZ's core values of service, excellence, and human dignity; (2) its stated corporate drive for market leadership, superior execution, and high teamwork; (3) explicitly articulated operational principles; and (4) other desired cultural characteristics. A gap analysis was performed, and areas for improvement were identified. Based on this assessment, appointed evaluators determined that formal mentoring of emerging leaders would be generally accepted as part of a total solution for enhancing XYZ Western Services' culture and leadership.

2. Securing Executive Sponsorship

The composite results of the focus groups were shared with divisional senior management along with specific action plans. As objectives of the mentoring process became formalized, senior management was requested to formally promote and express public support for the rollout. As an attempt to pilot the project, emerging leaders were initially tracked at the executive level only, and the program included an extremely limited number of high-potential candidates. Over time, the program was expanded to include successive layers of management and the general employee population. Every line manager in the organization was eventually tasked to identify high-potential employees at the department level for inclusion. Explicit guidelines and selection criteria were provided by senior management for evaluating possible candidates, such as identifying employees who might have the potential for significant future technical, business, and/or managerial impact. Candidates were evaluated for inclusion based on their leadership potential, teaming ability, communication/interpersonal skills, drive/personal passion, creativity, customer-centeredness, and competency-based acumen/subject-matter expertise.

3. Establishing Appropriate Expectations

In order to effectively implement the emerging leader mentoring program as a supplement to the corporate mentoring offering (rather than as a replacement for it), the program was closely aligned with XYZ's corporate strategy and guidelines for developing executive resources. In addition, once identified as part of the emerging leaders program, the protégés themselves were expected to drive the mentoring relationship. A policy of confidentiality was established to ensure mutual trust among participants, and managers were expected to foster an environment conducive to mentoring. Time was afforded to employees for engaging in mentoring activities, appropriate resources were dedicated as necessary, and administrative assistance in facilitating the mentoring process was provided. Furthermore, a general policy was established that mentors should be solicited exclusively from within XYZ Western Services. However, establishing external mentoring relationships was allowed with senior management concurrence. The scope and nature of the program thereby became explicitly and effectively articulated.

4. Cultivating Cultural Acceptance

As the program expanded from exclusive senior management mentoring to the widespread mentoring of high-potential employees in general, externalization seemed to simultaneously transpire (Nonaka & Takeuchi, 1995). That is, through a process of engaging thought leaders (usually participants in the mentoring program) in providing feedback for program improvement, acceptance of the emerging leader program spread via word-of-mouth. These thought leaders actually became known as cultural champions within XYZ Western Services, and they ensured diffusion of awareness about the emerging leaders mentoring program throughout the organization, advocating buy-in at the local grassroots level. "Brown bag" educational sessions were conducted to disseminate information to stakeholders as appropriate. In addition, the mentoring program was aligned with other strategic organization-wide efforts, including diversity initiatives. For example, promoting and publicizing diversity representation in the mentoring program helped to ensure greater acceptance within the organization.

5. Leveraging Technology Effectively

Technology became a powerful enabler for facilitating the pairing of mentors and protégés (Tahmincioglu, 2004b). For example, by using in-house company software technology and local development expertise, the organization created a central repository for maintaining data about emerging leaders. The database was incrementally expanded for greater functionality over time. As aligned with the program's objectives, availability of this emerging leader database was initially provided only to senior managers or their designated delegate(s). However, functional and line manager access gradually followed suit as appropriate security policies and business rules were defined and coded. Organizational application administrators were trained, and several division-wide program coordinators were eventually appointed. A process was created whereby managers would nominate their emerging leader candidates and enter their information into the database, including demographic, personal, and other data to track developmental activity against predefined leadership competencies. To facilitate pairing, mentors input relevant personal data directly into the database as well.

6. Measuring Program Effectiveness

Once emerging leaders were identified and incorporated into the XYZ Western Services mentoring program, protégés were formally notified and provided an opportunity to select appropriate mentors. Senior management conducted regular quarterly reviews of the program to assess its effectiveness and usage. Managers were required to review their candidates on a regular monthly schedule in preparation for the senior executive reviews. Moreover, focus groups were conducted on a bi-annual basis with the cultural champions, and feedback was solicited as a qualitative measurement of the program's progress and overall success. Tracking the emerging leaders program with appropriate database technology yielded metrics that facilitated not only better program management but also important organizational reporting. For example, it was determined that over time, between 8 and 12 percent of the organization was included in the emerging leaders mentoring database. Senior management reviewed statistics such as the percent of promotions that occurred from among candidates in the emerging leaders mentoring pool/database and how well the program reflected the diversity composition of the organization as a whole.

Outcomes

In the case of XYZ Western Services, a structured mentoring program for emerging leaders assisted in establishing operational continuity, key employee retention, and business stability over time. It helped to ensure that the entire resources of the XYZ Corporation were brought to bear in helping high-caliber individuals achieve greater potential and have the most impact possible on the organization's success. Grooming the organization's pipeline of next-generation leaders in this manner became a key strategy for sustaining customer responsiveness amid rapid business growth.

The six-step process that the firm implicitly followed not only helped in developing and implementing the emerging leaders mentoring program, but, over time, helped to ensure that the program became scalable in its applicability to other new hire, intern, and job-specific mentoring initiatives. The process thereby served as a starting point for creating customized formal mentoring programs in other venues, contexts, and organizational settings. Integrating the program with diversity and culture change initiatives also became essential for ensuring the internalization of mentoring as part of the group's holistic "human activity system" (Checkland, 1999).

Eventually, the emerging leader mentoring program contributed to a significant strategic competitive advantage for XYZ Western Services because it helped to build a culture that became an attractive selling-point subsequently marketed to potential customers. As customers outsourced their technology businesses to XYZ, the organization's climate of authentic care and concern for employees became a visible strength and an important consideration for many customers in their purchase decisions. According to XYZ senior leadership, the emerging leaders program thereby evolved into an organizational legacy that enhanced the division's marketplace profitability and long-term competitive success.

Summary

"None of us has gotten where we are solely by pulling ourselves up by our bootstraps. We got here because somebody . . . bent down and helped us. . . ."

—Hon. Thurgood Marshall, U.S. Supreme Court Justice, 1908–1993, as cited in Mujtaba, 2006

When properly applied and supported, formal mentoring in corporations may facilitate greater access to available growth prospects, applicable career development activities, educational opportunities, and more effective skills transfer. In the case of XYZ Corporation, the implementation of a formal mentoring program by its Western Services Division integrated technological, cultural, structural, business, and human capacities into an effective and well-integrated supplement to the company's existing passive corporate tools. The corporate-wide mentoring program also subsequently embraced a similar approach in developing a more robust strategy that included partnerships with external mentoring alliances such as MentorNet. The six-step framework for establishing mentoring programs tacitly followed by the XYZ Services Division reflected a process whereby formal mentoring could become rapidly institutionalized and incrementally improved via localized innovation—a process of cyclical socialization, externalization, combination, and internalization. As demonstrated through this case study, mentoring not only facilitates learning in large and complex organizations but may likewise assist in translating that learning into effective and sustainable competitive advantages.

References

Ambrose, L. (2000). *A mentor's companion*. Chicago, IL: Perrone Ambrose.

Anderson, W.T. (1992). *Reality isn't what it used to be.* San Francisco, CA: Harper and Row.

Anonymous. (2002, November/December). Making the most of mentoring. *Human Resource Management International Digest, 10*(7), 30–31.

Anonymous. (2003). Welcome, grasshopper: Corporate mentoring in practice. *Human Resources.* Retrieved May 31, 2005, from www.humanresourcesmagazine.com.au/articles/5E/0C019E5E.asp?Type=60&Category=877

Blake-Beard, S.D. (2001). Taking a hard look at formal mentoring programs: A consideration of potential challenges facing women. *The Journal of Management Development, 20*(4), 331–345.

Checkland, C. (1999). *Systems thinking, systems practice*. Chichester, England: John Wiley & Sons.

Clark, A.T. (1981). *The influence of adult developmental processes upon the educational experiences of doctoral students.* (Doctoral dissertation, The Humanistic Psychology Institute, 1980). Dissertation Information Service (UMI No. 8106952).

Cook, S.D., & Yanow, D. (2001). Culture and organizational learning. In J.M. Shafritz & J.S. Ott (Eds.), *Classics of organization theory* (5th ed.) (pp. 400–413). Fort Worth, TX: Harcourt.

Corporate Leadership Council. (2003). *Maximizing returns on professional executive coaching*. Washington, DC: Corporate Executive Board.

Davis, M. (2004, June). eMentoring. *Triangle Business Journal, 19*(40), 3.

Fitz-enz, J. (2000). *The ROI of human capital: Measuring the economic value of employee performance.* New York: AMACOM.

Friday, E., & Friday, S.S. (2002). Formal mentoring: Is there a strategic fit? *Management Decision, 40*(1/2), 152–157.

Friday, E., Friday, S.S., & Green, A.L. (2004). A reconceptualization of mentoring and sponsoring. *Management Decision, 42*(5/6), 628–644.

Garfinkel, P. (2004, January 18). Executive life; putting a formal stamp on mentoring. *NewYork Times*. Retrieved January 18, 2007, from http://query.nytimes.com/gst/fullpage.html?res=9507E1D91F30F93BA25752C0A9629C8B63&sec=&spon=&pagewanted=1

Herrera, C., Vang, Z., & Gale, L.Y. (2002). *Group mentoring: A study of mentoring groups in three programs.* Philadelphia, PA: Public/Private Ventures [prepared for the National Mentoring Partnership].

Huang, C.A., & Lynch, J. (1995). *Mentoring: The tao of giving and receiving wisdom.* New York: HarperCollins.

Jacques, R. (1996). *Manufacturing the employee: Management knowledge from the 19th to 21st centuries*. Thousand Oaks, CA: Sage.

Katzenbach, J.R. (1998). *Teams at the top: Unleashing the potential of both teams and individual leaders.* Boston, MA: Harvard Business School Press.

Katzenbach, J.R., & Smith, D.K. (1999). *The wisdom of teams: Creating the high-performance organization*. New York: McKinsey.

King, C. (2005). *Mentoring and being mentored on the technology track.* Santa Clara, CA: Sun Microsystems. Retrieved May 31, 2005, from http://developers.sun.com/toolkits/articles/mentor.html

Klagge, J. (2001). *Organization theory: Structural conventions of the industrial paradigm.* Lectures presented for the University of Phoenix Doctor of Management in Organizational Leadership program, ORG 700 course [online].

Lashway, L. (1995). Can instructional leaders be facilitative leaders? *ERIC Digest, 98*, 3.

MentorNet. (2005). *The e-mentoring network for diversity in engineering and science.* Retrieved January 18, 2007, from www.mentornet.net/

Morgan, G. (1998). *Images of organization* (Executive ed.). San Francisco, CA: Berrett-Koehler.
Mujtaba, B. (2006). *The art of mentoring diverse professionals.* Hallandale Beach, FL: Aglobe.
Muscatello, J.R. (2003). The potential use of knowledge management training: A review and directions for future research. *Business Process Management Journal, 9*(3), 382–394.
Nonaka, I., & Takeuchi, H. (1995). *The knowledge-creating company: How Japanese companies create the dynamics of innovation.* New York: Oxford University Press.
Perrow, C. (1986). *Complex organizations: A critical essay* (3rd ed.). New York: McGraw-Hill.
Raabe, B., & Beehr, T. A. (2003). Formal mentoring versus supervisor and co-worker relationships: Differences in perceptions and impact. *Journal of Organizational Behavior, 24*(3), 271–273.
Reingold, J. (2001). Want to grow as a leader? Get a mentor. *Fast Company*. Retrieved May 31, 2005, from http://pf.fastcompany.com/magazine/42/instill.html
Rogers, C. (1969). *Freedom to learn*. New York: Macmillan.
Shea, G.F. (1997). *Mentoring*. Menlo Park, CA: Crisp.
Smith, W.J., Howard, J.T., & Harrington, K.V. (2005). Essential formal mentor characteristics and functions in governmental and non-governmental organizations from the program administrator's and mentor's perspective. *Public Personnel Management, 34*(1), 31–58.
Starcevich, M.M., & Friend, F.L. (1999). *Attributes of effective mentoring relationships: Partner's perspective.* Retrieved May 30, 2005, from www.coachingandmentoring.com/mentsurvey.htm
Tahmincioglu, E. (2004a). Group mentoring: A cost-effective option. *Workforce Management*. Retrieved May 31, 2005, from www.workforce.com/section/11/article/23/89/50.html
Tahmincioglu, E. (2004b). Looking for a mentor? Technology can help make the right match. *Workforce Management, 83*(13), 63–65.
Taylor, F.W. (2001). The principles of scientific management. In J.M. Shafritz & J.S. Ott (Eds.), *Classics of organization theory* (5th ed.) (pp. 61–72). New York: Harcourt. (Original work published 1916)
Weber, M. (2001). Bureaucracy. In J.M. Shafritz & J.S. Ott (Eds.), *Classics of organization theory* (5th ed.) (pp. 73–78). New York: Harcourt. (Original work published 1922)

Arthur L. Jue, Ph.D., *is a director of global organization and talent development at Oracle. He has served in management capacities at technology companies such as IBM and Hyperion, and he currently serves on the board of directors of educational and financial services institutions. Dr. Jue attended Brigham Young University, received a B.S. in marketing with a music minor from San Jose State University, has an MBA with* *emphasis in technology management, and earned a doctorate in leadership. In addition, he has attended executive programs at London Business School, Harvard, and Oxford. Dr. Jue teaches at the University of Phoenix, serves on the editorial board of the* Journal of Management, Spirituality, and Religion, *and is chair of the International Leadership Association's Global Business Leadership Forum. He also recently co-authored* Leadership Moments: Turning Points That Changed Lives and Organizations *(Trafford, 2007).*

Leadership Coaching

The Developmental Power of the One-on-One

Maggie W. Dunn

Summary

Many corporations manage their leadership development investments in three buckets: experience-based/on-the-job development, education/training, and feedback/relationship-based development. This article looks at the investment in feedback and relationship-based leadership development, specifically the value that can be derived from a coaching relationship and what to consider when deciding whether to engage an internal coach, an external coach, or both.

The Unique Value of Coaching

There is something especially powerful about a one-on-one developmental relationship. The depth of discussion, focus, and unguarded sharing can lead to particularly meaningful discoveries about oneself. Exploring observations and perceptions through coaching can help to identify what is most important and meaningful for the client, the crux of the issue, and the leverage point for development.

While completing my second leadership coach certification process, I benefited from just such a feedback-stimulated "aha" moment. "Are you aware that you didn't pick up on any of the client's references to her family . . . that you exclusively focused on organizational issues?" was the question posed as the director of coaching and I were debriefing a coaching session I had just completed. "What do you mean?" I asked. She responded, "When a client mentions, for example, that the same pattern of tension develops with her spouse as does with her boss, you consistently focus on what happens with her boss and don't explore what happens with her spouse." As we talked about it, I realized that my orientation toward organizational issues likely stems from my background as an HR business partner

The 2009 Pfeiffer Annual: Management Development.

and internal coach in a Fortune 100 corporation. In the context of the corporation, family relationships were typically touched on as part of the rapport-building part of our internal coaching sessions, but not so much during the actual work of our sessions, where our focus was on increasing self-awareness and enhancing performance for success within the organization.

Follow-up research on the concept of "whole person coaching" confirmed the value of integrating this into my coaching approach. Elizabeth and Gifford Pinchot (2000), for example, in their article, "Roots and Boundaries of Executive Coaching," describe working with an executive whose biggest developmental boost came from coaching and behavioral development that extended beyond workplace issues to his personal life. Their focused conversations about including his wife and children in decision making at home translated into more effective participative leadership behaviors at work. Others on his staff began to use these more team-based behaviors as well, and the organization benefited as a result.

Some readers may question the line between coaching and therapy when discussing personal, family, or non-work issues. In coaching, we tend to focus on specific behaviors and their implications, with an emphasis on practical application. While we may cover the intent of the behaviors relative to the impact of the behaviors, we typically do not get into exploring the underlying reasons for the behaviors, as is more common in therapy.

Behavioral patterns at work are often consistent with behavioral patterns and relationship issues outside of work. Makes perfect sense, now that I am aware of and have focused on it. And this awareness came as a gift—in the form of constructive, one-on-one feedback about my coaching approach. It was the kind of "aha" moment that we strive to achieve with coaching—identifying meaningful discoveries about our clients that can lead to enhanced effectiveness and overall satisfaction.

Internal and External Coaching

Increasingly, large corporations are augmenting their investment in external coaching services with an investment in developing a cadre of internal coaches (Pomeroy, 2007). The logic is that internal coaching is less costly and can therefore be made available to a greater number of leaders. This investment in the development of internal coaches also provides members of the internal HR and OD community the opportunity to enhance their professional capabilities.

Motorola, for example, developed its cadre of internal leadership coaches with the help of RHR International. The certification process for coach candidates included months of assessment and feedback, training, reading, receiving leadership coaching from professional external coaches, providing coaching while being supervised by the external leadership coach, and evaluation and feedback from clients. During the program, and for years after completing it, I worked with leaders identified as "key talent" in Motorola businesses around the globe to support their development in the organization.

Internal coaches typically offer a deep understanding of the organizational context, the culture, and "how things really work around here," insights about organizational politics and career options, and a broad-based perspective on how the individual is viewed within the organization. Given their roles inside the organization, internal coaches are typically better positioned to observe the client's behavior in a variety of circumstances (with bosses, peers, staff members, in both high- and low-stress situations), and to solicit and share real-time feedback from key work partners.

External coaches typically offer the comfort of complete objectivity and confidentiality, a safe relationship for exploring both work and non-work issues, and a breadth of experience with a variety of industries, organizations, and clients. The "out of the box" thinking that an external coach brings to the relationship can lead to real "ahas" for the client. External coaches may also find it easier than internal coaches to support clients' exploration and discovery through a balance of inquiry and advocacy. With inquiry, the coach uses a process of open-ended questioning to help the client explore possibilities, develop broader awareness, and then make choices and take personal responsibility for specific actions to move forward. With advocacy, the coach takes a position and speaks in favor of specific actions. When advocacy is over-used, insights and alternatives are easily overlooked. Because internal coaches are often involved themselves in the inner workings of the organization, there may be a greater tendency to advocate for particular decisions and to use less inquiry and open exploration during the coaching process.

Some developmental needs lend themselves best to work with an internal coach, while others are best suited to working with an external coach. The key is matching coaching resources to each leader's development needs.

In the next sections, several actual coaching examples will shed additional light on coaching needs that lend themselves to internal or external coaching or to a blended approach.

Internal Coaching Example

Motorola, similar to many organizations today, is focused on accelerating the development of talent in emerging markets. Based in Chicago at the time, I was asked to coach one of our rising leaders in Tianjin, China. The goals of our coaching relationship were to develop his confidence and capability in working with our U.S.-based leadership team—specifically to coach him on organizational politics, how to surface issues proactively, to request support when needed, and to bring problems and recommended solutions to the table.

An external coach could not have effectively addressed this need because it required an understanding of the unique organizational culture and dynamics. Also, being positioned inside the organization enabled me to observe his behavior in meetings, to gauge reactions, and to solicit and share real-time feedback and encouragement with him.

One additional significant and unanticipated benefit for the organization was that, through the development of our coaching relationship, our rising Chinese leader shared with me some important feedback about his experience with the organization. Although he felt uncomfortable about sharing this feedback, he was able to do so because of the trust-based relationship we had developed and the knowledge that I was positioned to influence change. He shared the real challenges of working with the U.S. team (many of the staff calls being late at night for him, sensing impatience when he was trying to communicate his messages to the rest of the staff, being "forgotten" on the conference calls while those sitting together in the Chicago conference room discussed and debated the issues with each other, and lack of timely follow-up when the team in China was waiting for a response). The U.S. team got some helpful feedback and coaching as a result of this initial coaching engagement, originally designed to develop a key Chinese leader, yet ultimately effective in developing a more globally astute leadership team.

External Coaching Examples

External coaching made more sense for a new vice president in a mid-sized technology company. When we first met, she was struggling with whether to stay with the company or to move on. She likely would not have revealed this to an internal coach. She was feeling typecast as a functional leader and wanted to move into a general management role. We talked about how she could position herself for general management candidacy within her current organization, how to pick up profit and loss management experience on the job, and how to demonstrate the talents that she could bring to bear to help one of their struggling businesses. Now that she has decided to stay and is energized by the prospect, we are focusing on her leadership in establishing a more process-oriented organization. She uses me as a trusted and objective sounding board with subject-matter expertise. In this case, full disclosure and the ability to talk completely candidly was important to her and, given her level (she reports to the CEO), she did not feel that internal coaching would offer this. Second, she appreciated my experience with more process-oriented businesses and subject-matter expertise that was not available internally.

External coaching also made more sense for a senior executive at an automotive company in the Midwest who received feedback that he needed to be less task-focused and more relationship-oriented in general. As we were reviewing his 360-degree feedback, as part of our process to really hone in on the behavioral issues, he explained to me that he has a relatively weak team and that he therefore needs to use an autocratic style. We talked about the effect that his leadership style could have on his team (that is, shutting them down).

One of the interventions that skilled coaches offer is honest real-time process consultation, in other words, the commitment to vocalize what we are experiencing with the client is the intervention. When we see or experience something that may be useful, it becomes a question of how to present it in a way that will be helpful. The magic is in tempering the honest feedback with wisdom from past experience about what the individual is ready to hear.

My sense in this case was that he needed a real "wake-up call" on the impact of his behaviors on others. I pointed out to him that it was rare to see him smile, that he had a very focused (some might call it "intimidating") way of looking at people, and that his questioning technique felt like interrogation (no acknowledgement of responses, just rapid-fire questioning). In this case, he was surprised, but appreciative of the honesty.

I asked him whether he would be willing to experiment with his approach for a bit, to see whether he might notice any changes with his team members' behavior. He agreed. In this coaching relationship, he relies on me to challenge him and to give him "brutally honest" feedback (feedback he had not received internally), and then to explore alternative approaches with him.

Blended Coaching Example

In some cases, a blended coaching arrangement, tapping into the capabilities and perspectives of an internal and external coach partnership, can be the ideal formula. We used this approach with a senior director being groomed for a vice-presidential-level position. The organization made the decision to invest in leadership coaching to help her develop "executive presence." Recognizing that she could benefit from both a broad-based perspective on how others have overcome this issue and from ongoing observation and feedback, we opted to establish an internal and external coaching partnership on her behalf. The role of the external coach was to help to define the perceived gap in behavioral terms—not always an easy task. Perceived executive presence can be a combination of appearance, demeanor, voice, impact, credibility, maturity, courage, and astuteness. We defined the gap in behavioral terms by developing a structured interview, which we conducted individually with the key decision-makers in the organization (those who ultimately had to agree she was ready for a vice-presidential promotion). The internal coach had the lead, watching for the defined behaviors, soliciting feedback from key work partners, and providing feedback.

In this case, we were reminded that one of the most meaningful steps with behavior change is becoming conscious of the specific behaviors to be changed. Then, as in this case, a motivated leader is positioned to begin experimenting with the new behaviors (consciously and with support and feedback for a period of time) until the new behaviors ultimately become part of the innate behavioral repertoire—also known as unconscious competence.

Conclusion

Asking for help and admitting vulnerabilities is something with which many leaders struggle. Many leaders have a sense that they should be able to figure it out on their own.

It generally feels safer to reveal sensitive concerns and vulnerabilities one-on-one than with an audience. Having more people in the room determines how comfortable one is when hearing difficult feedback, and there may be more defensiveness (not to mention distractions).

Often the issues are subtle and require the full and undivided attention available in a one-on-one interaction to identify assumptions, underlying patterns of behavior, and to fully explore alternatives. Whether internal, external, or a blend between the two, a skilled coach can offer a uniquely effective development intervention.

References

Pinchot, E., & Pinchot, G. (2000). Roots and boundaries of executive coaching. In M. Goldsmith, L. Lyons, & A. Freas (Eds.), *Coaching for leadership* (pp. 43–63). San Francisco, CA: Pfeiffer.

Pomeroy, A. (2007, September). Internal mentors and coaches are popular. *HR Magazine*, p. 12.

Maggie W. Dunn, D.B.A., *has many years of experience as both an internal and an external leadership coach. She was on Motorola's HR team for sixteen years, where she coached leaders around the world. She now leads a Fort Lauderdale-based HR consulting practice, specializing in leadership coaching. Dr. Dunn is a faculty member at Nova Southeastern University, where she teaches HR, OD, and leadership courses in the master's programs.*

What Happened to the Other 20 Percent?

How Addressing the 20 Percent of Effects Left Aside by the Pareto Principle Can Increase Management Performance

Alejandro Palacios

Summary

This article looks at the most common application of the Pareto Principle and challenges the fact that 20 percent of effects are often left unaddressed by managers. Considering the fact that competitive differentiation and even profitability are increasingly defined by the smallest of strategic and financial calibrations, it seems apparent that leaving opportunities on the table for the sake of moving on to the next topic of the month may not be a very wise approach.

Real-life arguments are presented to support both why this is relevant and how implementing this approach may require less time and resources than one may think.

The Pareto Principle, also known as the 80/20 Rule, the Law of the Vital Few, and the Principle of Factor Sparsity, states that, in many cases, 80 percent of effects come from 20 percent of causes. This concept is widely used in business as well as many other settings; in fact, it has become an unwritten standard for "good enough," one of those terms that are tossed around by many people as a justification for making decisions solely based on approximations calculated on a 2-inch by 3-inch sticky note.

This article will focus on challenging the current application of the Pareto Principle, where—by solely focusing on 20 percent of the causes—the remaining

The 2009 Pfeiffer Annual: Management Development.

20 percent of effects are ignored. Often, managers never go back and address these effects because they are in a hurry to move on to new topics. I suggests that addressing the remainder of the opportunities in a second wave may open the door to hidden opportunities.

Business leaders could significantly improve their performance and results by better understanding when and how to apply the Pareto Principle, as well as understanding when to go beyond the 80/20 Rule.

The Pareto Principle

The Pareto Principle is not without merit and provides an easy and practical way to segregate the "vital few" from the "trivial many" (Levine, Stephan, Krehbiel, & Berenson, 2005).

Basically, when limited time and resources prevent us from focusing on all possible causes, opportunities, or alternatives for action (e.g., materials, products, markets, customer segments, facilities), we rank one common variable (e.g., revenue, size, number of employees, number of pieces processed) in descending order to visually highlight the areas that should be prioritized.

As an example, let's say that a company wants to reduce the number of thefts in its processing plants. To accomplish this, they decide to install a sophisticated surveillance system in each one of their eight facilities. This solution is optimal from the perspective of solving the problem, but not practical because it would be too costly. Because of the expense, the organization has decided to invest its limited resources in those plants that show the largest amount of theft.

As shown in Figure 1, by applying the Pareto Principle, management will be able to decide which plants should receive the surveillance systems first, thus maximizing the impact of their investment by achieving large reductions in theft.

As you can see in Figure 1, the options with the greatest value on the Y-axis are easy to identify as they appear on the left-hand side of the X-axis.

The origins of this principle date to 1906, when economist Vilfredo Pareto developed a mathematical formula to describe the unequal distribution of wealth in nations; his finding was that 80 percent of the wealth is concentrated in 20 percent of the population. Regrettably, although Pareto did not intend to extrapolate his observations to the field of business management, a plethora of creative and watered-down versions of this principle have evolved over the years.

For example, while most authors recommend that managers focus most of their time on the 20 percent of topics that drive 80 percent of the results (Craft & Leake, 2002, and Munshi, 2002, among many others), others propose that business leaders should focus on managing the 20 percent of employees who produce

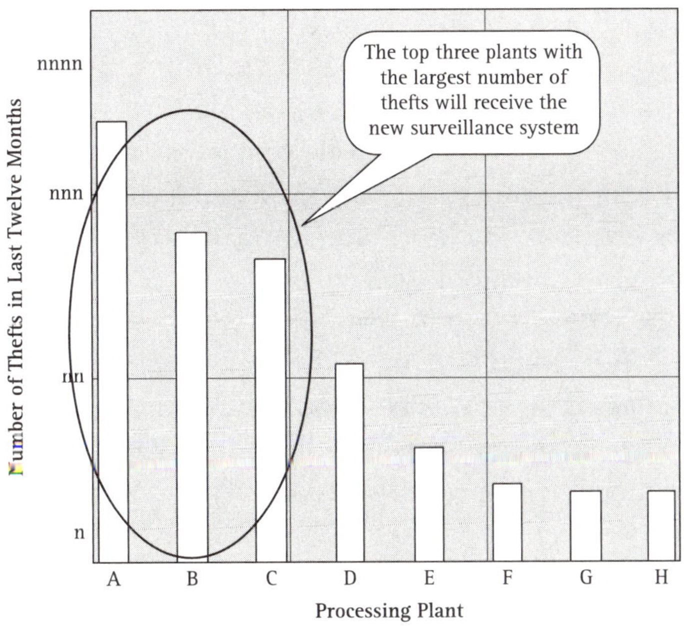

Figure 1. Application of the Pareto Principle (A)

80 percent of the results, also known as Superstar Management (Reh, 2005). The recurring themes of these approaches are efficiency gains, time management, and stress reduction, but taken as a one-size-fits-all rule for managers, the risk of these applications is an enormous amount of waste and missed opportunities.

One of the main limitations of the principle is that it is static, not dynamic. As described by Sanders (1988), the 20 percent that requires focus today may not be what requires focus tomorrow. Because the business environment changes constantly, any Pareto chart has only a limited application.

Considering the pace at which senior executives work and the broad scope of responsibilities and issues they face, it is logical to hypothesize that very few people ever go back to look at the 80 percent of causes that were not addressed.

Within an economic framework, Kaplow and Shavell (2000) also address the weaknesses in some applications of the Pareto Principle. These authors state that some policies that would be chosen by following the Pareto Principle, would make everyone worse off.

Illustrative Business Case

A large multinational organization has decided to launch a regional savings program for their Central American, South American, and Caribbean operations, aiming at finding "low-hanging fruit" that would ultimately have a positive impact on their bottom line. From over fifty countries in the region, the initial wave of efforts focused on the six largest countries (Mexico, Brazil, Argentina, Venezuela, Chile, and Colombia), which represented 80 percent of the regional revenues; furthermore, most of the resources were allocated to the two largest countries (Mexico and Brazil), which accounted for around 65 percent of total regional revenues. After running for a full year, the initiative was considered a success, and significant savings opportunities were both identified and implemented.

At this stage, in most situations, the program would have been shut down and the attention of management would have shifted to other business imperatives.

In this case, however, when looking at the countries left aside more closely, the company found a large array of missed opportunities that it could still take advantage of. Additionally, management realized that making it happen was much easier than they initially thought; some of the reasons were

- Several cost savings initiatives implemented in the largest countries could be easily transferable to many other countries; development time and costs had already been incurred so incremental implementation expenses would be marginal.
- Since the Pareto Principle has been consistently applied by this organization, there could be additional cost savings initiatives that were implemented in the largest countries a long time ago that had never reached the smaller countries.
- Due to the fact that senior management's attention seldom reached smaller countries, local management could see a golden opportunity to outperform and gain visibility by succeeding in the execution of various cost-saving initiatives.
- Because smaller countries frequently develop their own local initiatives, even the smallest improvement could be the difference between missing and meeting their annual budget requirements. These local practices could also be extrapolated and developed into replicable improvements for the largest countries.

Obviously, the type of second-wave implementation suggested in this case is not applicable in every instance because it could be a waste of resources and have high opportunity costs. This is why business leaders must be selective and practical when considering the other 20 percent.

In this particular case, the organization dedicated the second year of this program to both tracking the sustainability of the initiatives implemented in the larger countries and acting on opportunities that were identified in all small countries.

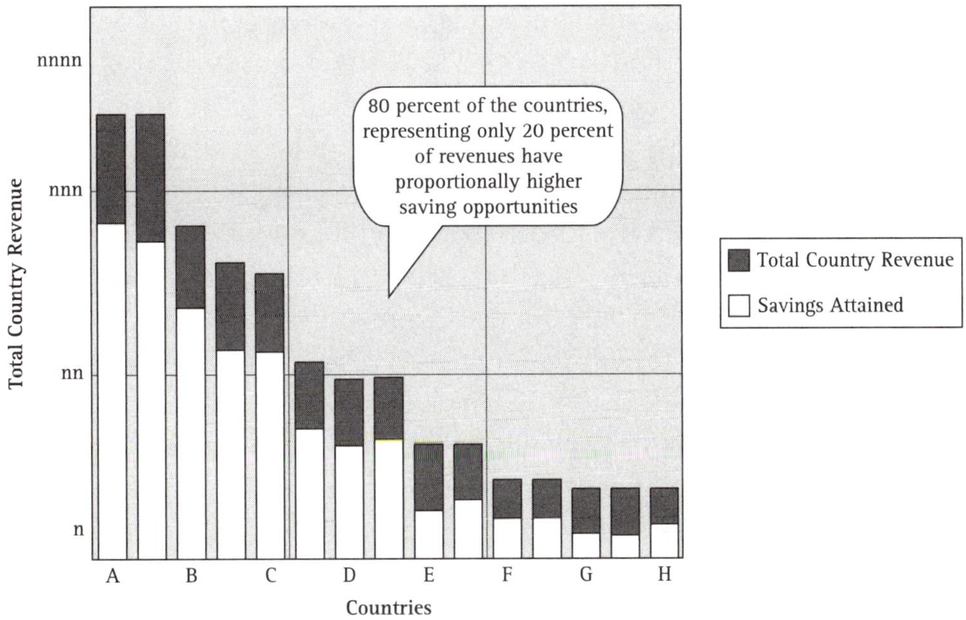

Figure 2. Application of the Pareto Principle (B)

Ultimately, this approach translated into a 40 percent increase in savings for the organization. As seen in Figure 2, although the proportions seem odd, countries adding up to 20 percent of revenues ultimately accounted for 40 percent of savings.

Because of the reasons mentioned above, the contribution ratio ($ saved/$ revenue) of the smaller countries was significantly higher than that of the larger countries.

Addressing the 20 Percent Can Increase Management Performance

Focusing on 20 percent of opportunities left on the table can increase management performance, significantly improve business results, and shape competitive differentiation. Following are some ways to use this approach.

Spend sufficient time in the planning stage of a program, documenting project fundamentals, approach, and lessons learned in such a way that the knowledge developed can be transferred with the smallest learning curve possible.

Dedicate 10 percent of program resources to identify missed opportunities for improvements during all stages of the project. In reality, the tail end of the planning phase of a program continues throughout the implementation stage, so there is room for small adjustments.

Maintain updated versions of maps for core processes in the organization in order to identify areas in which knowledge transfer can be applicable. This will also help standardize processes, thus enhancing improvements throughout the business.

Identify opportunities for grandfathering and creating shared service centers where operations can take on processes that currently run in several smaller entities.

Avoid having "flavor of the month" projects be the drivers of business decisions. Too often, projects are phased out or never brought up because management attention is focused on one big theme. Worse, many large projects are never 100 percent completed because they gradually lose management attention.

Design a rewards and recognition scheme that stimulates thoroughness, creativity, and opportunity-oriented behaviors; tie it to measurable results.

Be willing to take risks by volunteering aggressive goals and high (but attainable) expectations.

Make sure you understand the Pareto Principle and can identify the elements that cause problems and their effect on the organization.

Finally, learn how and when to use the Pareto Principle as a tool in your management toolbox and not as a way to cut corners!

Conclusion

Business leaders justify focusing only on the "vital few" by arguing that the pace of business is much too fast, and that there is no time to stop and be thorough. Ironically, this is the very reason why many organizations lose their competitive edge and why very few organizations are consistently successful in the long run. The remaining 80 percent of causes may not always be so "trivial"; in many cases, they are the key to competitive differentiation, the place where root causes are hidden, and the corner of the garden where low-hanging fruit have been growing for years without anyone ever collecting it!

Focusing solely on the largest buckets is the obvious approach and everyone does that. Stretching resources and capabilities, identifying creative solutions for squeezing the last drop of benefit from a program, and understanding the importance of marginal improvements is not an easy route. Having said that, with well-documented lessons learned from addressing the "vital few" and creative approaches to maximize resource utilization, addressing the "trivial many" may be highly rewarding!

References

Craft, R.C., & Leake, C. (2002). The Pareto principle in organizational decision making. *Management Decisions, 40*(7/8), 729.

Kaplow, L., & Shavell, S. (2000, November). Notions of fairness versus the Pareto principle: On the role of logical consistency. *The Yale Journal, 110*(2), 237.

Levine, M.D., Stephan, D., Krehbiel, T.C., & Berenson, M.L. (2005). *Statistics for managers*. Englewood Cliffs, NJ: Pearson Prentice Hall.

Munshi, P.P. (2002, December 30). The Pareto principle at work. *Business Line* (Chennai), p. 1.

Reh, F.J. (2005, July/August). Pareto's principle-The 80/20 rule. *Business Credit*, p. 76.

Sanders, R. (1988, Summer). The Pareto principle: Its use and abuse. *The Journal of Business and Industrial Marketing, 3*(2), 37

Alejandro Palacios *is an associate partner with the business consulting organization of Deutsche Post World Net, the world's largest transportation and logistics group. He manages projects involving business strategy, continuous improvement, organizational design, change management, and business processes. He is a doctoral candidate in international business administration and has an MBA from Nova Southeastern University's H. Wayne Huizenga School of Business and Entrepreneurship; he holds additional degrees in business management and organizational psychology.*

Why People with Disabilities Might Really Be Leaving Work

An Exemplar Case with Lessons for Managers

Margaret H. Vickers

Summary

This article presents a case study of one disabled woman's experience in organizational life. Miranda is a woman with multiple sclerosis (MS) who was discriminated against by her employer, ultimately resulting in her leaving the organization. Qualitative interview data is interspersed with the researcher's interpretations of her journey away from the workplace. Lessons for managers are shared as to why this might have happened and how managers might respond differently in the future.

This article presents one disabled woman's story of discrimination. The case was extracted from a much larger qualitative study in which lengthy interviews were held with people with multiple sclerosis (MS) to learn what was "really going on" in their lives and at work as a result of having MS. This case was deliberately presented from the disabled woman's perspective to show her view, given that most of the literature of this kind offers a managerial or human resources perspective instead.

Some respondents had finished work permanently; others had reduced their working hours; still others were continuing to work full time. While a few respondents did report positive and supportive workplaces, many reported quite a different picture—an ugly picture. In response, I have presented this stark example of what managers should *not* do when dealing with staff with a chronic illness or disability.

The 2009 Pfeiffer Annual: Management Development.

Multiple Sclerosis (MS): Some Background

Multiple sclerosis is one of the most prevalent neurological disorders in the world (Rumrill, Roessler, & Cook, 1998; Rumrill, Tabor, Hennessey, & Minton, 2000). In 2001, there were an estimated 2.5 million people in the world with MS. It is also one of the most common chronic illnesses in the West, affecting as many as 500,000 in the United States alone (Rumrill, Roessler, & Cook, 1998). In Australia, the National Health Survey of 2001 indicated that there were approximately fifteen thousand Australians with MS (MS Australia, 2003).

Multiple sclerosis is an often unpredictable, progressive, degenerative disease of the central nervous system (Kraft, Freal, & Coryell, 1986; Rumrill, Roessler, & Cook, 1998) that is characterized by damage to the myelin sheath that insulates white matter tracts within the brain and along the spinal cord (Rumrill, Tabor, Hennessey, & Minton, 2000). Kraft (1981) compared the demylenation process in people with MS as the breakdown of rubberized coating that surrounds electrical wires, with the breaks in the coating interfering with the transmission of electrical impulses. In people with MS, the slowed or impeded neurological impulses result in uncoordinated or awkward physical responses to their environment (Kraft, 1981).

For the majority of people with MS—around 70 percent—the course of the disease is characterised by seemingly random cycles of exacerbations (relapses) and remissions (Rumrill, Roessler, & Cook, 1998). Not only is the person with relapsing/remitting MS unable to predict when (or for how long) an exacerbation will occur, but he or she cannot anticipate with any certainty which symptoms to expect. For others, the disease may present as a very gradual progression of disability from the outset, or shift to that form over time.

The most common physiological symptom is fatigue, followed by balance and coordination problems, diminished strength and stamina, motor dysfunction, bowel or bladder dysfunction, visual impairment, depression, anxiety, pain, cognitive difficulties, sexual dysfunction and speech impairment (Koch, Rumrill, Roessler, & Fitzgerald, 2001; Rumrill, Roessler, & Cook, 1998). MS can cause problems in virtually every area of physical and cognitive functioning. The problems that stem from the existence of unseen symptoms such as fatigue, pain, diminished strength and stamina, and cognitive difficulties can create great confusion in the workplace. MS is a disease that is almost always confusing and frustrating for everyone exposed to it; it is certainly likely to be confusing for employers and colleagues of people who have it.

Unfortunately, retention of employment for people with MS is even lower than figures for other people with disabilities in general, and lower than would be expected even for people with very severe physical disability (Roessler & Rumrill, 1994). More than 90 percent of people with MS have employment histories, with most (60 percent) still working at the time of diagnosis (La Rocca, 1995; Rumrill, Tabor, Hennessey, & Minton, 2000) and yet as few as 25 or 30 percent of people with MS are able to retain employment as their illness progresses (Jackson & Quaal, 1991; Jongbloed, 1998; Roessler & Rumrill, 1994). Women are significantly less likely to be employed than are men. In the United States, 80 percent of women and 60 percent of men with MS were unemployed (La Rocca, Kalb, Scheinberg, & Kendall, 1985). In Canada, the figures were similar: 70 percent of women and 58 percent of men with MS were unemployed (Edgley, Sullivan, & Dehoux, 1991).

Once the person disengages from work, several threats to their continuing career identity become evident: there may be potential disincentives from Social Security support payments; they may assume the "sick role," which does not encourage a return to independence or work; and they may socially detach from former co-workers (Rumrill, 1996). People with MS who leave the workforce are unlikely to return (Rumrill, Tabor, Hennessey, & Minton, 2000).

Physical limitations are the most commonly cited reasons why people with MS leave the workforce (see, for examples, Duggan, Fagan, & Yateman, 1993). However, others have claimed that the variation in employment status seems to be due not to the severity of the disease or to educational, gender, or other demographic differences but, instead, to factors such as premorbid personality, coping style, characteristics of the workplace, and social support systems (LaRocca, Kalb, Kendall, & Scheinberg, 1982). Still others have argued that the capricious disease course—the cyclic ebb and flow of symptoms and disability—are what constitute the most prominent impediment to adjustment following diagnosis (Rumrill, Roessler, & Cook, 1998) and, thus, the biggest hurdle to continuing employment.

What is clear is that the severe and pervasive impact of the disease is just one reason for the low rate of post-diagnosis employment (Roessler & Rumrill, 1994). Indeed, several authors have pointed to the fact that the levels of disability do not equate directly or comfortably with the levels of employment in people with MS, compared to others with disabilities in the community (LaRocca & Hall, 1990; Roessler & Rumrill, 1994). Physical disability is not the only, or even the primary, cause of unemployment in people with MS (LaRocca, Kalb, Kendall, & Scheinberg, 1982). People with MS often leave the work force for non MS-related reasons (Rumrill, Tabor, Hennessey, & Minton, 2000).

So, while there has been some recognition that people with MS may be leaving work for a variety of reasons that may or may not be directly associated with the disease process and associated disability, there has been little written about the potential role of employers and colleagues in this passage away from work (Vickers, 2007). I claim that it may not always be the progression of MS, the coping abilities of the person diagnosed, a lack of open communication, or physical barriers that are responsible for some people with MS leaving work prematurely. Instead, institutional phenomena such as stigma, discrimination, excessive managerialism, and the hijacking of legitimate organizational processes for less than legitimate purposes may be responsible for some people with MS leaving their places of work either unnecessarily or prematurely.

Methodology

To date, no exploratory, qualitative studies of the experiences and reasoning of people with MS who have left the full time workforce have been conducted. There have been studies conducted about people with MS and associated employment issues (for example, Dyck & Jongbloed, 2000; Gulick, 1992; Ketelaer, 1993, Roessler & Rumrill, 1994; Salomone & O'Connell, 1998; Sumner, 1995). However, none of these studies has been situated in Australia, none has been purely qualitative, and none has addressed the specific reasons why people with MS have left their place of work. Most studies implicitly assume that the disease process or some other physical, psychological, or environmental impediment is responsible.

This qualitative study was intended to explore the subjective experiences of people with MS. Contact was made with potential respondents through the MS Society of New South Wales. I was invited to contact members of support groups, which included attending meetings to explain the study and recruit potential respondents. I interviewed twenty-one respondents, with twenty-two interviews being conducted in total. Interviews ranged from ninety minutes to three hours in duration and were guided by focus areas that shifted according to what respondents said as the interview process continued. In all, there were over forty-three hours of interview data that translated into thirty-five tapes, 335,258 words, and 1,222 pages of verbatim transcribed data. One of those interviews forms the case study shared here.

This case is deliberately presented from the perspective of a woman, Miranda, who has MS. The case is presented to explore Miranda's individual lived experience of working with MS and is not intended to be neutral or unbiased in its presentation. The value of the case is in its ability to share her perspective, meanings, and experiences so that managers and practitioners might learn how their (often unintended or ill-considered) behaviors might impact those with disabilities who work with them.

A Case Study: Miranda

Miranda was a thirty-eight-year-old woman, single, and living alone. She had no children, but both her parents were still alive, as were her two sisters. Miranda made it clear that neither of her sisters offered her any support. Of interest, Miranda's mother also had MS and was diagnosed when Miranda was just ten years old. Miranda achieved a high school education and was working as a flight attendant in the airline industry at the time she learned she had MS. Although her MS had commenced in a more benign, relapsing/remitting form (meaning that she had discrete episodes of disability after which she either partially or wholly recovered), at the time I met with her, the MS had clearly shifted to the secondary progressive form (meaning she was experiencing a gradual but constant deterioration in her level of ability).

Miranda's journey with MS began when she lost vision in one eye. She described her frightening introduction to the disease that would change her life:

> Miranda: I had a headache for about ten days . . . and basically I just got up to shower and go to the toilet. So I got up and I sat here [indicating her lounge room] and made myself a cup of tea. And I just covered my eye and then I looked out of one eye and thought, "Oh, I can't see!" And it was pitch black. It was like thick black smoke and I thought, "I can't see out of that eye!"

Miranda rang her GP, who immediately referred her to a neurologist and she was hospitalized. Miranda believed, at that time, that she would just go to the doctor and get some tablets or have some treatment that would fix her up. Unfortunately, it didn't work out that way. She was admitted to the hospital and given drug therapy for seven days in an attempt to bring back her sight:

> MV: And did it?
>
> Miranda: It took about five months.

I asked her what happened with work when she lost her sight.

> Miranda: I had five months off. They told me I'd used all my sick leave, and they told me that I had to use my long service leave and I used a few months of my long service leave. And that was [MV is making a face, looking astonished]—yes—and then I later found out I didn't have to use it, and because they felt so bad they gave it back to me.
>
> MV: Right, and who did you tell? Like how did that unfold?
>
> Miranda: I didn't tell anybody; I didn't really speak to anyone at [name of employer].

After having the five months off work—over which time she didn't disclose to her employer that she had MS, just that she had an eye problem—Miranda continued to work for another three years without incident. It was only after she disclosed that she had MS at work that her problems started.

Miranda: I spoke to a manager and I was signing on for a trip and I got emotional . . . and then I said, "Oh, I think I've got MS." I was a bit emotional. Then he said, "Are you ok? Do you want to talk?" and I said, "No, it's alright." And I was about to sign on and fly out to, I don't know, London or something, and nothing was said. And then I went away on a trip and a disgruntled passenger wrote a report about me. It was my first bad letter in ten years of my flying and he wrote in his letter that I seemed to be off my face.

MV: Off your face?

Miranda: And they took me out of the sky, grounded me. [Miranda is weeping].

MV: Did you think you were?

Miranda: No! No!! So not. I wish I was, in a way. I had a slight limp, if anything. This was just one of the passengers who wasn't happy. I didn't bow down to him or whatever, and he wrote this stupid letter and that letter then made the [human resources manager] click and he thought, "She talked about MS" . . . so they pretty much stood me down, brought me into the office, took me out of flying.

One report from a disgruntled passenger was used as the initial leverage to get Miranda to cease her flying duties. She had, by this stage, developed a very slight limp, but she reported that this was barely noticeable and did not affect her being able to do her job.

Miranda: You really couldn't tell . . . and I didn't really talk about it that much. It was, you couldn't tell. You really couldn't tell that I had it and nothing was wrong with me.

MV: You didn't think it was a problem?

Miranda: No, I didn't think it was a problem.

MV: So, you didn't see the doctor at that point?

Miranda: No, or throughout all this time. I'd seen neurologists and that. They noticed the left leg weak, but, you know, I was fine.

MV: Ok, but you could still walk and you had a bit of a limp, and you could still do all of your work.

Miranda: All of my duties, yes. Everything.

After disclosing the MS, Miranda found herself facing not one, but three further negative reports about her—after a decade of none. When she complained about being grounded, management told her that it was because of their concerns for her well-being. I saw evidence of the beginnings of a discriminatory process being used to leverage her out of the organization. It was also a process carefully disguised as a legitimate organizational process. (See, for a discussion about bullies doing the same thing, Hutchinson, Vickers, Jackson, & Wilkes, 2005.) Miranda was asked to take sick leave based on medical advice from her employer's doctor.

> Miranda: Like the managers would say, "We are concerned for you, for your welfare, a duty of care." They would rip me out of the sky for any report that was written. This happened once, this happened twice, and this happened three times. I've got copies of all of them where this happened. The fourth time I saw the [employer's] doctor . . . and I said, "Doctor Smith, I've got a limp and I'll show you. Here it is" because my left leg is weak. And I said, "The day I can't take my peers and passengers out of that aircraft, I'll be going." He said, "Miranda, I know. You are the talk of the town in the company now, because you've got MS and it's just, you know how [employer] is, when they start the rumors." And he said, "Would you agree to an ergonomics testing? The company pays a lot of money to do it."
>
> MV: Is this to test to see if you were fit to still fly, is that right?
>
> Miranda: Yes. I agreed with that.

Miranda agreed to do the ergonomics testing and passed all the tests. However, pressure remained on her in the months that followed as she awaited the results. During this time, she was still not allowed to fly. Miranda had this to say about management's protestations of innocence when she suggested that the problems she was experiencing had only come after her disclosure of the MS.

> Miranda: The managers were trying to calm me down, having interviews telling me, "No. No, we are not. No, we are not. No, we are not. No, we are not." And then they just kept denying it and saying that they are not. And I'm saying [Miranda is emotional], "Well, how come you only bring me in the office when I've talked about it [meaning the MS]? How come not any other time? There's no other time. You haven't pulled me out of the sky—only if someone writes about it."

Miranda was alone, financially vulnerable, and her health was deteriorating. While she did explore the possibility of legal action in response to what was happening, she realized that participating in a lawsuit would be likely to further exacerbate her illness, most likely result in further disability, and have a likely outcome—if she won—of a relatively small financial compensation. Employers who wish to divest themselves of employees they don't want are in the driver's seat in such situations, especially if the employee is emotionally, physically, and financially vulnerable (Vickers, 2006a).

Miranda then described a special test that she—and only she—had to do, which was designed to test her physical abilities during an emergency. While she also passed this test, she felt the need to call in the union to support her beforehand, as she felt she had been singled out. Not only did she have to do an extra test that others didn't have to do, but she had to do it alone, rather than as part of a normal group situation, and with more physical exercises than were usually required.

Miranda: Then you have what we call [emergency testing]. Now, you used to have to do [the tests] once a year ... where you guard the door, you pretend there is a fire. "Evacuate, evacuate." Plus, you know, it's the one thing you have to do every year and you hated it, because you have to pretty much get 97 percent to pass. They gave me "one-on-one" [usually these tests are done in groups], and I wrote a report to the union. My union's saying, "I smell a rat in here." They do a huge report about everything . . . what happened, the sequence of events, and saying, "Why are they giving you a one-to-one?"

MV: Yes, did they give you a reason at the time?

Miranda: No. They basically told me, "We want this girl to have one-on-one." And then I rang the manager and I said, "Why am I having one-on-one?" like, "What is it that I have to have one-on-one?" and "We just, well, the [emergency testing department] has been advised that it's just what we've got to do." So I rang the [emergency testing department] and asked them why I am doing this. They made out the guy who was giving it to me one-on-one had no idea. And I thought, "Bullshit!" *"Bull shit!"* He knows. And then two representatives from the union came with me. You have to go down a slide, a blown-up slide, and go down the slide. They made me do this too and the union stepped in and said, "Hang on a minute. This girl doesn't have to go down a slide."

MV: No one else had to do that, did they?

Miranda: No . . . I went down the slide twice. They also . . . a few weeks beforehand . . . the smaller mockup aircraft, when you have to open that door to get the over-wing slides. You push the door in and you throw it

> out. And because of injuries to people's backs and things like that . . . the union stepped in, and you didn't have to open it now. You could pretend that you were opening the door out, because of too many injuries. Not me. I had to throw the door out. So that was huge discrimination. [Miranda's voice is emotional].

Miranda was asked to do more physical activity than other staff would have been asked to do, and more than she had been asked to do during previous testing, and she still passed both this test and the ergonomics test with flying colors. However, in the months that followed, she believed that the stress she experienced as a result of all this scrutiny and pressure to perform exacerbated her condition. Even though she passed all the tests, by the time the results were in and she was allowed to return to flying again, she had deteriorated considerably and she was then no longer able to do her job as a flight attendant.

> Miranda: I thought, "This is the way the company wants me out. This is how they are going to find a way to discriminate against me, make me sign on a dotted line." They'd probably prefer to see the back of me. I thought, "Yep. This is the way the company's going to do it . . . it's going to look like they are not discriminating and they're doing the right thing." And yes, extremely stressed, and knowing I had a mortgage to pay off. . . . And it was like, "Oh, my God, I'm going to lose my job!" And so panic, scared . . . and I just had no idea what they were going to do. . . . I was, yes, really scared. I thought, "I'm out of here now. This is the way the lovely company's going to get rid of me."

Once Miranda's level of disability had progressed to a point where she could no longer fulfil her duties, she asked her employers if there was any other work she could do on the ground. She was still quite capable of answering phones, doing scheduling, and liaising with staff, and had over ten years of knowledge and experience in the industry and with this organization to offer. However, rather than offering to assist her in finding an alternative role, Miranda had to ask about the possibility—and she was not supported when she did.

> Miranda: Before I signed on the dotted line, I said, "Is there anything I can do on the ground?" I said, "I can sit behind a desk or whatever." They said, "You have to apply for the jobs." I said, "Ok." A couple of jobs came up. I applied for a cargo job on the ground, sitting behind the desk, pretty much, it was. When I walked in to do that interview, I lost it. I couldn't even speak. I was so nervous and remembering I hadn't been in an

> interview for about ten years, I hadn't done all this. I had two [interviews]: one was on the ground again, picking up telephones and stuff like that, like a scheduling job, where you answer when crew rings in sick, when crew ring you for different things, and I didn't get that job or the cargo one because I was so nervous. I just shitted myself. . . . They made me go for these jobs, and I didn't get the job. So, basically, they pretty much then said, "We can't help you anymore."

I could understand completely why Miranda was nervous. She was desperate to find work now, knowing that her days as a flight attendant were over. It had been over a decade since she had been in a job interview, she believed that her employer wanted her to leave, and she had received no encouragement to apply. Despite the very real possibility that some kind of work could have been found for her, her employers chose not to assist her in finding alternative work arrangements.

On Miranda's last day, her employers had a morning tea for her farewell. She indicated that this was a rare thing indeed—very special. She was presented with a plaque for her ten years' service. However, all Miranda was thinking about was how she was going to pay the mortgage.

> MV: How were you feeling at the morning tea when they gave you the little plaque and they were making all the right noises?
>
> Miranda: I guess I wasn't really thinking about it. It was more, "It's really happening." I was sad, sad that, "This is really it. This is it; I'm losing my job." It happened so quickly, that morning tea, and I guess I just . . . until I got home and the depression just really hit.
>
> MV: Yes, what were you thinking when you got home?
>
> Miranda: How am I going to pay my mortgage off?

Discussion: Lessons for Managers

What we have seen is an employee with a highly stigmatized illness who chose to disclose it to management at a time when it was not affecting her ability to perform her duties. Management responded in a manner designed to defend the organization at all costs—regardless of the impact on the person involved and at a time when no action was necessary. Their actions were discriminatory and unlawful; they were also insensitive and lacking in compassion. Why might managers do this, and what might be a better approach?

First, I would suggest that stereotypes and associated stigma for people with disabilities in general, and for people with MS in particular, are quite commonplace and likely to be responsible for a large part of the motivation to get rid of people with MS. If you ask the average person who is not well informed about MS what he or she does know, highly negative media images of people in wheelchairs with significant physical and cognitive disability are likely to emerge (Vickers, 2000, 2001). It is quite likely that these kinds of images played in the minds of Miranda's managers when she disclosed her diagnosis.

However, as noted above, for around 70 percent of people with MS, the disease is characterized by relapses that may be wholly or partly recovered from. In many cases, people with MS are physically able to work for many years after diagnosis. However, it has long been recognized that, for many with chronic illness and disability, stigmatization is a part of life (see Goffman, 1963; Nijhof, 1995; Scambler, 1984; Scott, 1974; Vickers, 2000, 2001, 2006b). Miranda was experiencing a negative, even punitive response from her employer as a result of the stigma that attached to her illness (Vickers, 2000).

There are also many misunderstandings about MS and the unpredictable trajectory of the disease. While Miranda's employer may well have had a duty to protect her, their other staff, and the passengers on their flights, at the time she disclosed her diagnosis, she reported that she was able to safely perform her duties. The physical tests she undertook at the time confirmed this. It would appear that Miranda's employer was making flawed assumptions about her illness, which may or may not have proven accurate in the longer term and were certainly not accurate at the time. They appeared to have wanted to be rid of her based on what they expected would happen, whether that was accurate or not.

It is often assumed that, because anti-discrimination legislation now exists to protect people with disabilities in many parts of the Western world (for example, the Americans with Disabilities Act in the United States; the Disability Discrimination Act in Australia, and the Disability Discrimination Act in the UK), then discrimination against people with disabilities in those countries no longer takes place. (See, for examples of such assumptions, Duggan, Fagen, & Yateman, 1993; Huebner, 2000; Roessler & Rumrill, 1994, 1995; Rumrill, Roessler, & Cook, 1998; Rumrill, Tabor, Hennessey, & Minton, 2000). However, that discrimination does still exist; it is just more covert and may come in the form of the manipulation of legitimate organizational processes being used with a different, darker, and less explicit intent than was originally intended.

In the case presented here, the organization employed ergonomic and other physical testing for Miranda, perhaps believing that the additional scrutiny would expose any physical weaknesses and enable them to dispense with her services. However, she passed all the tests. It was only after she passed all the tests and suffered all the additional stress and scrutiny associated with the threat to her continued employment that her disease did deteriorate to a point at which she could not continue with her duties.

One reason why employers might routinely disregard legislative imperatives is that people with disabilities are likely to be more financially vulnerable than most. It is unlikely that they will take on the might of large, well-financed organizations with specialist company lawyers experienced in litigating such cases in the interests of protecting the organization. Employers know this. As long as the burden of proof remains with victims of discrimination, rather than with those accused, the difficulty of proving such events, combined with the stress and expense of court cases, is likely to provide a strong disincentive for people with MS not to litigate, especially when the likely payouts are relatively small (Vickers, 2006a).

Another motive for employers to follow the path described by Miranda is the recent (1980s on) orientation toward "rabid" managerialism in organizations, both public and private (Vickers, 1999). The human costs of managerialism (Britton, 1995; Rees, 1995; Solondz, 1995) can be high, as Miranda's case demonstrates. Miranda herself commented on the obsessive organizational pursuit of dollars and cents, and the inevitable corollary that managers are encouraged to leave their humanity, compassion, and emotional intelligence at the door when they arrive at work. When I asked Miranda what she would have preferred her managers to do differently, she said this.

> Miranda: The managers, those people are taught differently, trained differently. It's all about the money. Like, "What if it was your child or something?" You think, "I hope your child doesn't get cancer or get something like this" . . . but they'd be more understanding if they did.

So what to do? Miranda believed, as I do, that it is often the case that those who are the most understanding and compassionate tend to be those touched by illness, disability, or other hardship. While we won't all have experienced this, there is another way, which Miranda alluded to. Miranda remarked about one person who helped smooth an especially painful separation by convincing another manager to change his approach.

> Miranda: There was a female. . . . She was so understanding. And she actually pushed him into being understanding and I did notice a difference to his tone of voice. I had rung her . . . and I said to her, "What did you do?" because I said, "His attitude really changed." She said, "You know what I did, Miranda? I sat there, had a meeting with him before we were to meet you and said, 'You know what? That could be me or you. '" I said,

> "Thank you so much for making him realize that situation," because it's just, even though things didn't work out, there was a tone of difference in all those meetings. . . . He softened down and it was good because she was in there and I felt more at ease because she brought it to his realization and said, "That could be me or you."

While it is recognized that our ability to imagine the illness experience and to empathize with those who are ill is limited (Morse & Johnson, 1991; Vickers, 2001, 2006b), it can be achieved—with a little effort.

I recommend that you take a moment now and put yourself in Miranda's shoes. Think about how you would feel learning that you had a serious, chronic, disabling illness. Consider waking up one day and not being able to see out of one eye and then think about how or what you might tell your current employer. Take a moment and ponder, realistically, how they might respond. Finally, consider how a serious chronic illness might impact your future career aspirations and then consider what you would do—right now—if you found yourself permanently retired as a result of having a disability.

What I am advocating is the simple, humane, compassionate, and appropriate recognition of the needs of others, especially those with illness or disability in our workplaces. This will enable an orientation toward flexibility and compassion for those among us who are "damaged workers." Policy makers, human resource professionals, and line managers can also find ways to ensure that workers remain productive for as long as possible.

Ask people with disabilities what they need, what they can and cannot do, and what you can do to assist them in continuing to do their jobs. Avoid making assumptions about levels of ability, especially for conditions that are not obvious to the casual observer (which includes most chronic conditions). Also, avoid projecting what little knowledge you might have about an illness or disability onto the bearer of that condition. What is better is to become informed, either by asking the person or by asking people who do know. Striving to keep people with disabilities employed, or at least, employed for longer, will enhance their quality of life through allowing them to continue living full and productive lives. It also makes good business sense not to lose that vital corporate memory, significant experience, and the goodwill that can follow a compassionate response.

Compassion and consideration are effective tools to move forward with employees who are damaged or troubled, not just those with disabilities. Work histories tell us a lot about staff motivations and loyalty. If you employ compassion in your dealings with those who have been loyal to the organization, you will engender trust, compassion, and support from those around you—the classic win-win.

References

Americans with Disabilities Act of 1990 (ADA): Title 1–Employment. U.S. Department of Labor, Employment Standards Administration, Office of Federal Contract Compliance Programs. www.dol.gov/esa.

Britton, S. (1995). Some health costs of managerialism. In S. Rees & G. Rodley (Eds.), *The human costs of managerialism: Advocating the recovery of humanity* (pp. 221–228). Sydney: Pluto Press Australia.

Disability Discrimination Act. (1992). Sydney, Australia: Government Printing Office.

Disability Discrimination Act. (2005). London, UK: Crown Copyright, Controller of HMSO, Queen's Printer of Acts of Parliament, The Stationery Office.

Duggan, E., Fagan, P., & Yateman, S. (1993). Employment factors among individuals with multiple sclerosis. Unpublished manuscript. New York: National Multiple Sclerosis Society.

Dyck, I., & Jongbloed, L. (2000). Women with multiple sclerosis and employment issues: A focus on social and institutional environments. *The Canadian Journal of Occupational Therapy, 67*, 337–346.

Edgley, K., Sullivan, M.J.L., & Dehoux, E. (1991). A survey of multiple sclerosis. Part 2. Determinants of employment status. *Canadian Journal of Rehabilitation, 4*, 127–132.

Goffman, E. (1963). *Stigma: Notes on the management of spoiled identity*. Harmondsworth, Middlesex, England and Ringwood, Victoria, Australia: Penguin Books.

Gulick, E.E. (1992). Model for predicting work performance among persons with multiple sclerosis. *Nursing Research, 41*, 266–272.

Huebner, C. (2000). On the job with multiple sclerosis. *Inside MS, 18*, 12–16.

Hutchinson, M., Vickers, M.H., Jackson, D., & Wilkes, L. (2005). "I'm gonna do what I wanna do!": Organisational change as a vehicle for bullies. *Health Care Management Review, 30*, 331–338.

Jackson, M., & Quaal, C. (1991). Effects of multiple sclerosis on occupational and career patterns. *Axon, 13*, 16–22.

Jongbloed, L. (1998). Disability income: The experiences of women with multiple sclerosis. *The Canadian Journal of Occupational Therapy, 65*, 193–201.

Ketelaer, P. (1993). *Multiple sclerosis and employment: Synthesis report*. Brussels, Belgium: Multiple Sclerosis Society.

Koch, L.C., Rumrill, P.D., Roessler, R.T., & Fitzgerald, S.M. (2001). Illness and demographic correlates of quality of life among people with multiple sclerosis. *Rehabilitation Psychology, 46*, 154–164.

Kraft, G.H. (1981). Multiple Sclerosis. In W.C. Stolow & M.R. Clowers (Eds.), *Handbook of severe disability*. Washington DC: United States Department of Education and Rehabilitation Services Administration.

Kraft, G.H., Freal, J.E., & Coryell, J.K. (1986). Disability, disease duration, and rehabilitation service needs in multiple sclerosis: Patient perspectives. *Archives of Physical and Medical Rehabilitation, 67,* 164–168.

LaRocca, N., Kalb, R., Kendall, P., & Scheinberg, L. (1982). The role of disease and demographic factors in the employment of patients with multiple sclerosis. *Archives of Neurology, 39,* 256–260.

LaRocca, N., Kalb, R., Scheinberg, L., & Kendall, P. (1985). Factors associated with unemployment of patients with multiple sclerosis. *Journal of Chronic Disability, 38,* 203–210.

LaRocca, N.G. (1995). *Employment and multiple sclerosis.* New York: National Multiple Sclerosis Society.

LaRocca, N.G., & Hall, H.L. (1990). Multiple sclerosis program: A model for neuropsychiatric disorders. *New Directions for Mental Health Services, 45,* 49–64.

Nijhof, G. (1995). Parkinson's disease as a problem of shame in public appearance. *Sociology, 17,* 193–205.

Morse, J.M., & Johnson, J.L. (1991). Understanding the illness experience. In J.M. Morse & J.L. Johnson (Eds.), *The illness experience: Dimensions of suffering* (pp. 1–12). Newbury Park, CA: Sage.

MS Australia Website: www.Msaustralia.Org.Au/MSinformation/Faqs/Htm#1.

Rees, S. (1995). The fraud and the fiction. In S. Rees & G. Rodley (Eds.), *The human costs of managerialism: Advocating the recovery of humanity* (pp. 15–28). Sydney: Pluto Press Australia.

Roessler, R.T., & Rumrill, P.D. (1994). Strategies for enhancing career maintenance self-efficacy of people with multiple sclerosis. *The Journal of Rehabilitation, 60,* 54–59.

Roessler, R.T., & Rumrill, P.D. (1995). The relationship of perceived worksite barriers to job mastery and job satisfaction for employed people with multiple sclerosis. *Rehabilitation Counseling Bulletin, 39,* 2–14.

Rumrill, P. (1996). Employment and multiple sclerosis: Policy, programming, and research recommendations. *Work: A Journal of Prevention, Assessment and Rehabilitation, 6,* 205–209.

Rumrill, P.D., Roessler, R.T., & Cook, B.G. (1998). Improving career re-entry outcomes for people with multiple sclerosis: A comparison of two approaches. *Journal of Vocational Rehabilitation, 10,* 241–252.

Rumrill, P.D., Tabor, T.L., Hennessey, M.L., & Minton, D.L. (2000). Issues in employment and career development for people with multiple sclerosis: Meeting the needs of an emerging vocational rehabilitation clientele. *Journal of Vocational Rehabilitation, 14,* 109–117.

Salomone, P.R., & O'Connell, K.R. (1998). The impact of disability on the career development of people with multiple sclerosis. *Journal of Career Development, 25,* 65–81.

Scambler, G. (1984). Perceiving and coping with stigmatizing illness. In R. Fitzpatrick, J. Hinton, S. Newman, G. Scambler, & J. Thompson (Eds.), *The experience of illness* (pp. 203–226). London: Tavistock.

Scott, R.A. (1974). The construction of conceptions of stigma by professional experts. In D.M. Boswell & J.M. Wingrove (Eds.), *The handicapped person in the community* (pp. 108–121). London: Tavistock Publications in Association with The Open University Press.

Solondz, K. (1995). The cost of efficiency. In S. Rees & G. Rodley (Eds.), *The human costs of managerialism: Advocating the recovery of humanity* (pp. 211–220). Sydney: Pluto Press Australia.

Sumner, G. (1995). *Project alliance: A job retention program for employees with chronic illness and their employers*. Denver, CO: National Multiple Sclerosis Society.

Vickers, M.H. (1999). "Sick" organisations, "fabid" managerialism: Work-life narratives from people with "invisible" chronic illness. *Public Voices, 4*, 59–82.

Vickers, M.H. (2000). Stigma, work, and "unseen" illness: A case and notes to enhance understanding. *Illness, Crisis and Loss, 8*, 131–151.

Vickers, M.H. (2001). *Work and unseen chronic illness: Silent voices*. London: Routledge.

Vickers, M.H. (2006a). Towards employee wellness: Rethinking bullying paradoxes and masks. *Employee Responsibilities and Rights Journal, 18*, 267–281.

Vickers, M.H. (2006b). *Working parents of children with chronic illness: Disconnected and doing it all*. London: Palgrave Macmillan.

Vickers, M.H. (2007). Why People with MS are really leaving work: A Clayton's choice and an ugly passage: A phenomenological study. *Proceedings of the 15th Annual International Conference of the Association on Employment Practice and Principles (AEPP)*, 4–6 October, 2007, Fort Lauderdale, Florida, 171–176.

Margaret H. Vickers, Ph.D., *is an associate professor and director of research, School of Management, College of Business, University of Western Sydney. She researches individuals experiencing adversity and trauma at work and is the author of over one hundred international refereed publications, including two books,* Work and Unseen Chronic Illness: Silent Voices *(Routledge, 2001) and* Working and Caring for a Child with Chronic Illness: Disconnected and Doing it All *(Palgrave MacMillan, 2006).*

Provision of Outplacement Services During Redundancy

Lessons from Australian Executives

Melissa A. Parris and Margaret H. Vickers

Summary

The increasing prevalence of organizational downsizing has been matched by the growth in the number of outplacement service organizations. It has been argued that the provision of outplacement services to employees who have been made redundant can have benefits for both the individual and the downsizing organization. Yet there has been limited research on either the effectiveness of these programs or the experience of individuals using them. The experience of using outplacement services was explored by the authors in a qualitative study investigating the experiences of Australian executives who had been made redundant. In this article we compare their experiences to some of the espoused benefits of outplacement services, while highlighting lessons for managers. We present four themes, two of which were positive—use of office services and proactive provision of support—and two of which were negative—absence of counseling skills and impersonal exit from the organization.

These findings highlight the need for managers to choose carefully when considering the use of outplacement services and to give attention to how these services might be most effectively incorporated into the redundancy process.

Organizational downsizing now impacts an increasing cross-section of organizations, occupations, and countries (Donnelly & Scholarios, 1998). Since the 1980s, issues such as deregulation, decline in organizational growth, and intensified global competition have all placed pressure on organizations to reduce costs (Dopson, Risk, & Stewart, 1992; Goffee & Scase, 1986). Thus, organizations have restructured and downsized, essentially "cutting back" on employee numbers. At the start of the 21st Century, the pace of organizational downsizing has continued unabated. Furthermore, reductions in the workforce are not only occurring in organizations in which it is deemed necessary for immediate survival, but in "healthy" companies endeavoring to pre-empt future economic difficulties (Cascio, 2002). While termination of employment has always been present due to cyclical economic conditions, organizational downsizing today impacts a greater number of white-collar workers, including middle- and senior-level managers and executives.

The increased use of organizational restructuring and downsizing has many impacts for managers today, not least of which is increased concern for their own positions and careers (Armstrong-Stassen, 2006; Ebadan & Winstanley, 1997). Importantly, it has also required many managers to be involved in the removal of others from the organization—both in deciding who is made redundant and in communicating this to those affected. Wright and Barling (1998) report the experience of "downsizers" as being professionally demanding, incorporating significant role ambiguity and overload, and being a source of profound guilt. This article provides insight for managers who may be undertaking redundancies and focuses attention on the provision of outplacement services that can provide benefits to both the downsizing organization and the person who has been made redundant.

Outplacement has been broadly defined as any planned efforts provided (or paid for) by an organization in order to assist employees who have been made redundant to seek new employment (Mendleson, 1975). As the number of people experiencing redundancy has increased, there has been a concurrent growth in the provision of outplacement services (Butterfield & Borgen, 2005). This increasing emphasis on outplacement services means that managers today require both an understanding of the range of services that can be offered and of the reasons for choosing these. Yet there is a dearth of current literature to assist managers in gaining this knowledge (Tzafrir, Mano-Negrin, Harel, & Rom-Nagy, 2006).

Most commonly, outplacement services are provided by an external firm (Papalexandris, 1996). However, the level of assistance provided by outplacement services can vary greatly, from short group workshops to long-term individualized attention (Westaby, 2004). Practical assistance and support may be provided through a variety of resources, such as career assessment, skills identification and training, office support services, and the development of job-search strategies, including networking, resume writing, interview training, and image development (Butterfield & Borgen, 2005; Doherty, 1998; Westaby, 2004). Proponents of outplacement services highlight the stress and anxiety associated with the redundancy process and emphasize the need for psychological support through the provision of counseling services (Arslan, 2005).

Much of the literature endorsing outplacement services has emphasized the benefits for the downsizing organization. These potential benefits include a reduced chance of litigation, improved morale for remaining employees, and an enhanced organizational image within the community (Fulmer & Fryman, 1985; Simon, 1988; Soukup, Rothman, & Brisco, 1987). It is argued that these benefits are realized because outplacement services are viewed as being a humane and just approach to the redundancy process (Doherty, 1998). The benefits for people being made redundant are often expressed using similar language—to assist those who have been made redundant in "managing" their transition process and "moving forward" in their new career path (Butterfield & Borgen, 2005; Doherty, 1998).

However, despite the proliferation of outplacement services in many countries, there has been limited research on either the effectiveness of these programs or the experience of individuals involved in them (Butterfield & Borgen, 2005; Westaby, 2004). This paucity of research reflects the limited attention that downsizing research has focused on those who are made redundant—often called the "victims"—when compared to those remaining in the organization (Vickers & Parris, 2007). These individuals continue to be considered as "out of sight, out of mind" (Simon, 1988, p. 52), fading into obscurity (Appelbaum, Close, & Klasa, 1999). Yet, if managers want to see the organizational benefits outlined above realized, attention needs to be given to how outplacement services are experienced by the individuals who use them.

Stories of redundancy can have impact on both the morale of remaining employees and the community's image of the organization. In this article, we focus on the outplacement experiences of Australian executives who have been made redundant and consider how these compare to some of the espoused benefits found in the outplacement literature. Our discussion highlights lessons for managers, both in choosing outplacement service organizations and in how to best incorporate their use into the redundancy process.

Research Methodology

The stories presented here come from a larger exploratory study focused on the individual experience of being made redundant. An interpretive qualitative approach guided the study, emphasizing lived experience (Oiler, 1982) and the meaning that experience holds for the individual (Drew, 1989). Using this approach, our understanding was developed through examining the "network of meanings and significances" (Skoldberg, 1998, p. 78) individuals created and shared about their experiences.

Purposive sampling was used in the selection of the ten respondents to the study; all had experienced being made redundant (see Creswell, 1998). Focused, in-depth interviews were conducted with each respondent, exploring multiple facets of their experiences. All interviews were transcribed verbatim, and thematic analysis was conducted, identifying patterns in the data (Taylor & Bogdan, 1998), which revealed the meaning of individuals' experiences (Benner, 1994). The analysis sought to explore both the shared and unique stories to better understand the experience of being made redundant.

All respondents were middle- and senior-level executives. Nine males and one female participated and, reflective of the increased number of individuals experiencing multiple redundancies over their working lives, four of the respondents had been made redundant twice and two had experienced redundancy three times. While the level of outplacement services received varied, all respondents had had an opportunity to use outplacement services in their most recent redundancy, with the time period of access ranging from three months to "indefinite" (i.e., longer than a year). In the following discussion, respondents have all been given pseudonyms to protect their privacy and confidentiality.

Executive Experiences of Outplacement Services

When analyzing these executives' stories, it became apparent that there were mixed feelings about the value of outplacement services. While respondents spoke positively about some of their experiences, they also shared negative perspectives. These ambivalent responses demonstrated recognition of the potential value that outplacement services might provide, making clear that many of their expectations were not met. Shen's remarks encapsulated the views of many respondents:

> Shen: The bit that I did use, I was happy about that; I just didn't use it that much at all.

Most respondents found some services offered were limited in terms of the help they provided; these tended not to be used for that reason. However, in many cases, there were elements of the outplacement services that were actively avoided, not only because they did not provide the benefits advertised, but because they had the potential to cause more stress and anxiety for the executive.

The following discussion highlights this sense of ambivalence by focusing on the four key themes discussed by respondents. Of the four, two were positive—use of office services and proactive provision of support—and two were negative—absence of counseling skills and impersonal exit from the organization.

Use of Office Services

When outplacement services were originally developed, the elements of office support, such as telephones, fax machines, computers, and secretarial support, were a primary component (Kirk, 1994; Mendleson, 1975). When needing to find new employment, these tools aid individuals in their job search. Office support equipment still forms part of most outplacement services to varying degrees. However, we note that, as more people have computers and other resources in their homes, the physical need for these services may not be as great as in the past. Some respondents mentioned this specifically:

> Shen: I've got all the connections, the Internet, at home. I didn't need any of their facilities.

Nevertheless, provision of office support services was identified as an important outplacement service offering. It became apparent from respondents' stories that the utilization of office support services had greater significance beyond the use of equipment. Even if respondents had home offices, many still travelled to the outplacement office as it provided a sense of structure and a "place" to go:

> Tony: Part of the counseling that they give here is, "Try and keep your life as normal as possible." Which is pretty much what I've been doing. And I tend to come in here to work rather than try and work from home. I find the distractions at home are more than in here. It's a bit more like a work environment, which is helpful.

The interview with Tony was actually conducted at the outplacement firm and, at the time of our interview, Tony noted that he was coming into the office two or three times a week. Other respondents also spoke about this need for structure, and how they appreciated being part of an office environment. This was described as providing a sense of normality, where "normal" was going to work, rather than being at home. Ben shared how important this feeling was for him, and how it was absent from his outplacement experience during his second period of unemployment after redundancy. On that occasion, he was given that desired sense of belonging from a person outside of the outplacement service:

> Ben: A guy I didn't really know that well gave me his boardroom and his secretary to help me—fax, telephone, and so forth. It was only a small environment, so there were only three people in the office, but the other two were extremely friendly. I mean, even little things like they used to buy

> lotto tickets each week; if I was in there, they'd buy me one just so I felt part of the team. That guy, I have *huge* admiration for and huge gratitude too, because he really went out of his way.

When choosing an outplacement service, managers should ensure that office support is offered—not only the physical equipment but a structured and accessible space where individuals can go to feel "normal" and be more productive in their search for future employment.

Proactive Provision of Support

Within the counseling literature, some attention has been given to what constitutes an exemplary model of outplacement counseling. These models commonly recognize the grief process involved (e.g., Aquilanti & Leroux, 1999; Kirk, 1994; Mirabile, 1985), with individuals who have been made redundant experiencing shock, denial, and anger. As any or all of these emotions can be felt at the point of being made redundant, attention has been drawn to the value of an outplacement consultant or counselor playing a role from the initial notification of redundancy (Arslan, 2005). The outplacement consultant can potentially provide support for individuals as they deal with their initial reactions to the news. Some executives confirmed these findings, reporting a positive experience as a result:

> Ben: I think the biggest thing that helped in that particular case was that I was able to talk with him [the outplacement counselor] because he didn't know me and he was independent. I found it much more difficult to talk it through, well, particularly with my wife; it was harder to talk through your feelings and what you were going to do with people who knew you than it was with someone who didn't know you but was sympathetic. So, at that particular point in time, he was certainly invaluable to me.

Those executives who spoke positively of the counseling service frequently used the word "comfortable" to describe this relationship. This is of interest—and value—when considering the discomfort many respondents expressed with respect to sharing their experiences of redundancy with family, friends, and former colleagues. This appeared particularly relevant for the men in this study, some of whom were reluctant to discuss their feelings with others, as Ben's comments above confirm.

This discomfort was also evident when relating to the manager who delivered the news of redundancy, particularly if a positive working relationship had previously been present. Having an outplacement counselor present at this time can be helpful—and managers should consider doing this. Indeed, it is important for managers to recognize that the outplacement "service" should begin before the point of making an individual redundant. Managers need to meet with the outplacement consultant to plan and discuss how the meeting with the employee will be conducted and the specific roles both the manager and the outplacement consultant will take.

When discussing the role the outplacement counselor played in their experiences, some respondents also pointed to the proactive nature of their counselor:

> Anthony: [The outplacement counselor] was very proactive. He actually phoned me and said, "When are you coming to see me?" So I think the following week—I can't remember precisely—I went around there and we started a program.

This element of proactivity from the counselors proved invaluable for many, especially given the level of emotionality associated with the redundancy journey. It is the emotional highs and lows of the redundancy journey that are often most vividly recalled after the fact and that are most likely to impact the individual's long-term view of the overall process. The experiences of these executives also mirrored the findings of a study conducted in Belgium on the effectiveness of outplacement services. Participants in the Belgian study also expressed an appreciation for the "psychological respite" that early interventions and proactive responses can provide (De Witte, Vandoorne, Verlinden, & De Cuyper, 2005, p. 153).

While being made redundant will never be an easy experience, sensitivity from managers and proactivity from outplacement counselors can aid in ameliorating the personal impacts, as Jake confirms:

> Jake: The outplacement fellow was very helpful. He even rang me at home the following day to see whether I was OK, and we had a quick chat. So that sort of restored some of my faith in people to a certain degree.

For Jake, there was still a long way to go in the journey of recovery, but this sign of caring from an outplacement worker was remembered.

When choosing an outplacement service, managers should not only consider whether counseling services are offered, but how "active" the support is. To provide a valuable service, it may not be sufficient for services to "be there" when the individual asks for them. Rather, recognition of the individual's practical and emotional needs is required. Furthermore, attention is required to be directed to the quality of the counseling skills offered by outplacement service organizations, as these can vary dramatically.

Absence of Counseling Skills

While the provision of counseling is often put forward as a key benefit of outplacement services—and as a way for terminated employees to speak with someone more "experienced" in working through the redundancy process—experienced counselors are not always present in outplacement firms. What some agencies label as counseling does not always incorporate the experience required to support people dealing with the anger, fear, and anxiety that often follows being made redundant. Indeed, a key concern raised about outplacement services has been the lack of trained counsellors (Butterfield & Borgen, 2005). However, worse are the use of impersonal computer-based questionnaires administered in place of the intervention of a qualified practitioner:

> Jake: I remember it was a PC-based questionnaire. That was their form of counseling. It was no real sit in a room with a cup of coffee and just basically chat through it to work through the process and, you know, try and work out and get to an end result so you can move on. There was none of that. It was sit down and work through this PC-based questionnaire so we can put you in a database with all these other people so we can work out programs to manage your type of situation.

Jake's experience stands in stark contrast to the proactive counseling he experienced after his second redundancy. It also challenges the putative "humane" nature of an outplacement service, with "support" in this instance being provided by a computer. However, merely including another person in the process is not sufficient; strong counseling skills and experience are required. Clarkson (1995) shares this concern, relating an example from a training program she was involved with that offered similarly inadequate training for those living with the emotional responses that traditionally attach to involvement with one's own or another's job loss.

Researchers have emphasized the importance of outplacement counselors having strong interpersonal skills, empathy, warmth, caring and understanding (Aquilanti & Leroux, 1999; Kirk, 1994; Soukup, Rothman, & Brisco, 1987). However, these skills are just a beginning. With outplacement counselors playing a role both at the initial point of redundancy and in the days and weeks (and possibly months) that follow, they must have the skills to deal with the various emotional stages their clients will move through. For the few executives who believed they did receive skilled counseling support, it was their subsequent reflections that allowed recognition of the value of what had transpired, which could then be incorporated into their subsequent discussions:

> Anthony: Being a psychologist, he probably knew what I was going through, knew the behaviors and all that sort of thing, but we really got straight into doing some psychometric testing. I just found he was a fairly nice sort of a person, and we spoke about a lot of my personal interests. I'm a fairly obsessive-compulsive perfectionist, so we were talking a lot about that sort of stuff. Then we were talking about his family and what he's done, so there was a lot of—how can I say it—not bonding, but there was a lot of personal stuff that we were talking about. I was feeling very comfortable with him as a person and, I suppose, he was trying to do that. And probably just seeing that I was sort of psychologically moving forward.

These stories highlight the need for managers to give attention to the level of counseling qualifications of counselors and consultants. While an empathetic and caring outplacement consultant is a basic requirement, adequate skill and experience are also essential.

Impersonal Exit from the Organization

Much of the literature endorsing outplacement services has traditionally applauded them as being a "humane" organizational response (Fulmer & Fryman, 1985; Hill & Fannin, 1991; Soukup, Rothman, & Brisco, 1987). This can be an appealing benefit for organizations as they seek to reduce the negative impacts on those employees who remain after downsizing (Hopkins & Weathington, 2006; Lee & Corbett, 2006). It has been argued that having an outplacement consultant present at the point of redundancy can "soften the initial impact of the termination" (Hill & Fannin, 1991, p. 15). However, this study confirmed that the presence of an outplacement consultant was, in itself, not sufficient to alleviate the negative impacts of redundancy. Respondents described feeling "bundled along" the redundancy path, with outplacement service provision being described by them as merely another step in the process:

> Jake: And then the following day they came out and said, "No, you're all gone." And then we were moved down into some meeting rooms, given our formal letter in one room, and then moved next door to the outplacement.

Doherty (1998) argues that outplacement is often used by organizations as a "bolt-on tool" to help smooth the path of redundancy for managers, as much as it is designed to support those being made redundant. However, the presence of an outplacement consultant might have little or no beneficial impact on either party if the process has not been given sufficient sensitive consideration and pre-planning:

> Anthony: They were sort of like joint executive directors for what they call the customer service group. One of them did all the talking, and she was basically saying, "Look, unfortunately there's nothing for you moving forward. You didn't choose to look at some of the alternatives. Blah, blah, blah. Here's your package. Here's the HR person. Now you're going to be taken down to the psychologist on the thirteenth floor and he'll talk you through it." And that was it.

This "handing off" of the employee to the outplacement consultant reinforces the notion of the employee feeling "out of sight, out of mind" (Simon, 1988, p. 52). The expedient and impersonal manner in which this occurred did little to assuage the painful emotional impact for the individual affected—nor enhance their perception of the organization they were leaving.

While the previous three themes provide some valuable insights into choosing a quality outplacement service, including the need to offer extensive office support, high-quality and proactive counseling skills, as well as attention to individuals' particular needs, it must be emphasized that the benefits gained from doing this will be lost if the point of exit from the organization is not handled correctly. Kamal spoke of his experience on the day of being made redundant:

> Kamal: There were no complaints with anything; fax machine, mobile, telephone, car, the whole lot was kept for me, *and* they gave me outplacement for twelve weeks. Which was the best thing I did. So in one sense they treated me with dignity—I even went out for a meal with a couple of directors—and *yet* the whole act was done in such a nasty way. I was frog-marched out of the building.

If employees are to be treated with consideration, managers need to also consider the whole manner in which the redundant person exits from the physical workplace. We recognize that this experience can also be emotionally difficult for managers and, indeed, recommend that managers should also seek support in dealing with their reactions (Wright & Barling, 1998). However, as Kamal's story demonstrates, respectful treatment at the point of exit is an essential part of a successful redundancy strategy. Negative experiences can have a lasting effect on the person being made redundant and on remaining employees.

Conclusion

The proliferation of outplacement service organizations has led to a greater expectation that such services will be provided when employees—particularly executives—are made redundant. However, there can be a great deal of variation in the level and quality of the services provided. For managers who have the task of managing the redundancy process, it is not sufficient to merely arrange provision of an outplacement service for exiting employees. Attention should be given to both the services offered and how the outplacement counselor is involved in the redundancy process.

The stories of executives presented in this article highlight the importance of having skilled (and proactive) psychological support available for individuals as they deal with the shock, grief, and anger resulting from being made redundant. When choosing an outplacement service, managers should investigate carefully the expertise and professional qualifications held by those in the outplacement organization and speak with consultants about the level of active support to be provided to their clients.

In addition to providing office support, outplacement organizations need to create a "place" for individuals to go where they will feel comfortable as they seek re-employment. Managers should investigate this and ensure that the outplacement services provided are more than impersonal job-search tools or group-based workshops. Attention to these details prior to the commencement of the redundancy process will improve the experience of the person to be made redundant. A positive experience with outplacement services will not only be beneficial to the individual involved, but the organization will also benefit as positive stories are subsequently shared with remaining employees and others in the community.

Managers also need to ensure that they do not rely on the outplacement consultant entirely and take care to maintain the quality of their own interactions with individuals being made redundant. As the executives in this study highlighted, the potential benefits of a good outplacement service can be lost if the individual's exit from the organization is not handled with sensitivity and care. While an outplacement counselor can provide a valuable contribution at the point of redundancy, managers need to avoid creating an impression of "handing off" their involvement and responsibility too soon. We also argue that careful consideration should be made as to how redundant employees should ultimately leave the physical workspace. While security and confidentiality are of concern, managers should consider how their actions will be perceived by those departing and those watching others depart. Avoid situations in which an exiting employee feels shame and humiliation. Attention must be given to maintaining both the redundant person's dignity as well as preserving the image of the organization for the benefit of remaining employees.

It is people, not merely positions, that are affected by redundancies. It is vital that the emotions of all involved—managers implementing redundancies, employees who have been made redundant, and employees who remain—be taken into account at every stage.

References

Appelbaum, S.H., Close, T.G., & Klasa, S. (1999). Downsizing: An examination of some successes and more failures. *Management Decision, 37*(5), 424–436.

Aquilanti, T.M., & Leroux, J. (1999). An integrated model of outplacement counseling. *Journal of Employment Counseling, 36*(4), 177–192.

Armstrong-Stassen, M. (2006). Determinants of how managers cope with organizational downsizing. *Applied Psychology: An International Review, 55*(1), 1–26.

Arslan, H.B. (2005). Where can outplacement be placed? Offering a broader role to assistance: A theoretical approach. *Problems and Perspectives in Management, 3*, 137–146.

Benner, P. (1994). The tradition and skill of interpretive phenomenology in studying health, illness, and caring practices. In P. Benner (Ed.), *Interpretive phenomenology: Embodiment, caring, and ethics in health and illness* (pp. 99–127). Thousand Oaks, CA: Sage.

Butterfield, L.D., & Borgen, W.A. (2005). Outplacement counseling from the client's perspective. *The Career Development Quarterly, 53*(4), 306–316.

Cascio, W.F. (2002). Strategies for responsible restructuring. *Academy of Management Executive, 16*(3), 80–91.

Clarkson, P. (1995). Redundancy counseling. *Employee Counseling Today, 7*(7), 7–13.

Creswell, J.W. (1998). *Qualitative inquiry and research design: Choosing among five traditions*. Thousand Oaks, CA: Sage.

De Witte, H., Vandoorne, J., Verlinden, R., & De Cuyper, N. (2005). Outplacement and re-employment measures during organizational restructuring in Belgium: Overview of the literature and results and qualitative research. *Journal of European Industrial Training, 29*(2), 148–164.

Doherty, N. (1998). The role of outplacement in redundancy management. *Personnel Review, 27*(4), 343–353.

Donnelly, M., & Scholarios, D. (1998). Workers' experiences of redundancy: Evidence from Scottish defence-dependent companies. *Personnel Review, 27*(4), 325–342.

Dopson, S., Risk, A., & Stewart, R. (1992). The changing role of the middle manager in the United Kingdom. *International Studies of Management and Organization, 22*(1), 40–53.

Drew, N. (1989). The interviewer's experience as data in phenomenological research. *Western Journal of Nursing Research, 11*(4), 431–429.

Ebadan, G., & Winstanley, D. (1997). Downsizing, delayering and careers: The survivor's perspective. *Human Resource Management Journal, 7*(1), 79–91.

Fulmer, W.E., & Fryman, C. (1985). A managerial guide to outplacement services. *S.A.M. Advanced Management Journal, 50*(3), 10–13.

Goffee, R., & Scase, R. (1986). Are the rewards worth the effort? Changing managerial values in the 1980s. *Personnel Review, 15*(4), 3–6.

Hill, C.J., & Fannin, W.R. (1991). Management of the corporate layoff: Developing an effective outplacement program. *Business Forum, 16*(1), 14–17.

Hopkins, S.M., & Weathington, B.L. (2006). The relationships between justice perceptions, trust, and employee attitudes in a downsized organization. *The Journal of Psychology, 140*(5), 477–498.

Kirk, J.J. (1994). Putting outplacement in its place. *Journal of Employment Counseling, 31*(1), 10–18.

Lee, J., & Corbett, J.M. (2006). The impact of downsizing on employees' affective commitment. *Journal of Managerial Psychology, 21*(3), 176–199.

Mendleson, J.L. (1975). Does your company need outplacement? *S.A.M. Advanced Management Journal, 40*(1), 4–12.

Mirabile, R.J. (1985). Outplacement as transition counseling. *Journal of Employment Counseling, 22*(1), 39–45.

Oiler, C. (1982). The phenomenological approach to nursing research. *Nursing Research, 31*(3), 178–181.

Papalexandris, N. (1996). Downsizing and outplacement: The role of human resource management. *The International Journal of Human Resource Management, 7*(3), 605–617.

Simon, D.R. (1988). Outplacement: Meeting needs, matching services. *Training & Development Journal, 42*(8), 52–57.

Skoldberg, K. (1998). Heidegger and organization: Notes towards a new research programme. *Scandinavian Journal of Management, 14*(1/2), 77–102.

Soukup, W.R., Rothman, M., & Brisco, D.R. (1987). Outplacement services: A vital component of personnel policy. *S.A.M. Advanced Management Journal, 52*(4), 19–23.

Taylor, S.J., & Bogdan, R. (1998). *Introduction to qualitative research methods. A guidebook and resource* (3rd ed.). Hoboken, NJ: John Wiley & Sons.

Tzafrir, S.S., Mano-Negrin, R., Harel, G.H., & Rom-Nagy, D. (2006). Downsizing and the impact of job counseling and retraining on effective employee responses. *Career Development International, 11*(2), 125–144.

Vickers, M.H., & Parris, M.A. (2007). "Your job no longer exists!": From experiences of alienation to expectations of resilience: A phenomenological study. *Employee Responsibilities and Rights Journal, 19*(2), 113–125.

Westaby, J.D. (2004). The impact of outplacement programs on reemployment criteria: A longitudinal study of displaced managers and executives. *Journal of Employment Counseling, 41*(1), 19–28.

Wright, B., & Barling, J. (1998). "The executioner's song": Listening to downsizers reflect on their experiences. *Canadian Journal of Administrative Sciences, 15*(4), 339–355.

Dr. Melissa A. Parris *is a lecturer in management at Deakin University. Her research is concerned with individuals' workplace experiences and the personal effects of these. Dr Parris' research projects to date have included a focus on both middle managers and individuals within organizational teams and have resulted in several refereed journal articles and international conference papers.*

Associate Professor Margaret H. Vickers, Ph.D., *is director of research, School of Management, College of Business, University of Western Sydney. She researches individuals experiencing adversity and trauma at work and is the author of over ninety international refereed publications, including two books,* Work and Unseen Chronic Illness: Silent Voices *(Routledge, 2001) and* Working and Caring for a Child with Chronic Illness: Disconnected and Doing it All *(Palgrave Macmillan, 2006).*

Affirmative Action

Tool for Diversity or Favoritism

Sean T. Foley and Kristie J. Loescher

Summary

The purpose of this article is to examine the legal history of affirmative action and provide guidance to firms wishing to increase the diversity of their workforce while remaining in compliance with EEO laws. The initial legislation enacting affirmative action is discussed, along with the court cases that limited its scope and the most recent legal decisions in this area. Guidance is provided to help companies determine whether discrimination exists in their hiring practices, as well as the components of an Affirmative Action Plan to increase the hiring of qualified members of "underutilized" groups.

Since President John F. Kennedy first uttered the words "affirmative action" on March 6, 1961, the landscape of hiring has evolved to ensure that no class of America's workforce is discriminated against. Affirmative action has had a very deep and colorful history in the forty-six years since its inception.

President Nixon's Philadelphia Order of 1969 laid out, for the first time, clear goals and timetables (Kleiman, 2007). Affirmative action grew over the next few decades to encompass all designated protected classes for admission to school, as well as in hiring.

From a manager's perspective, affirmative action is a tool to increase diversity in workplaces. However, the majority of workplaces and hiring decisions should continue to follow the EEO-mandated "color-blind" philosophy that focuses on each applicant's skills, abilities, and fit for the position.

The 2009 Pfeiffer Annual: Management Development.

The Birth of Affirmative Action

On March 6, 1961, President John F. Kennedy became the first president to reference "affirmative action." Executive Order 10925 created the Committee on Equal Employment Opportunity and mandated that projects financed with federal funds "take affirmative action" to ensure that hiring and employment practices are free of racial bias (Curry, 1996).

A little over three years later, on July 2, 1964, President Lyndon Baines Johnson signed the precedent-setting Civil Rights Act, broadening the scope of bias-free hiring practices. The Civil Rights Act prohibited discrimination of all kinds based not only on race, but color, religion, and national origin (Kleiman, 2007). On June 4, 1965, in a speech to the graduating class at Howard University, President Johnson provided a practical framework for the Act:

> "You do not wipe away the scars of centuries by saying: 'now, you are free to go where you want, do as you desire, and choose the leaders you please.' You do not take a man who for years has been hobbled by chains, liberate him, bring him to the starting line of a race, saying, 'you are free to compete with all the others,' and still justly believe you have been completely fair. . . . This is the next and more profound stage of the battle for civil rights. We seek not just freedom but opportunity—not just legal equity but human ability—not just equality as a right and a theory, but equality as a fact and as a result." (Curry, 1996, p. 17)

Roughly one year later, on September 24, 1965, Johnson established Executive Order 11246 (Kleiman, 2007), mandating employers to take specific measures to ensure equality in hiring and to document their hiring practices. On October 13, 1967, the order was amended to cover discrimination on the basis of gender.

In 1969, Richard Nixon initiated The Philadelphia Order. This plan was the most forceful yet with regard to fair hiring practices. It focused on construction jobs in the Philadelphia area, which were "openly hostile toward letting blacks into their closed circle" (Curry, 1996, p. 27). The Philadelphia Order laid out clear goals and timetables for affirmative action.

Limiting the Scope of Affirmative Action

In June of 1978, the issue of affirmative action was brought to the Supreme Court in the case of Regents of the University of California v. Bakke, a case that required that affirmative action to provide greater opportunities for minorities must not come at the expense of the majority. Allan Bakke, a white job applicant, had been rejected for admission twice, even though minority applicants with significantly lower scores were admitted. Bakke claimed this was a violation of the Equal Protection Clause of the Fourteenth Amendment. The Supreme Court ruled that, while race was a legitimate factor in school admissions, the use of inflexible quotas was not (the school reserved sixteen of every one hundred places for minorities).

On July 2, 1980, the Supreme Court addressed the case of Fullilove v. Klutznick. In this case, the Supreme Court ruled that some quotas were, in fact, constitutional. The Court upheld a federal law requiring that 15 percent of funds for public works be set aside for qualified minority contractors. The Court deemed there to be no "allocation of federal funds according to inflexible percentages solely based on race or ethnicity" (Brunner, 2007).

On May 19, 1986, the case of Wygant v. Jackson Board of Education again addressed the issue of reverse discrimination. Wygant challenged a school board's policy of protecting minority employees at the expense of the non-minority by laying non-minority teachers off first, disregarding seniority. In this case, the Supreme Court ruled against the school board:

> "We have previously expressed concern over the burden that a preferential layoff scheme imposes on innocent parties. In cases involving valid hiring goals, the burden to be borne by innocent individuals is diffused to a considerable extent among society generally. Though hiring goals may burden some innocent individuals, they simply do not impose the same kind of injury that layoffs impose. Denial of a future employment opportunity is not as intrusive as loss of an existing job." (Brunner, 2007)

In July 1970, a federal court found that the State of Alabama Department of Public Safety discriminated against black minorities in hiring (Brunner, 2007). In the thirty-seven-year history of the Alabama Department of Public Safety, there had never been a black trooper. The court ordered reform in its hiring practices. Seventeen years later, on February 25, 1987, the case of United States v. Paradise addressed the department's hiring practices, as they still had not promoted any blacks above entry level. The Supreme Court ordered specific quotas that for every white hired or promoted, one black would also be hired or promoted until at least 25 percent of the upper ranks of the department were composed of blacks. The Supreme Court rationalized this strict quota system to combat the department's obvious racism.

Strict Scrutiny

Two years later, the subject of "strict scrutiny" was addressed, meaning that any affirmative action taken in the workplace was deemed unconstitutional unless racial discrimination could be proven to be "widespread throughout the industry" (Brunner, 2007). For example, in the case of The City of Richmond v. Croson (1989), a local Richmond program set aside 30 percent of city construction funds for black-owned firms. The court ruled that undocumented assertions of past racial discrimination were insufficient to support a racial quota system. Where Croson dealt with state- and local-run affirmative action programs, the case of Adarand Constructors, Inc. v. Peña on June 12, 1995, was its federal counterpart. The Court again called for "strict scrutiny" in determining whether discrimination existed before implementing a federal affirmative action program (Brunner, 2007).

On July 19, 1995, President Clinton called for the elimination of any program that "(a) creates a quota; (b) creates preferences for unqualified individuals; (c) creates reverse discrimination; or (d) continues even after its equal opportunity purposes have been achieved" (Fischer, 2007). This decision in effect upheld the "strict scrutiny" mandate of the Supreme Court and ensured fair practices in affirmative action.

After Clinton's order, on March 18, 1996, affirmative action was addressed in Texas public universities. In Hopwood v. University of Texas Law School, Cheryl Hopwood and three other white law-school applicants challenged the school's affirmative action program, asserting that they were rejected because of unfair preferences toward less-qualified minority applicants. As a result, the 5th U.S. Court of Appeals suspended the university's affirmative action admissions program and ruled that the 1978 Bakke decision was invalid (Brunner, 2007). Hopwood rejected the legitimacy of diversity as a goal, asserting that "educational diversity is not recognized as a compelling state interest" (Moses, 1997). The Supreme Court allowed the ruling to stand. In 1997, the Texas Attorney General announced that all "Texas public universities [should] employ race-neutral criteria" (Brunner, 2007). Texas public universities now rely on the "top 10 percent" rule, which automatically admits any student in the top 10 percent of his or her high school class to the public university of his or her choice to encourage diversity on campuses (Selingo, 2000).

On November 3, 1997, a state ban on all forms of affirmative action was passed in California: "The state shall not discriminate against, or grant preferential treatment to, any individual or group on the basis of race, sex, color, ethnicity, or national origin in the operation of public employment, public education, or public contracting" (Brunner, 2007). This rule was referred to as Proposition 209. On the heels of this legislation came Washington State's Initiative 200 (Brunner, 2007). On December 3, 1998, Washington became the second state to abolish state affirmative action measures. On February 22, 2000, Florida, too, banned race as a factor in college admissions (Brunner, 2007). The Florida legislature approved Governor Jeb Bush's "One Florida" initiative, aimed at ending affirmative action in the state (Graves, 2000).

Current Legal Direction

In a retreat from both the California and Washington acts, on December 13, 2000, the case of Gratz v. Bollinger (2003) was brought to court. A federal judge ruled that the use of race as a factor in admissions at the University of Michigan was constitutional. The University argued that, just as preference "is granted to children of alumni, scholarship athletes, and other groups for reasons deemed beneficial to the university, so too does the affirmative action program serve 'a compelling interest' by providing educational benefits derived from a diverse student body" (Brunner, 2007). On March 27, 2001, the University of Michigan Law School was the subject of another historic case, Grutter v. Bollinger. In this case, a different federal judge came to a different conclusion, invalidating the law school's in-place affirmative action policies and ruling that "intellectual diversity bears no obvious or necessary relationship to racial diversity" (Brunner, 2007). However, this decision was reversed on May 14, 2002 (York, 2007).

June 23, 2003, was the date of the most important and comprehensive affirmative action decision on admission policies since the Bakke case of 1978. In a very heated and tight decision, the Supreme Court (five to four) upheld the University of Michigan Law School's policy (Grutter v. Bollinger, 2003). The Court ruled that race can be one of many factors considered by colleges when selecting their students because it furthers "a compelling interest in obtaining the educational benefits that flow from a diverse student body" (Brunner, 2007).

It is important to note that this article does not provide an exhaustive list of the history of affirmative action in the United States. Instead, the authors have included what they believe to be landmark legislation in the ever-changing landscape of equal hiring practices and fair admission processes. Landmark cases involving universities have resonating impacts regarding management practices in the workplace. These cases provide a bell-weather for employers of the likely focus for future state and federal legislative action.

In the next section, we provide specific recommendations for managers on implementing affirmative action in the workplace.

Recommendations for Managers

Kleiman defines affirmative action in the workplace as "an approach to eliminating employment discrimination by taking proactive initiatives to ensure proper minority group representation within an organization" (2007, p. 35). According to Kleiman, firms should make conscious efforts and special provisions to recruit, train, retain, and promote members of protected classes—those people who are legally protected from discrimination in the workplace. In theory, the overarching goal of affirmative action in the workplace is identical to Equal Employment Opportunity (EEO): hiring decisions should be free of discrimination from factors such as race, gender, age, and disability. However, where EEO promotes the practices of "color-blind" initiatives, affirmative action gives managers the mandate to be "color-conscious" in their practices.

Increase Your Awareness of Potential Discriminatory Practices

Putting into action EEO practices without an affirmative action plan may lead to varying degrees of discrimination in environments in which there is a historically dominant gender or racial majority (Curry, 1996). First, information on most job opportunities travels through informal networks of friends, family, and neighbors. In a work environment dominated by one gender or race, people outside of that majority are left out of the information loop (Thaler-Carter, 2001). This tendency can limit the number of minority candidates available for interviewing.

Second, even when minority candidates are interviewed, employers will gravitate toward candidates they feel most comfortable around and who will "fit" with the dominant culture of the workplace. Workplaces with a culture driven by one race or gender will naturally be more attracted to individuals who will easily fit into that culture. Without dominating qualifications, minority candidates receive a minority of job offers (AHA News, 1999; Columbia, 2000).

Thus, even after over forty years of EEO legislation, systemic discrimination still exists (Clemons, 2004). Next we will outline how to identify unintentional discrimination in your company.

Conduct a Utilization Analysis

Given the legal expectation of "color-blindness" in hiring decisions, coupled with the business advantages of a diverse workforce, the first step for a company trying to identify its diversity challenges is to conduct a utilization analysis. This statistical procedure compares the percentage of each protected group within a given firm to that of the entire available labor market (Kleiman, 2007). A group may be categorized as "underutilized" when there are large discrepancies between the labor population and the employee profile without any bona fide occupational qualifications (e.g., only women can model for Victoria's Secret) (Kleiman, 2007). All federally protected classes should be evaluated, as well as the classes protected in your state.

For larger companies, software tools such as Comprehensive Affirmative Action Management Software (CAAMS) developed by People Clink Inc. exist to help evaluate areas of potential adverse impact that hiring policies or recruiting methods could have on protected classes. Smaller companies can compare their employee racial and gender profiles against local demographics (e.g., if the high school graduate population in the area is 30 percent Hispanic, the employees in jobs requiring only a high school diploma should be about 30 percent Hispanic) (Gruer, 1994).

Rely on Qualifications and Abilities in Hiring

Where no "underutilized" groups are found, a "color-blind" approach should be followed: focus recruitment and selection solely on qualifications and abilities (Attorneys from Goodwin Guber LLP, 2003). The key to successfully avoiding a discrimination lawsuit is to document your recruitment and selection processes to substantiate your reliance on common and objective measurement requirements for all hiring decisions (Columbia, 2000). An excellent resource, *Hiring Compliance Guidelines* by Jerome Bennett (2003), is provided on the Society for Human Resource Management's website (www.shrm.org).

However, where "underutilized" groups are identified, a firm should develop an affirmative action plan (AAP).

Develop an Affirmative Action Plan

An AAP is required of most firms with federal contracts. The Office of Federal Contract Compliance Programs is charged with enforcing contractor affirmative action mandates. Employers without federal contracts may institute voluntary AAPs to remedy past discrimination if certain conditions are met. These are set forth in EEOC (2008) guidance on the subject and should be strongly considered as a proactive anti-discrimination measure by any firm with a significant diversity challenge. An AAP should set objective, measureable targets in three main areas (Clemons, 2004):

- Increasing the number of people belonging to the targeted "underutilized" groups that are recruited, interviewed, and hired
- Increasing the size of the qualified applicant pool
- Increasing retention of new hires in the target groups

To avoid discrimination against majority members, AAPs should specifically avoid the use or discussion of quotas or designating a specific number of member employees to hire. AAPs should also be evaluated regularly and be limited in scope and duration (Kleiman, 2007). Once the AAP efforts result in an increase in member recruitment, selection, and/or promotion, the official plan should be terminated and basic hiring guidelines should be followed. Finally, qualifications and abilities must remain at the heart of all hiring decisions. Anyone benefiting from affirmative action must have relevant and valid job or educational qualifications (Clemons, 2004). Specific action steps to consider for each AAP goal include:

Recruiting

- Meeting with employees to identify how best to market job openings and communicate attractive features of the employer (Kleiman, 2007)
- Focus on diversity in recruitment ads (e.g., Morgan Stanley: "Diversity. It's Not an Obligation—It's an Opportunity") (Thaler-Carter, 2001)
- Implement employee referral programs (reward current employees for suggesting a potential candidate) (Kleiman, 2007)
- Cultivate a positive employer image within the community (demonstrate an understanding of the culture through communication, advertising, etc.; become involved in the community through sponsorship of events, etc.) (Thaler-Carter, 2001)
- Review personnel policies, benefits, and employee relations programs to determine how these programs help employees meet their responsibilities to their families, promote the acceptance of diversity, and enhance employee productivity and loyalty (Gruer, 1994)
- Increase the candidate pool (Kleiman, 2007)
- Meet with member employees to identify education and skill barriers (Kleiman, 2007)
- Establish training programs to provide missing skills
- Provide targeted scholarships to increase the pool of group members who meet job-related education requirements (Gruer, 1994)

Hiring

- Review current selection procedures to determine job relatedness (e.g., physical, education, and experience requirements) (Kleiman, 2007)
- Provide training and documentation guidelines for hiring managers to decrease inadvertent bias in hiring decisions (e.g., review resumes/applications without names, use panel interviews) (Kleiman, 2007)

- Ask applicants to voluntarily self-identify on application forms (report their gender, race, handicapped status, and/or veteran status) (Kleiman, 2007)

Organization

- Don't skip the basics. Supervisors should give new employees a tour of the office, introduce them to colleagues, and explain security procedures. (Galbreath, 2006)
- Keep your messages consistent. The ideas conveyed in orientation should reflect those expressed during recruitment and how the company presents itself externally (Galbreath, 2006)

Retaining

- Initiate a mentor program to coach new employees (Kleiman, 2007)
- Install a new, less subjective performance appraisal system (Kleiman, 2007)
- Design and implement a career counseling program for lower-level employees to encourage and assist in planning occupational and career goals (Kleiman, 2007)
- Give employees from every segment of the workforce a non-threatening medium to express their concerns (Gruer, 1994)
- Allow employees to organize cultural networks to facilitate discussion of group-specific issues and as a forum to educate the entire workforce by arranging multicultural events both within the organization and in the community (Gruer, 1994)

Promoting

- Review current promotion procedures to determine job relatedness (Kleiman, 2007)
- Implement a succession planning process that enables managers at a certain level to nominate themselves for senior or executive-level jobs (Babcock, 2004)

Your AAP must be communicated—internally and externally—with particular care to identify the context and limited scope and duration of the plan as well as the anti-discrimination safeguards in place for majority member employees (Nail, 1999).

On a final note, workplace diversity should be evaluated beyond protected classes. Both cultural and gender diversity can represent a competitive advantage, as firms can attract a wider, perhaps better, pool of applicants who bring original ideas and new approaches to the workplace. This diversity can result in better results for a firm (Miller & Katz, 2002).

Conclusion

This article has examined the legal history of affirmative action and provided guidance to firms wishing to increase the diversity of their workforce while remaining in compliance with EEO laws. Based on past and present court decisions, affirmative action plans are tools with limited use when a color-conscious hiring priority is required to introduce diversity in a workplace. However, all hiring decisions must continue to focus on each applicant's skills, abilities, and fit for the position.

References

Adarand Constructors, Inc. v. Peña (515 U.S. 200 1995).

Attorneys from Goodwin Guber LLP. (2003). Xerox affirmative action plan runs out of toner. *Texas Employment Law Letter, 14*(3).

Babcock, P. (2004). Diversity down to the letter. *HR Magazine, 49*(6).

Bennett, J. (2003). *Hiring compliance guidelines*. SHRM. Available: www.shrm.org/hrresources/whitepapers_published/CMS_003042.asp.

Brunner, B. (2007). *Timeline of affirmative action milestones*. Pearson Education. Available: www.infoplease.com/spot/affirmativetimeline1.html.

City of Richmond v. J.A. Croson Co (488 U.S. 469 1989).

Clemons, H. (2004). *Affirmative action...Is it still necessary?* SHRM Workplace Diversity Library. Available: www.shrm.org/diversity/library_published/nonIC/CMS_012385.asp.

Columbia, K. (2000). *Discrimination and harassment pitfalls in hiring*. SHRM whitepaper. Available: www.shrm.org/hrresources/whitepapers_published/CMS_000332.asp.

Curry, G.E. (1996). *The affirmative action debate*. New York: Basic Books.

EEOC. (2008, January 25). *About the EEOC*. Washington, DC: U.S. Equal Employment Opportunity Commission.

Execs split over barriers to minority hiring. (1999). *AHA News, 35*(6).

Fischer, C. (2007, October 31). *What is affirmative action? Five decades of rhetorical discussion*. Available: www.missouricri.org/the_point_10_31_07.html.

Fullilove v. Klutznick (448 U.S. 448 1980).

Galbreath, R. (2006, January). *Profiting through employee orientation*. SHRM whitepaper. Available: www.shrm.org/hrresources/whitepapers_published/CMS_000456.asp.

Gratz v. Bollinger (539 U.S. 244 2003).

Graves, E. (2000). Florida's Trojan horse. *Black Enterprise, 30*(10), 13.

Gruer, W. (1994, November). *Diversity*. SHRM whitepaper. Available: www.shrm.org/hrresources/whitepapers_published/CMS_00234.asp.

Grutter v. Bollinger (288 F. 3d 732 2001).

Grutter v. Bollinger (539 U.S. 306 2003).

Hopwood v. University of Texas Law School (78 F.3d 932 (5th Cir.) 1996).

Kleiman, L. (2007). *Human resource management: A managerial tool for competitive advantage* (4th ed.). Mason, OH: Thomson.

Miller, A., & Katz, J. (2002). *The inclusion breakthrough*. San Francisco, CA: Berrett-Koehler.

Moses, G. (1997). *Texas backlash: Dismantling affirmative action with all deliberate speed.* Available: http://pages.prodigy.net/gmoses/moweb/txback.htm.

Nall, I. (1999). *Affirmative action plan for persons with disabilities and veterans*. SHRM whitepaper. Available: www.shrm.org/hrresources/whitepapers_published/CMS_00319.asp.

Regents of the University of California v. Bakke (438 U.S 265 1978).

Selingo, J. (2000). George W. Bush's mixed record on higher education in Texas. *Chronicle of Higher Education, 46*(42), A32.

Thaler-Carter, R. (2001). Diversify your recruitment advertising. *HR Magazine, 46*(6).

United States v. Paradise (480 U.S. 149 1987).

Wygant v. Jackson Board of Education (476 U.S. 267 1986).

York, G.E. (2007, January 18). *Documents in the news 1997-2003: Affirmative action in college admissions*. The University of Michigan Documents Center. Available: www.lib.umich.edu/govdocs/affirm.html.

Sean T. Foley *is a second-year MBA student at the McCombs School of Business at the University of Texas at Austin, where his concentration is entrepreneurship. Prior to McCombs, he led business development efforts for the Olympics Sports Division at Octagon, an agency specializing in the representation of professional athletes. He is a 2003 graduate of UT's undergraduate program, where his major was economics.*

Dr. Kristie J. Loescher *is a lecturer in the Management Department of the McCombs School of Business at The University of Texas at Austin, where she teaches management, leadership, and business communications. She has her doctorate in business administration from Nova Southeastern University, specializing in human resources management. Prior to her career in academia, she earned an MPH from the University of Michigan and worked in the healthcare industry for fifteen years in the areas of quality assurance, utilization management, and clinical research. Her academic publications focus on ethical education, organizational ethics, change management, and diversity management. Dr. Loescher is also a co-author of the book,* Communication Matters: Write, Speak, Succeed *published by Kendall Hunt in 2007.*

Leveraging Your Human Resources Partner

Leaders at All Levels Must Become Effective Talent Managers

John E. DiBenedetto

Summary

The human resources function has evolved over the years to the point at which it can truly drive business performance. The days of having a personnel clerk processing payroll tickets are long gone. Great HR professionals are born out of the business operations and matriculate into HR generalist and specialist positions. They are trained in root-cause analysis and add value as performance consultants, partnering with their internal business clients/stakeholders to actually help navigate the business. The organization and the customer always win when business strategy and objectives are enabled by solid talent planning, acquisition, and development practices.

One of the most interesting and powerful discoveries I have had as a human resources (HR) professional is the need to continually educate line leaders and senior executives about the importance of leveraging their relationships with the HR department. The HR profession has undergone significant change and redefinition in recent years (Noe, Hollenbeck, Gerhart, & Wright, 2005). Only recently have companies looked at the HR function as a means to drive business performance and contribute to overall profitability, quality, and other business goals.

One of the key HR issues is talent management. What is the value of talent in your organization? How is talent measured? Who helps you place a price tag on talent? Managers must leverage their talent. "Leaders at all levels must recognize the criticality of investing in a talent management strategy to identify, attract, and engage high performers" (Tarquinio, 2006, p. 119). HR can play a key role in this.

The 2009 Pfeiffer Annual: Management Development.

The HR/Management Partnership

The HR department plays four key roles in the planning, acquisition and development of strategic human resources (Ulrich, 1988). Your HR partner can provide tremendous value as:

- *Strategic Business Partner*—aligning HR strategies with organizational objectives to drive business performance and help the company achieve its business strategies through talent.
- *Employee Advocate*—managing the commitment and contributions of talent by ensuring development, engagement, productivity, and retention.
- *Change Agent*—transforming talent and organizations to meet new competitive conditions.
- *Administrative Expert*—designing and delivering HR systems, processes, and practices to optimize talent investments, through selection, compensation, training, and performance management.

Prior to becoming an HR professional in 1993, I spent many years in operations and sales management with AT&T. In each of those roles, I ran large organizations and led geographically dispersed teams that either sold or serviced multi-million-dollar voice and data communications networks for AT&T's largest global clients. I could never have achieved my goals in those assignments without the help of my HR business partners. AT&T had a very robust HR infrastructure that was designed to add value to its business units, including the deployment of geographic and functional HR managers to support line organizations. That's how I came to know and love the human resources profession, and ultimately become a member. As a leader, I had a competitive edge because many of my peers just did not understand or appreciate what HR brought to the table.

Many examples could be described of our successful partnership, but one in particular was helping to facilitate numerous team-building events to help define and put clarity to each person's role in the organization. My HR partner helped the team craft a realistic and attainable mission statement, as well as create objectives for the performance year. My HR partner served as a neutral facilitator and worked offsite with the team for two days to accomplish the stated goals. I could never have done this alone because of my need to participate with the group. The result was the creation of a clear, concise team mission statement, role clarity for each functional group, and SMART objectives that the entire team could agree to and be held accountable for. Apart from the business aspects of the session, we had a heck of a lot of fun participating in exceptional outdoor team-building exercises that consisted of trust walks, trust falls, and storytelling.

Talent Planning

Great people make up great workforces. Best-in-class companies such as GE, IBM, and Microsoft have well-developed systems for managing and motivating their high-performance and high-potential employees. They also have proven and tested methods for eliminating dead wood from the organization (Huselid, Beatty, & Becker, 2005). Bossidy, in his best-selling book *Execution*, refers to this sort of differentiation among employees as "the mother's milk of building a performance culture." Talent planning, the first of three elements in an integrated talent management framework, helps to build that performance culture.

HR's strategy should be aligned with corporate objectives and help to drive business performance. HR's plans are developed once strategic plans have been created. The HR plan consists of both a "workforce plan" and a "talent plan." Workforce planning is simply a forecast of talent needs, that is, a talent demand chart. The role HR plays with workforce planning spans activities such as coordinating college and professional recruiting, internship programs, and inclusion/diversity hiring.

While at Limited Brands, I helped to create the company's first Talent Development Center of Excellence. Part of my responsibilities included the appointment to the company's Inclusion Leadership Steering Committee, which was a team consisting of senior leaders from each business unit and select HR executives. Limited Brands valued inclusion/diversity and worked hard to ensure that it existed at every level within the organization. One of the most exciting projects I participated in was helping business unit leaders increase workforce diversity, either through recruitment or promotions from within. I worked primarily with business unit and division HR partners to administer an Inclusion Readiness Survey Instrument. This tool was designed to help the leadership teams understand the power behind diverse hiring and promotions and to gauge how ready each leadership team was to execute its workforce diversity plan. The survey instrument was completed by the HR partner and business unit CEO and recorded as a baseline score. I aggregated the scores together to represent inclusion readiness for the entire company. The survey was administered every six months thereafter to see whether progress was being made toward predetermined hiring and promotional goals. HR partners added significant value to the process by working with their leadership teams to educate them on the power behind diversity and inclusion, as well as helping them create realistic and attainable workforce diversity plans.

From a talent planning perspective, HR partners added value by identifying and developing high-potential/high-performing leadership talent. This process, often referred to as succession management, generally begins with identification of the critical few positions that an organization just cannot do without. From there, A-, B- and C-level players are identified using some type of formula and/or grid. A players are generally considered high-potential and groomed for upward progression. B players are usually your "steady-Eddies" who perform well but don't have the potential to move to more senior roles. C players are the "up or out" crowd, that is, they must quickly move their performance to acceptable standards or be separated from the company. Your HR partner plays a critical role in this very labor-intensive succession planning process.

While I was vice president of talent planning and development at Wal-Mart Stores, members of my team would align themselves with division presidents and their HR vice presidents. From there, they would educate the line executives and HR managers on the succession management process and how to identify A, B, and C players. The goal was to build leadership bench strength at every level of management by identifying who was deemed "high potential" and then accelerating development of that top talent so they would be ready to fill critical positions.

The team would use a modified version of GE's nine-box grid and place targeted audiences, by job family, into the grid. Last, individual development plans would be created for the critical A players, and A players would be tracked for progress against plan. Without the help of the HR partners, line managers would not be able to conduct such comprehensive talent audits to prepare for succession planning purposes.

Talent Acquisition

The second critical area HR partners can help with is talent acquisition. Like a baby to a bottle, organizations need to provide incentives that attract and retain top talent. Generation Y candidates think they should be paid the highest possible compensation because they have the highest skill set. Thus, organizations need to ensure that line managers understand the culture of the organization and can convey it to new hires.

While at Limited Brands, I recall seeing many talented executives enter the company, many spinning out months later because they didn't become "students of the culture." In the early 2000s, Limited Brands, Inc., was a large fashion apparel and consumer products portfolio of companies with very eclectic organizational cultures. Many talented individuals joined, but not all took the time to learn and meld into the culture. To combat high executive turnover, my team built a robust eighteen-month on-boarding program designed for successful assimilation into the organization (DiBenedetto, 2005). Each executive was assigned an on-boarding coach, who was usually the division HR leader, responsible for ensuring that the new hire or promoted individual actually did the things he or she was assigned to do, including attending training and completing a mandatory community service event. In order to be productive in this type of business, the main requirement was to "fit in with the group" (Tarquinio, 2006, p. 119). The best results in a case like this can only be attained from a joint line/HR partnership.

Aside from attracting the best talent through a compelling organizational culture, HR partners help managers understand that economic conditions in recent years have made U.S. employees more likely to switch jobs quite often. Changes in global and local economies have created a market for talent, and employees are often eager to search for a new job if they are not achieving what was promised at their place of employment.

Keeping employees engaged requires an involved management and a plethora of talent development tools and programs. Some very frightening statistics exist on workforce engagement. According to the Gallup (2007) management journal's semi-annual Employee Engagement Index:

- 29 percent of employees are actively engaged in their jobs.
- 54 percent are not engaged at all.
- 17 percent are actively disengaged.

With over 70 percent of employees falling into the high-risk zone, what should line managers do to reduce turnover? Engaged workers produce more, make more money for the company, and create emotional engagement—leading to loyal internal and external customers. Engaged employees contribute to working environments in which people are happy, productive, ethical, and accountable. These individuals stay with organizations longer and are more committed to quality and growth than are non-engaged and actively disengaged workers. My experience has shown there to be a direct correlation to engagement when employees have:

- A strong relationship with their managers
- Clear communication from their managers
- A clear path set for focusing on what they do best
- Strong relationships with their co-workers
- A strong commitment to their co-workers, which enables them to take risks and strive for excellence

Your HR partner can assist you with these tactics to elevate employee engagement and can provide strategies and action plans to mitigate turnover.

Great managers don't leave their excellent employees alone. They spend most of their time with the most productive and talented people because these people have the highest potential (Olney, 2007).

In that spirit, your HR partner can help you identify who is at risk of leaving the organization. This is generally done through the administration of an employee climate survey. Many HR consulting organizations provide such tools. *Workforce Management* magazine published Gallup's (2007) Q12, a twelve2-question survey that identifies strong feelings of employee engagement. Results from the survey show a strong correlation between high scores and superior job performance. Here are the twelve questions:

- Do you know what is expected of you at work?
- Do you have the materials and equipment you need to do your work correctly?
- At work, do you have the opportunity to do what you do best every day?
- In the last seven days, have you received recognition or praise for doing good work?
- Does your supervisor, or someone at work, seem to care about you as a person?
- Is there someone at work who encourages your development?
- At work, do your opinions seem to count?
- Does the mission/purpose of your company make you feel your job is important?
- Are your fellow employees committed to doing quality work?
- Do you have a best friend at work?
- In the last six months, has someone at work talked to you about your progress?
- In the last year, have you had opportunities at work to learn and grow?

Based on the results of a survey like this one, your HR partner can use root-cause analysis techniques to determine the key reasons for employee dissatisfaction and non-engagement. Many HR people are specially trained in ASTD's Performance

Improvement Model and other tools that help to quickly identify problems and find solutions. "The biggest challenge faced by an organization today is not one of growth or profitability. Rather, it is about retaining one's best employees" (Chugh, 2007). Your HR partner can help you develop creative strategies to identify and retain top talent. Line managers often utilize incentives such as training, benefits, and other perks in addition to competitive compensation as a means to retain good employees.

Talent Development

The third critical function of talent management is talent development, which is referred to as the acquisition of knowledge, skills, and abilities that improve employees' ability to perform given job tasks, handle changes in job requirements, and satisfy customer demands (Noe, Hollenbeck, Gerhart, & Wright, 2005). Retaining knowledge within the organization is one of the largest concerns leaders have today due to the high number of baby boomers planning to retire in the next few years. By implementing an HR strategy to develop and retain knowledge workers, a company can understand how to create, transfer, and use that knowledge effectively (Jayne, 2006).

Organizational knowledge can be thought of in two categories: (1) knowledge that is explicit and codified and (2) knowledge that is codified but exists only within the minds of employees or tacit knowledge (Nonaka, Takeuchi, & Umemoto, 1996). "The distinction between organizational explicit and tacit knowledge is the difference between "know-what" and "know-how" in which organizational "know-how" puts "know-what" into action" (Jayne, 2006). Tacit knowledge is intuitive, often difficult to express, and gained through experience—not shared with others through day-to-day interactions. So think of tacit knowledge as that precious commodity that drives an organization's work processes and product/service development. Employees generally hold such information above and beyond what the organization has documented (Droege & Hoobler). Explicit knowledge is not at risk when employees exit a company.

Knowledge workers are "capital" (Drucker, 2002), and thus knowledge has emerged as a firm's most strategically significant resource (Grant, 1996; Penrose, 1959). As the number of knowledge workers increases, HR's partnership with line management becomes even more important. Finding ways to minimize turnover is a critical management problem (Alvesson, 2000). Line managers, in partnership with their HR leaders, should continually identify and invest in knowledge workers whose professional development should be accelerated so that knowledge can be cascaded to others. Line managers can use developmental assignments, formal training opportunities, and total reward systems to create new tacit and explicit knowledge.

Talent development is important for every employee but is particularly important for Millennials (Generation Y) who are seeking companies that will invest heavily in their professional development. "In too many organizations today, employees say that their skills and talent are underutilized as they experience barriers to mobility and opportunities within their companies" (Leighanne, 2006). So smart employers use training as a reward or incentive to keep bright young talent from seeking jobs outside the company (Power, 2007).

FMI Corporation, a management consulting firm, determined that employee retention is a key struggle for construction firms in the United States. The survey predicted a 35 percent loss of top executives over the next ten years. Over the same period, 24 percent of managers and 21 percent of project managers are also likely to depart from the field. According to FMI, the problem is that companies attract new people but don't provide a clear development path so they know what their career ladders are. FMI contends that companies that invest in the talent development function and provide clear development paths for employees experience higher retention rates. (Powers, 2007).

When I was asked to build the corporate education function for AT&T Global Markets, as well as when I took on the talent planning and development role at Wal-Mart Stores, I began with a clean sheet of paper. Both companies had very little in place, but wanted to bring best-practices programs, processes, and platforms to their organizations. While assimilating into the roles, I spent quite a bit of time with managers and associates at all levels. As I conducted my needs analysis, I hosted individual meetings and focus groups to fully understand what was working or not working—and what was missing. My teams served as a "center of excellence," assisting HR partners geographically dispersed. I, in turn, partnered with senior HR leaders throughout the business to get their perspectives, as they were the link to key stakeholders—division presidents and vice presidents.

We began by studying individual job families and the many job positions within said families. The goal was to determine what the "high-performance" knowledge, skills, and abilities (KSAs)were. The idea is that, once you understand what high-performance looks like, you can set out to build "competency models" or "success profiles."

Both AT&T and Wal-Mart teams followed the same protocol of mapping newly formed competency models to newly created, competency-based professional development curricula. Learning curricula was blended, consisting of experiential exercises, action-learning assignments, books, articles, internal workshops, and online and external training courses. The completed platform was housed on each company's existing learning management system and named A.I.M., for associate investment model.

The key components of each A.I.M. Toolkit included:

- Job descriptions
- Success profiles (functional and leadership competency model)
- Skills inventories/assessments
- On-boarding programs
- Foundational and advanced training tracks
- Career ladders

Best practices dictate considerable testing before piloting any new HR program. Successful outcomes required the endorsement of field HR partners who must market the new tools to line managers and executives. That's the value of having a solid, credible HR function who have the knowledge of their respective organizations' business challenges and the skills to bridge those gaps with proven and tested talent solutions. In other words, a key competency of any HR professional is the possession of marketing, negotiating, and influencing skills.

In both companies, my center of excellence teams partnered successfully with their respective field HR teams, who in turn sold line managers on the value of the A.I.M. platform. The successful outcomes at AT&T and Wal-Mart evidence the power of having solid relationships between HR partners and line management.

Conclusion

Managing talent has become a viable task and focus for managers and HR professionals since the first "war for talent" that began in 2000. Management now looks to its HR department as a key to helping attract, select, engage, develop, and retain top talent. The competitive advantage lies with those who actually lead companies and organizations.

Why the intense focus? In our information and knowledge-based economy, talent is the main source of competitive advantage. Thus, it is incumbent upon the company doing the hiring and/or assessing to know what talents they are looking for and to find ways to hire and keep those talents (Louis, 2006). Competitive advantage can only be gained by organizations that are effective at all three components of talent management (planning, acquisition, and development), and that provide managers with value-added HR partnerships.

References

Alvesson, M. (2000). Social identity and the problem of loyalty in knowledge-intensive companies. *Journal of Management Studies, 26.*

Brockbank, W., & Ulrich, D. (2005). *HR value proposition.* Cambridge, MA: Harvard Business School Press.

Chugh, M. (2007). *How to retain talent.* Available: www.123oye.com

DiBenedetto, J.E. (2005). Leadership on-boarding: Successfully assimilating new executives. In R.C. Preziosi (Ed.), *The 2005 Pfeiffer annual: Human resource management* (pp. 21–29). San Francisco, CA: Pfeiffer.

Droege, S.B., & Hoobler, J.M. (2003). Employee turnover and tacit knowledge diffusion: A network perspective. *Journal of Management Issues, 15*(1).

Drucker, P.F. (2002). Knowledge work. *Executive Excellence, 9*(10).

Gallup. (2007, September 10). 12 questions to measure employee engagement. *Workforce Management.*

Grant, R.M. (1996). Toward a knowledge-based theory of the firm. *Strategic Management Journal, 17,* 109–122.

Huselid, M.A., Beatty, R.W., & Becker, B.E. (2005, December). A-players or A-positions? The strategic logic of workforce planning. *Harvard Business Review.*

Jayne, R.L. (2006). *Knowledge worker: Human resource strategy to achieve a competitive advantage.* Available www.midwestacademy.org/Proceedings/2006/papers/paper9.pdf.

Leighanne, L. (2006). Organizing talent through competency-based management. Plateau (webcast). Available: www.plateau.com.

Louis, L. (2006, October 5). Everybody's doing it. *The Economist.*

Nonaka, I., Takeuchi, H., & Umemoto, K. (1996). A theory of organizational knowledge creation. *International Journal of Technology Management, 11,* 833–845.

Noe, R., Hollenbeck, J., Gerhart, B., & Wright, P.M. (2006). *Human resource management: Gaining a competitive advantage* (5th ed.). New York: McGraw-Hill.

Olney, M.D. (2007). *The power of employee engagement.* Available: www.leadershipadvangtage.com/employeeEngagement.shtml.

Penrose, E. (1959). *The theory of growth of the firm.* Oxford, England: Basil Blackwell.

Power, M. (2007, April). What price loyalty? *Professional Builder, 72*(4), 50–58.

Powers, E.M. (2007, May). Winning the "war for talent" is key challenge in growing industry, says new FMI report. *ENR, 258*(19), 133–134.

Tarquinio, M. (2006). Talent acquisition strategies: Sourcing and assessing the best of the best. *Human Resources, 52,* 119.

Ulrich, D. (1988). *From human resource champions.* Cambridge, MA: Harvard Business School Press.

John E. DiBenedetto, D.B.A., *is executive vice president, chief people officer, for General Parts International, Inc., in Raleigh, North Carolina, and adjunct professor of management with the H. Wayne Huizenga School of Business and Entrepreneurship at Nova Southeastern University. He has held senior human resources positions at Wal-Mart Stores, Inc., Limited Brands, Inc., Wachovia Bank NA, and AT&T Corporation. Dr. DiBenedetto was awarded the 2007 Elliott Masie Learning Leadership and Innovation Award for his accomplishments as vice president, talent planning and development, at Wal-Mart Stores, Inc. In 2006, the American Society for Training and Development (ASTD) awarded Dr. DiBenedetto and his Wal-Mart University team its coveted "BEST Award" for notable achievements in transforming talent at the world's largest retailer. Also, Dr. DiBenedetto's lifelong professional contributions were honored in 2006 by the Huizenga School when he received NSU's Alumni of the Year Award.*

The Strategic Manager

Success Competencies for Managing Organizations in the New Economy

Peter Vultaggio

Summary

The dynamics of the workplace have changed underneath us. What had been forewarned by business experts is upon us: global competition, aging global population, four generations in the workplace, and shifts in values about work and life. For organizations to adapt, those who manage them must adapt—must change their approach and style. Expanding their roles and adding new competencies is required. For example, in dealing with the speed of change, all managers must add foreseeing and anticipating the future to their lists of competencies, a role typically expected only from senior leadership in a company. The author focuses on three of the competencies a manager needs to master for his or her organization to remain competitive in this environment: strategic thinking and planning, delegation, and leading change. Although competencies such as delegation or leading change have been around for many years, they have new meaning and more strategy is involved today.

Promotions based purely on tenure or politics are a relic of the past. Now, managing is a profession. Organizations realize the need for strong managers, whom they ask to do much more with a lot less. Today, managers are responsible for a business environment in constant change, with evolving employee expectations, and seemingly impossible requirements from senior management. Many of the competencies that made managers successful in the past are outmoded. A new model—the Strategic Manager—embodies the requirements managers need to succeed.

Shifting Business Environment

Changes in the Workforce

The manufacturing orientation in many industries is giving way to a service orientation. Developing intellectual capital has turned into a top priority, making knowledge workers more valuable. Companies are moving away from traditional hierarchies. Organizations are flatter with fewer layers of management, using more complex, network-like matrix structures. More work is project-based, and most managers supervise cross-functional and virtual teams. Corporate "right-sizing" is forcing employees to do more with less. With the Baby Boomer generation retiring, managers are losing a wealth of talent and experience. The rate of growth for the U.S. labor force will likely decline (BLS, 2008) before 2016. There are as many as four generations in the workplace, and it's an era of global competition. Clearly, managers must increase their skills in dealing with employees of all generations and focus on keeping employees committed to the company.

Employees' Expectations

It is commonly known that employees disengage from their work or leave their companies because they lack trust in company leadership, they lack growth and development opportunities, and job fit is poor. Yet, a meta-analysis of twelve major studies by top research firms concluded that the strongest determinant of employee engagement level is the relationship between the employee and his or her immediate supervisor (Gibbons, 2006). The factors are related. How employees view senior leadership is influenced by their managers. Employees often seek to grow professionally and personally through their work. While it is the employees' responsibility to develop themselves, they often expect their managers to act as coaches, provide funding and time away from work, and give them the opportunity to exercise any new skills. Managers also play a major role in the employees' job fit.

Senior Management's Expectations

One commonly hears senior leadership wanting their managers to "think bigger" or "think outside the box." Although the management team may want to change their thinking, in fact, such change requires redefining and reeducating management. What senior leaders really want is for their managers to take a longer-term look at any current issues. They do not just want problem solving, which often looks more like a "band-aid" where there is only a symptom fix or a temporary fix, often causing more problems downstream.

The Strategic Manager

The "strategic manager" keeps employees engaged, meets senior management's expectations, and boldly faces the changing business environment. Managers need new competencies to achieve peak performance in this environment.

These competencies include delegation, coaching, engagement, and empowerment. Success means satisfying employees' desires for growth on the job. Employees want to increase their marketable skills and work in an environment that fosters their development.

Senior managers demand that managers become more strategic. They want managers to yield influence and practice systems thinking, creative thinking, and analytical thinking. Unfortunately, many managers don't have time to acquire these skills.

Here we will address three main areas of strategic competency: strategic business unit planning, strategic delegation, and leading change. Strategic business unit planning helps the strategic manager answer the call of senior management to "think outside the box" and "be more independent of their bosses." Planning competencies guide the strategic manager to more fully engage team members, make the vision and directives of senior management more tangible, and develop action plans to help the group implement changes to the business environment.

With strategic delegation, the manager engages employees and helps them with their personal and professional development. It's about delegating tasks that will enable employees to develop. Delegating tasks allows the strategic manager more time to "think bigger" and address longer-term issues, for example, how to direct the upcoming retirement of the Boomer generation.

Similarly, leading change competencies also address multiple issues. Change creates more work and stress on all levels of the organization. More than ever, senior management needs managers to be independent and take charge of implementing change. The strategic manager must translate what change means for his or her group and effectively enable a successful transition.

Strategic Business Unit Planning

It used to be the responsibility of senior leadership to set strategy. The further down the levels of management, the more directive the communications became. At the lower levels of management, strategy was practically nonexistent.

The strategic manager today is responsible for setting the direction of the business unit for long-term growth and survival. Only after the direction is set and agreed on can the focus for people and resources be established.

Having the business unit participate in the process allows for more ideas to be put forth and engenders a greater sense of commitment and ownership. Having

The 2009 Pfeiffer Annual: Management Development.

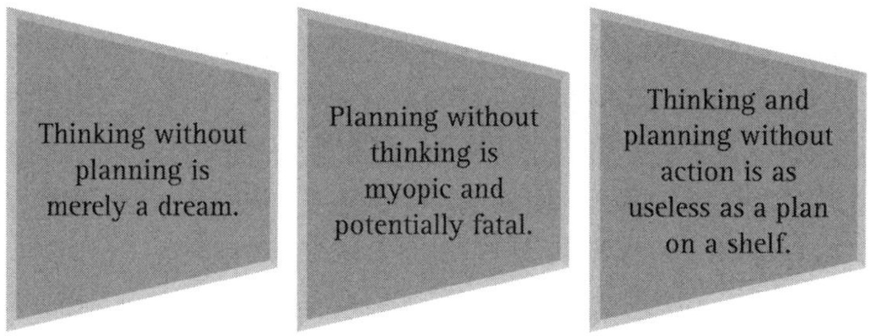

Figure 1. Thinking, Planning, and Action

every business unit create a plan empowers all employees to help the company achieve its vision.

The strategic manager uses both strategic thinking and strategic planning. Strategic thinking is the capability to foresee a future state and anticipate events before they occur. It requires creativity and information. Strategic thinkers can extrapolate future scenarios and envision entirely new possibilities and opportunities. The best strategic thinkers are very creative. Creative thinkers are able to question assumptions and make room for new ideas.

Strategic planning is the process of making business visions a reality and requires analytical thinking and information. Strategic managers use analytical thinking to determine whether their goals and actions are appropriate, relevant, achievable, specific, and measurable. They evaluate whether the action plan will lead to the fulfillment of the business plan. Figure 1 illustrates how thinking, planning, and action work together to advance an organization.

A business unit plan is the roadmap that defines the future state and spells out how to achieve it. It includes a vision statement, clear objectives, metrics, and an action plan. Metrics are established to determine whether objectives are being met, and the action plan states who is responsible for completing each step by when.

Strategic Delegation

Delegation is a continuous and integral part of a strategic manager's role. A strategic manager knows how to assign the right tasks, along with the appropriate decision-making power and autonomy, while still maintaining ultimate responsibility.

Strategic delegation is not only telling someone what to do or assigning jobs; it is the transference of the authority to act in the manager's behalf. This process involves planning, communication, and monitoring to empower others to succeed in the tasks they are given. Each strategic delegation is unique.

Strategic managers delegate, while myopic managers "dump" work on their subordinates, which can cause resentment and frustration and threaten employee self-esteem. True delegation builds confidence and aids employees in building skills.

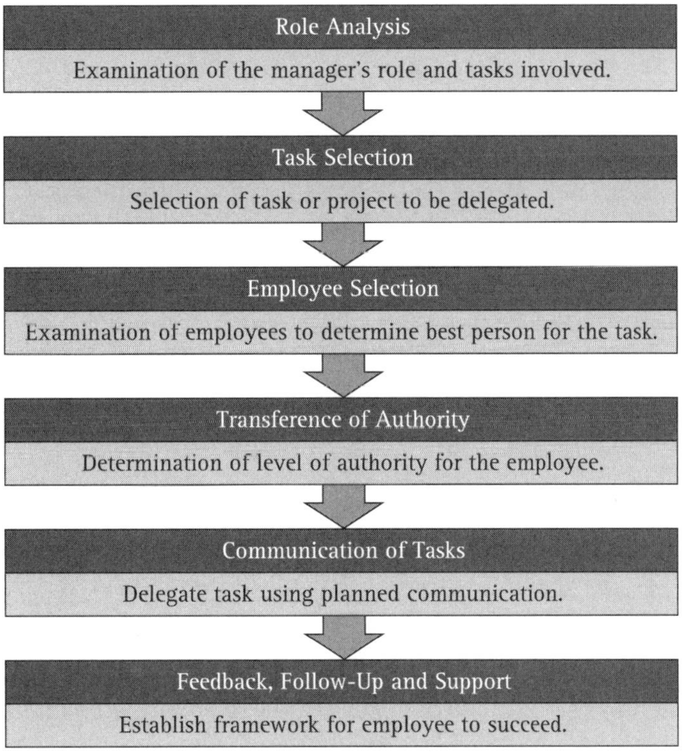

Figure 2. The Delegation Process

Strategic delegation gives managers more time for strategic initiatives, coaching, and staff development.

Strategic managers follow the delegation process shown in Figure 2: role analysis; task selection; employee selection; transference of authority; communication of task; and feedback, follow-up, and support.

Leading Change

Change is stressful for everyone. The more removed someone is from the top of the organization or the less decision-making authority someone has, the more difficult it can be to embrace change. The strategic manager contributes to the success of change processes by knowing the phases of change, leading by example, creating a supportive environment, reducing resistance, and communicating clearly.

The Phases of Change

There are four phases to any change process: ignore/surprise, resist/protect, investigate/consider, and adapt/commit. Phase 1, ignore/surprise, is characterized by denial and disbelief. Employees may avoid the topic of change or assume that everything is okay. When the change is undeniable, shock and surprise can be the result, and employees sometimes take the situation personally. Phase 2, resist/protect, finds employees responding with negativity and desiring to maintain the status quo. Anger, aggression, blame, finding fault, negative gossip, and resistance are common behaviors during this phase. Phase 3, investigate/consider, is where employees begin to turn the corner to a more hopeful outlook. People become more willing to test new approaches, consider possibilities, and determine how they can contribute. In addition, the questioning becomes more about information and clarity and not discrediting the change. Employees begin to bargain for their new roles. Phase 4, adapt/commit, is when employees accept the change. There is a desire for accomplishment, feelings of optimism, and accountability for new behaviors and actions. In addition, employees begin helping others through the change and act as change champions.

People can bounce from one phase to another, and each person transitions through the phases at his or her own pace. A strategic manager can determine which phase of change an employee is in by listening to what the employee says, and thus help him or her through the transition. Figure 3 lists common phrases heard in each step of the change process.

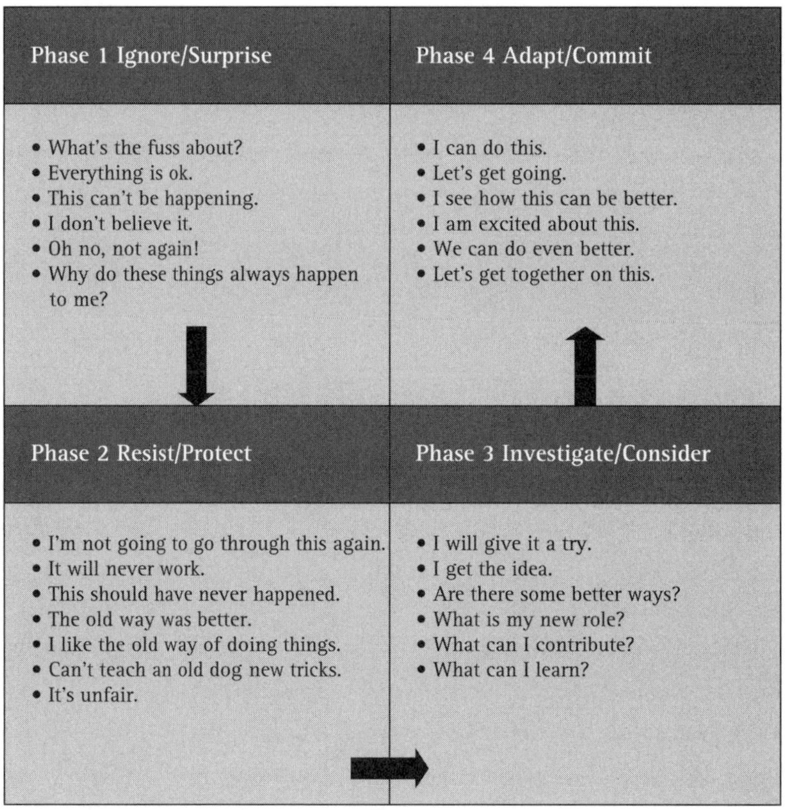

Figure 3. The Phases of Change and Related Language

Leading by Example

Change can cause many different reactions and emotions, from excitement and elation to anxiety, depression, or even hostility. The strategic manager wants to be a settling influence on employees, and thus models positive ways to adapt to change, using empathy to assist employees in overcoming their objections.

Creating a Supportive Change Environment

Leading by example is a powerful way that strategic managers create a supportive change environment. They involve the team early in the process and allow more people to be a part of the planning and implementation. They solicit ideas and are open to feedback. Strategic managers must ask the team what type of support they might need to successfully implement the change. They encourage team members to seek training and acquire new skills. They recognize employees who engage the change and demonstrate positive behaviors and encourage other team members to follow their lead. Strategic managers communicate early and often about the change and stay abreast of developments.

Handling Resistance

Just as change is an integral part of doing business in today's world, resistance is an integral part of the change process. Even if the change is for positive reasons, people still resist things that might disrupt their lives. They will need to pass through the phases of the change process at some point. Strategic managers are prepared to handle resistance and watch for signs of it. Sometimes it is necessary to let employees vent their feelings about the change. Strategic managers listen actively and deal with the concerns and fears that employees express.

Effective Communication

One of the key strategies in leading change is the strategic manager's ability to communicate the change, what the impact of the change will be, and what the expectations are for all involved. Employees want to feel that even minor aspects of the change are being addressed. How a manager communicates the change creates positive or negative perceptions.

After becoming aware of an upcoming change, strategic managers go through the following steps to effectively lead their teams.

The first step is to write a communication plan. Strategic managers use these plans to prepare what they will say. They anticipate and prepare responses to potential questions. The next step is to communicate the change with conviction. Third, they empower others to act by removing any obstacles that undermine the change. In addition, strategic managers support training and education as well as encourage risk taking and non-traditional ideas, activities, and actions that support moving forward. The last step they take is to plan for and create both short-term and long-term wins to help keep employees motivated.

Conclusion

Strategic business unit planning, strategic delegation, and the ability to lead change are three competencies essential for strategic managers to enable their companies to be successful in the new economy. By using these competencies, strategic managers can navigate the challenges of the shifting business environment, satisfy evolving employee expectations, and exceed senior management expectations. Strategic delegation enable managers not only to develop and empower their employees but also open up time to engage in strategic planning. Through strategic business unit planning, managers engage employees while meeting senior management's desire for self-sufficient managers. Leading change is an especially critical competency in today's shifting business environment.

References

Gibbons, J. (2006, November). *Employee engagement: A review of current research and its implications*. New York: The Conference Board.

U.S. Department of Labor, Bureau of Labor Statistics. (2008). Tomorrow's jobs. *Occupational Outlook Handbook* (2008–2009), 2.

Peter Vultaggio *is CEO and co-founder of The LUMI Company, LLC, a management and workforce development organization serving both major domestic and international clients. The high-caliber team of multi-lingual and multi-cultural LUMI consultants handles 21st Century needs of global organizations spanning leadership development to labor-management negotiations to strategic planning. Vultaggio has over twenty years of management and consulting experience from working predominantly with Fortune 500 companies in pharmaceuticals, semiconductor, software, banking and insurance, and defense. He is also a recognized author and speaker with multiple media appearances. He holds a bachelor's degree in biomedical engineering and a master's degree in human resources and organization development.*

Developing Leaders in the Federal Courts

The Federal Judicial Center's Leadership Development Program

Michael Eric Siegel, with Anthony Teke Quickel

Summary

The Federal Judicial Center's Leadership Development Program for U.S. Probation and Pretrial Services was launched in 1992 and has graduated some six hundred probation and pretrial services officers, specialists, and supervisors. From among the ranks of these alumni are 42 percent of the current U.S. Probation and Pretrial Services Chief Officers, with many other graduates having been promoted as well. The increase in leadership utilized by these participants and the changes they have affected have resulted in real costs savings. In these ways and others, the Leadership Development Program has played an important role in shaping the future of the federal courts.

This article describes the development of the program as a response to an anticipated leadership vacuum in probation and pretrial services agencies, analyzes its major components, describes its unique blending of academic and experiential instructional approaches to develop leadership skills, and assesses the impact of the three-year program on the participants and on the federal court system overall.

"There is nothing more difficult to take in hand, more perilous to conduct, or more uncertain in its success, than to take the lead in the introduction of a new order of things."

—Niccolo Machiavelli, *The Prince*

A Need for Leadership

The Federal Judicial Center's Leadership Development Program for Federal Probation and Pretrial Services Officers was born in January 1992 out of a necessity identified by the Judicial Conference's Committee on Criminal Law (the Judicial Conference of the United States being the main decision making body for the U.S. Courts). The committee was concerned about several issues: an anticipated vacuum in capable and prepared leaders in federal probation and pretrial services, as a significant number of chiefs would reach mandatory retirement age, which is set at fifty-seven; the changes that had taken place in federal probation and pretrial services offices stemming from Congressional statutes, Administrative Office of the U.S. Courts (AO) guidelines, and new automation applications; and the wide variation by which the probation and pretrial services officers were implementing the changes and the problem meant, in some cases, that things were not changing enough.

Program Goals and Design

According to Warren Bennis, "The first ingredient of leadership is a guiding vision. The leader has a clear idea of what he wants to do—professionally and personally—and the strength to persist in the face of setbacks, even failures" (2003, p. 35).

Keeping in mind the factors that the Judicial Conference cited as prompting a need for a leadership development program, the Federal Judicial Center envisioned the following goals for the program:

- To develop a personal approach to leadership and management;
- To develop new skills in the area of change management;
- To develop an ability to benchmark the achievements of federal probation and pretrial services officers;
- To broaden participants' understanding about judicial administration; and
- To learn from the best practices of other probation and pretrial services officers across the country.

Based on these goals, the Center staff began researching program design and techniques that were found effective in the pursuit of leadership development in other government agencies as well as in the private sector. From this study, the Center learned that the leadership development programs that achieved the greatest success were those that offered learning opportunities over an extended period and not just in the short term. Secondly, a study conducted by the Center for Creative Leadership confirmed that a broad range of leadership challenges, including completing a temporary work assignment outside of the person's area of expertise, contribute to the building and seasoning of effective managers (cited in Siegel & Vernon, 1994). Finally, research in program design found that focusing the program in the current realities of the actual organization, in this case the federal courts, was critical for program success. Based on this background information, the Center was now ready to develop a program.

The Plan

Utilizing the research conducted on successful leadership development programs and remembering the lofty goals of the Judicial Conference's committee, the Center launched its Leadership Development Program for Federal Probation and Pretrial Services Officers in the fall of 1992. The Center staff designed a three-year developmental program grounded in the actual needs of the system, sensitive to but not driven by current leadership literature, and responsive to the decision-makers and funders of the federal probation and pretrial services system. The Leadership Development Program was created to challenge the participating probation and pretrial services officers to complete a rigorous and dynamic program that included multiple projects (as elaborated below), to read course material, and to attend in-person leadership training. In addition, the Center appointed faculty members (college professors, consultants, leadership experts) to provide ongoing mentorship and feedback to participants.

A Discussion of Program Content

To garner a better understanding of the multifaceted nature of the Leadership Development Program, a thorough examination must be made regarding the program's three critical components: the Management Practice Report, the In-District Project, and the Temporary Duty Assignment.

Management Practice Report

The Management Practice Report is designed as a transition into leadership activity. Its purpose is to aid participants in gaining insight into leadership and how leaders and managers can impact their organizations. In doing this, participants review leadership literature and conduct interviews with at least three leaders in the private and public sectors. Leadership literature used in the completion of the Management Practice Report includes, among others, *Leadership*, by Rudolph Giuliani (2002), *Execution: The Discipline of Getting Things Done*, by Larry Bossidy and Ram Charan (2002), *Churchill on Leadership: Executive Success in the Face of Adversity*, by Steven F. Hayward (1998), and Warren Bennis's (2003) *On Becoming a Leader*. Regarding this portion of the Management Practice Reports, interesting feedback has arisen from the LDP's focus groups. "Hardened probation and pretrial services officers, who typically confront the most challenging realities of contemporary life daily, were delighted with the opportunity to read and reflect about broader management and leadership issues. Many of the officers indicated that they had not read or studied a 'serious' book outside of the technical area of their profession in several years and expressed appreciation for the chance to learn about the evaluation of leadership and management thinking in the private and public sector" (Siegel & Vernon, 1994, p. 5). The other critical portion of the Management Practice Report, interviewing public and private sector leaders, has also yielded positive results. These interviews include police chiefs, corporate executives, sport team coaches, and government leaders, and both LDP participants and faculty have felt this component of the Leadership Development Program to be of great benefit (Siegel & Vernon, 1994). This support may be seen in LDP graduate and Chief of Probation and Pretrial Services for the Northern District of Georgia Tom Bishop's (2007) statement that he was "exposed to different styles of leadership, both in the private and public sector. I especially enjoyed the opportunity to interview different leaders and learn what made them effective and the lessons which they learned over the years."

In-District Project

Around a year and a half into the three-year leadership development program, participants complete in-district projects. These reports require participants to take an issue or challenge in their district, analyze its root causes, propose a solution, and actually implement that solution with the input of the chief and the faculty advisor. The value of this project is in allowing participants to practically apply skills that they are beginning to develop, as well as confront head-on, the types of struggles with which a leader is faced. The types of projects completed can be divided into five broad categories, as shown below. Also provided are some examples of each to illustrate the diversity of opportunity:

1. Officer Orientation, Training, and Evaluation Job Satisfaction Survey
    - Time Management for Probation Officers
    - Orientation and Development Programs for New Officers

2. Probation/Pretrial Services Administration and Supervision Practices
    - Enhancement of Fine and Restitution Collection
    - Feasibility Study of Field Offices
    - A Pretrial Diversion Program for Juvenile Offenders on Military Bases
3. District Policies and Procedures
    - District Colloquium on Sentencing Guidelines Departures
    - Day Care for Federal Employees
    - Search and Seizure Policy and Procedures
4. Innovative Practices in the Supervision of Offenders
    - An Automated Risk Assessment Program
    - Criminal Debt Enforcement Monitoring
    - Specialized Gang Programs
5. Substance Abuse, Mental Health Issues
    - Linking Treatment Services: Mental Health Issues
    - Evaluation of a Drug After-Care Program
    - Enhancing the Monitoring Process for Contracting Services

(Siegel & Vernon, 1994)

The creation of an in-district project was not taken lightly by the participants. In their serious pursuit to change the climate of their district, many participants created needs assessment surveys, interviewed other district employees, and reviewed policies. This serious approach has yielded profound results and change within districts. "The Leadership Development Program participants have systematically studied the status quo, measured it, analyzed it, and made recommendations to improve it based on empirical data and not on a whim or fad" (Siegel & Vernon, 1994, p. 6). Furthermore, program participants have also learned that not all change is created equal. They have discovered that some innovations might bring more harm than good to a district, and when the officers did find useful ideas and changes, however, they practiced negotiating and persuasion skills with their chiefs and their colleagues.

As a result of this substantial undertaking, the system itself has gained much. Knowledge was created and gained and resistance toward change was lessened.

"The development of research and advocacy skills among aspiring leaders is itself a positive outcome. Another positive result for the system is its own capacity for change and ability to become a 'learning organization'" (Senge, 1990).

Perhaps the major benefit is that the probation and pretrial services system has learned how to learn. Some of this learning will promote increased efficiencies, and some will actually result in dollar savings. Now more than ever, there is a critical need for organizations to continually learn from their environments. When systems experience an enhanced capacity to learn from people at all levels, they also increase their capacity to adapt to change in their environment. A learning probation/pretrial services organization, therefore, will be more adequately equipped to adapt to the changes imposed by Congress, the Judicial Conference, the Administrative Office, or from wherever it comes (Siegel & Vernon, 1994). This is critical, as the ability to respond to change was one of the points on which the Judicial Conference identified a need for a leadership development program.

Temporary Duty Assignment

Bennis and Nanus, in their 1985 book, *Leaders: Strategies for Taking Charge,* evaluated ninety public and private sector leaders and found the following:

- Nearly all leaders are highly proficient in learning from experience;
- Most were able to identify a small number of mentors and key experiences that powerfully shaped their philosophies, personalities, aspirations, and operating styles. All of them regard themselves as "stretching," "growing," and "breaking new ground"; and
- Leaders have discovered not just how to learn, but how to learn in an organizational context.

Based on this premise of learning for leaders, the Leadership Development Program took on a temporary duty assignment (TDY) component, in which participants work briefly in another field, which may include other judicial districts, legislative and executive branch governmental agencies, or private corporations. During their assignments, participants observe new management techniques and leadership strategies, contribute short work projects, and interview relevant leaders and staff. The variety of the experiences gained by the participants is only surpassed by the plethora of sites at which the temporary duty assignments were conducted. Examples of past temporary duty assignments include various probation and pretrial services offices throughout the United States; local fire and rescue departments; the International Criminal Tribunal for the Former Yugoslavia in The Hague,

Netherlands; the United States Sentencing Commission; the Executive Office of the President, Office of National Drug Control Policy at the White House; Sacramento Intelligence Unit; Boston Red Sox baseball franchise; American Airlines; and several churches and research hospitals (Siegel, 2005).

In achieving the goal of the assignment, to give officers an opportunity to observe and experience leadership in an organizational context other than their own, it is clear that the temporary duty assignment has found successes. These achievements are not to the individual alone, but have also benefited the system as a whole. The officers in the program gained the opportunity to see new patterns of management and leadership, developed new perspectives on the entire judicial system, and formed new insights into the linkages among the different parts of the criminal justice system (Siegel & Vernon, 1994).

Implementation and Quantitative Results

Since the inception of its inaugural class in 1992, the LDP has seen great successes over its seven completed classes (Siegel, 2005). These successes can be seen in the quantitative results that are hereafter summarized and may be attributed to the aforementioned components of the program.

In understanding the trends of the successes incurred from the Leadership Development Program, a portrait of the participants of the program should be painted. Of 493 participants, 303 have been male and 190 female (Siegel, 2005). The breakdown of male to female participants of the program is important because it shows the increasing participation of women in a field in which leadership positions were heretofore dominated by white males.

Further, the distribution of participants' positions within the Federal Probation and Pretrial Services is varying, as shown in Figure 1.

This breakdown of positions illustrates an important point. Seeing that only 1 percent of participants are currently in the chief position, the other 99 percent, therefore, have room for promotion, and the skills learned in the Leadership

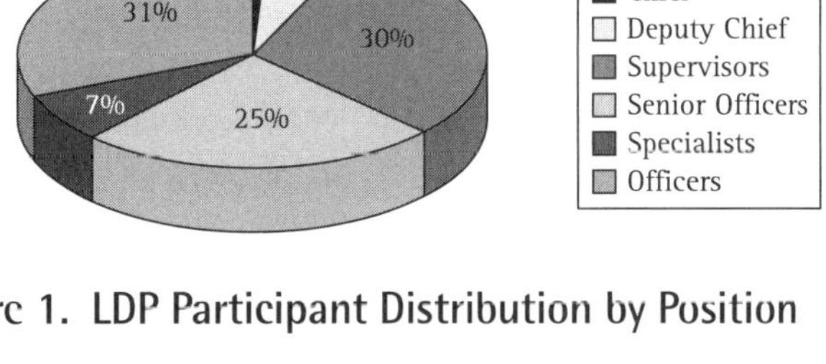

Figure 1. LDP Participant Distribution by Position

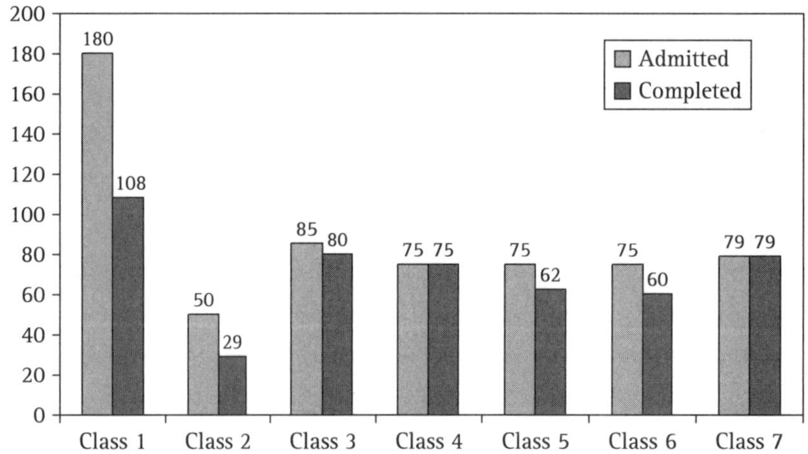

Figure 2. Admitted Versus Completed Participants by Class

Development Program can contribute toward that end as well. Further, being that they are not in the chief position, it is probable that there is room for leadership improvement and development in the participant. Thus, they are the perfect audience for the program's material. Last, the Leadership Development Program is based on the proposition that people can lead from anywhere!

During the course of the first seven classes of the LDP, 619 participants have been admitted to the program. From that admitted participant pool, 493 participants have graduated the program. That is a completion rate of 79 percent; 87 percent when excluding the first class, as shown in Figure 2 (Siegel, 2005).

The steep difference between admitted participants and completed participants in the first class may be attributed to several factors and illustrates a trend. In the first class, there was a significant dropout rate. This may be attributed to the fact that most inaugural participants did not understand the depth of the responsibilities to which they were obliged. Further, it is likely that many of the early participants were unaware or underestimated the time commitment required by the program. The decline in admitted students in the second class reflects the first class's comments to the court community regarding the challenging nature of the program. The second and third class spread news of the program in saying that the program was difficult but satisfying, and it is probable that this is why the subsequent classes have had both more participants and higher completion rates.

In addition to the notable success of participants in graduating from the LDP, which indicates that the process promotes success inside the program, one only has to look at external factors to see that the Leadership Development Program has cultivated leaders and that other people are taking notice. Looking at the promotion rates of past participants is one way of doing this.

The promotion rate experienced by Leadership Development Program graduates is around 30 percent. This illustrates the success of the program in fostering new leaders (Siegel, 2005). Further, women account for 24 percent of all of the promotions of past Leadership Development Program participants (Siegel, 2005). This shows that a proportional number of those being promoted from the program are women. Last, as of the start of 2008, forty-eight of the one-hundred and twenty chief probation and pretrial services officers are Leadership Development Program graduates. Signifying the substantial impact the program has had on leadership in probation and pretrial services, these 42 percent of chiefs testifies to the quality of leaders produced in the program (Siegel, 2005).

Qualitative Results

Numbers alone cannot tell the story of the Leadership Development Program's successes. For that purpose, only the words of past participants can do. From hearing personal perspectives, one can gain an understanding of the lasting implications the program has had on its participants, in their professional and private lives, and the court institution.

Regarding her experience, LDP graduate Elaine Terenzi (2007), who now serves as chief of U.S. probation in Tampa, Florida, said, "The Leadership Development Program improved my ability to view situations and issues from a variety of vantage points, rather than just from my own or my organization's interest. Also, the LDP provided an understanding of the strength that comes from a disciplined focus on the right goals. I believe the combination of these two skills helps me to think about issues and ideas with greater clarity."

A key lesson in the Leadership Development Program is the idea that someone can lead from wherever he or she is. This notion is expressed by LDP graduate Tim Goodman (2007), a senior probation officer in Greensboro, North Carolina: "I have had to remind myself that not all leaders are managers. By doing so, I have often challenged managers' preconceived ideas and have tried to provide new and innovative alternatives. While these ideas have not always been adopted by managers, my ability to provide leadership from a non-management position has been significantly enhanced due to the knowledge I obtained during participation in LDP."

Another attribute of the Leadership Development Program is its ability to allow participants to network with colleagues throughout the nation, which provides for a broader perspective of the court system. LDP graduate Danny Kuhn, deputy chief probation officer in Charleston, West Virginia, discusses this notion and how it helped him receive a promotion: "I was the only graduate at the time, and, as a senior officer, was promoted over the middle managers. While all were very experienced and good at what they did, the Court was looking for a broader perspective, and nationwide networking potential. The LDP provided both" (Kuhn, 2007).

Finally, Junie Richard, supervising probation officer in Birmingham, Alabama, details how she applies tools learned in the program to her work and how those utilities aid her every day: "I use 'emotional intelligence' when dealing with the probation officers who are faced with stringent deadlines and stressful jobs, whereas before LDP, characteristics such as patience and empathy were not tools in my 'leadership kit.' I strive to exercise concepts such as 'leadership by example' and 'servant leadership' on a daily basis" (Richard, 2007).

Conclusion

The successes of the Leadership Development Program can be seen both quantitatively and qualitatively in the statistics and responses of past participants. These triumphs serve not just the participants themselves or the program, but the judiciary as a whole.

The Leadership Development Program has built the capacity of individual probation and pretrial services officers and managers to assume leadership positions within the judiciary and has prepared them to improvise leadership in an institution (the judiciary) that is not necessarily hospitable to bold, forceful leadership (Siegel, forthcoming).

Another important impact of the LDP on the judiciary is in cost savings and an embracement of change. Cost savings are being realized in the judiciary because of the participants' increased ability to detect and change inefficiencies. In addition, the courts' more accepting attitude toward change prevents another slew of problems. With newly developed skills in leadership, participants are more able to embrace changes and implement them successfully. For instance, LDP graduates have been notably active in national committees and work groups organized in the past two years for the purpose of implementing cost containment strategies in the Federal Judiciary (Cost Containment . . ., 2007).

Perhaps the Leadership Development Program's greatest success is that the program has planted the idea that professionals in the courts can be "reflective practitioners," people who customarily accomplish their work responsibilities, but take the time to reflect on the work and the ways in which they can improve (Schon, 1987). Constant improvement through reflection, embracing change, and courage in adversity—these are the hallmarks of the LDP participant. Theodore Roosevelt summarized the traits of our participants best:

> It is not the critic who counts; not the man who points out how the strong man stumbles, or where the doer of deeds could have done them better. The credit belongs to the man who is actually in the arena, whose face is marred by dust and sweat and blood; who strives valiantly, who errs, and comes short again and again; because there is not the effort without error and shortcoming, but who does actually strive to do the deeds; who knows the great enthusiasms, the great devotions; who spends himself in a worthy cause, who at the best knows in the end triumphs of high achievement and who at the worst, if he fails, at least fails while daring greatly, so that his place shall never be with those cold and timid souls who know neither victory nor defeat.
>
> (Pfeffer, 1992, p. 9)

References

Bennis, W. (2003). *On becoming a leader*. New York: Basic Books.

Bennis, W.G., & Nanus, B. (1985). *Leaders: Strategies for taking charge*. New York: Harper and Row.

Bishop, T. (2007, October 17). Interview/survey by author. Washington, DC.

Bossidy, L., & Charan, R. (2002). *Execution: The discipline of getting things done*. New York: Crown Business.

Cost Containment and the Federal Judiciary. (2007). *The Third Branch, 39*.

Giuliani, R. (2002). *Leadership*. New York: Talk Miramax Books.

Goodman, T. (2007, October 17). Interview/survey by author. Washington, DC.

Hayward, S.F. (1998). *Churchill on leadership: Executive success in the face of adversity*. New York: Random House.

Kuhn, D. (2007, October 17). Interview/survey by author. Washington, DC.

Pfeffer, J. (1992, Winter). Understanding power in organization. *California Management Review*, pp. 29–50.

Richard, J. (2007, October 17). Interview/survey by author. Washington, DC.

Schon, D. (1987). *Educating the reflective practitioner*. San Francisco, CA: Jossey-Bass.

Senge, P. (1990). The leader's new work: Building learning organizations. *Sloan Management Review, 32*(1) pp. 29–50.

Siegel, M.E. (2005, June 1). Leadership Development Program. Presented at the Federal Judicial Center, Washington, DC.

Siegel, M.E. (forthcoming). Riding tall in a small saddle: The chief judgeship of Richard H. Chambers. *Western Legal History*.

Siegel, M.E., & Vernon, M.C. (1994). The Leadership Development Program for Federal Probation and Pretrial Services Officers. *Federal Probation, LVIII*, 3–9.

Terenzi, E. (2007, October 17). Interview/survey by author. Washington, DC.

Michael Eric Siegel, Ph.D., *serves as a senior education specialist at the Federal Judicial Center in Washington, D.C.. He teaches as an adjunct professor of government and management at The American University, The University of Maryland University College, and Johns Hopkins University. Having received numerous awards for teaching excellence and having published several articles and a book on leadership, management, and faculty development, Dr. Siegel is currently writing a book on the Presidency since Watergate.*

Anthony Teke Quickel *is an undergraduate student at the American University in Washington, D.C.. A Middle East enthusiast, Mr. Quickel has studied at the American University in Cairo and is majoring in international relations with a focus in economic development and a minor in Arabic studies. Having completed research on peace dialogue between the Abrahamic faiths, Mr. Quickel was recently published in the* Proceedings of the National Conference on Undergraduate Research.

Expatriation and Repatriation
Different Directions, Similar HR Concerns

Lincoln H. Marshall

Summary

This article reviews the human resource concerns and challenges encountered by expatriates during their initial introduction to a new environment. It also identifies several challenges residents encounter when repatriating.

A proactive model is presented to make the transitions from one country to another smooth, cost-effective, and efficient. The model highlights benefits for both the new employees and the host organizations. It also promotes the need to be flexible and respectful of culture as a catalyst for an uneventful transition from one country to another.

During the past ten to fifteen years, there has been much talk about globalization. The discussions occur in almost all segments of the economy. The banking, hospitality, nursing, and IT industries have been most involved in this globalization. These industries have been aggressively sending employees around the globe. Many managers see the need to move people from place to place because of the scarcity of supply and the high demand for individuals with specific expertise. Most managers agree to this practice of sending employees around the globe without giving it a second thought. There is a feeling that employees can be dispatched from one work site to another like a UPS overnight parcel. This insensitive practice is now resulting in many problems for both employees and employers. Managers are faced with the reality that globalization is not as easy as Scotty "beaming them down." Globalization, in its truest form, is a myriad of human resource and management challenges.

Briefly stated, globalization entails the freedom of movement of goods, services, and ideas across borders without any restrictions. There are several sides to globalization. In this article we will focus on the human resource side. Yes, it is possible to fly from New York to Paris, Madrid, or Frankfurt in six to eight hours and upon arrival be ready to work. Physically it is possible. The challenge many workers face is to adjust to the American, French, Spanish, or German culture and workplace when they arrive. After making the trip to a foreign country to work or visit, we realize it is not as easy as Scotty beaming us down. Managers must support the process.

When a multinational sends one of its employees to another country, there is a need to prepare the employee for the cultural difference and similarities he or she may encounter. Human resource managers must discard their ethnocentricity and make an attempt to accommodate the new culture. This will require a paradigm change.

This article identifies and highlights, in an anecdotal format, the human resource challenges encountered by foreigners working in a different land and also residents returning to their native lands after being away for as long as ten years. This article will look at some of the common human resource and management practices to accommodate expatriates and returnees. The challenges will be identified, and a model and recommendation will be made to make the transition from one country to another go more smoothly.

Terminology

Expatriates are "individuals who work in a country in which they are not citizens" (DeCenzo & Robbins, 1996, p. 177). It is important for human resource professionals to have a clear understanding of the implication of some of the challenges of living and working in another country. There are several types of expatriates. Figure 1 identifies three types, each having different needs.

Parent-country nationals (PCNs) are employees who were born and live in a parent country, that is, the country where the organization is headquartered.

Host-country nationals (HCNs) are employees who were born and raised in the host country, not the parent company, that is, they live in the country in which the organization has a branch.

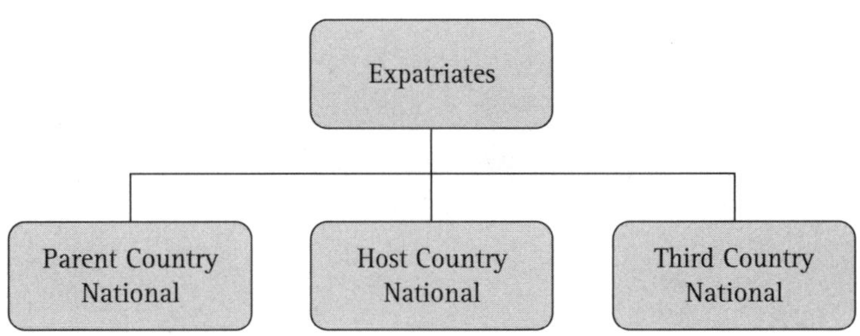

Figure 1. Types of Expatriates

Third-country nationals (TCNs) are employees born in a country other than the parent or host country.

Multinational organizations should design specific training programs for each type of expatriate. The parent country national has the advantage of understanding the culture of the organization's headquarters. Ostensibly, this person should not encounter any problems communicating with the main organization. On the other hand, if he or she is not properly oriented, this person may encounter challenges interacting with the residents of the host country. For example, a Japanese from Japan working for Toyota would be considered a PCN. If he or she is transferred to Kentucky to work for the Toyota company there, he may encounter problems with an American in Kentucky.

The training for parent country nationals should highlight how to deal with culture shock, ethnocentrism, and accommodations. The individuals chosen for an international assignment should be mature and have an appreciation of the new culture. Human resource professionals and recruiters should expend great energies to ascertain whether parent country nationals can adjust to the new environment of an international assignment, away from the corporate power base. This is also true for their managers.

A host country national who has citizenship in the country where an international company is located (Noe, Hollenbeck, Gerhart, & Wright, 2006) may be cognizant of the culture and the values of the parent country, but may have spent little time living in that country. These individuals should not be considered totally bi-cultural; they are comfortable with the culture of the host country, but not with the culture of the parent country.

More and more third country nationals are being recruited and placed on international assignments. These individuals may be ignorant of both the host and parent country's culture. They would likely have been selected because of technical expertise and should be given extra cross-cultural preparation.

Sample Expatriation Case

In considering how best to ensure successful repatriation, let's begin by reviewing a mini human resource case.

> A national company advertises internationally for a professional position. The selection process is completed overseas and an expatriate is offered the job without ever visiting the job site or the country. Fortunately, the only language spoken in the country is English and the native language of the expatriate is also English.

> The new employee is given an airplane ticket to fly to the foreign destination. He is met at the airport by a representative of his new place of employment and taken to a local hotel, which is paid for by the organization for two weeks. During his fortnight tenure, he was left on his own to find accommodations, local transportation, and acquire utilities. The new professional's family planned to join him one month after the start of his contract.

In the above case, the employee may be either a host country national or a third country national. In either case, genuine efforts should have been made to help with the employee's assimilation. The case is typical in many countries and highlights several of the problems encountered by expatriate employees.

What should the HR department have done? What can a human resource professional learn from the above expatriate case? What was not done correctly? What strategies could be used to provide a smooth transition from one country to another? What role(s) should the manager have played?

The Expatriate Cycle

It is essential for human resource practitioners to develop or be cognizant of the "Expatriate Cycle" (see Figure 2). In this model, seven steps are proposed to avoid the "warm body syndrome" for international placement, which contributes to a high turnover rate with many foreign assignments. Managers must also tend to the cycle.

The cycle begins with the selection of a suitable candidate. The easy part of the selection process is to ascertain whether the individual has the technical expertise

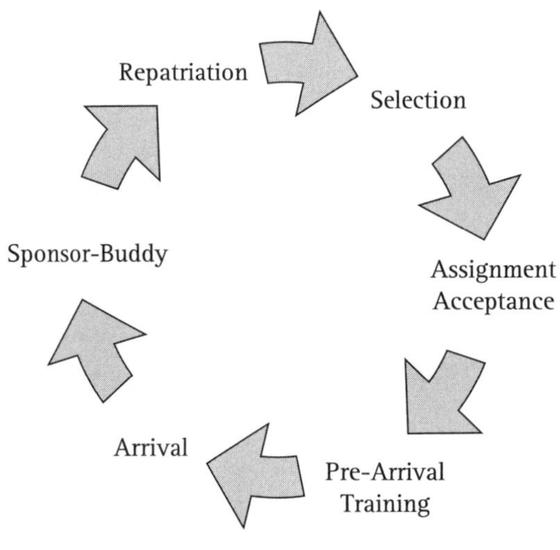

Figure 2. The Expatriate Cycle

necessary. This decision can be based on past job performance. However, one could debate whether that should be the most important criterion for an overseas selection. Care should be taken to determine whether the individual is flexible and willing to respect the new culture. Once that determination has been made, the candidate should be given some time to consider accepting the assignment. During this interim the company should perhaps sponsor a site visit for the candidate with his or her spouse.

Once the candidate has signed a contract, the human resource department should immediately begin a "pre-arrival training," consisting mainly of cross-cultural training. The new employee's manager must reinforce the training. New employees should obtain information about the culture, language, and values of the host country. See the list of concerns below that must be thoroughly addressed. Training or an orientation for an employee's family would also be invaluable.

Expatriate Human Resource Concerns

- Safety
- Benefits
- Career advancement
- Opportunity costs
- Housing
- Spousal adjustment
- Family
- Language
- Culture

Someone once said, "First impressions are lasting impressions." It is of paramount importance for the first arrival of a new employee to be smooth. A senior member of the human resource department should be responsible for the initial arrival. This task should not be delegated to a low-ranking subordinate. Attempts should be made to verify that all of the living arrangements have been made or to offer assistance if needed. The new employee should be assigned a "buddy" from his or her primary department and also a "sponsor" from the human resource department. If both of these individuals are responsible for the new employee, the employee would have more energy to focus on the new challenge of the job. The manager of the primary department should also be involved.

The expatriate cycle is not complete until the expatriate leaves the host country. Repatriation may be at the end of the contract or it may arise prematurely as a result of family or professional challenges. If repatriation is voluntary and planned, a strategy should be in place to create a smooth exit and to allow for a period of readjustment. If it were to occur involuntarily, the human resource department must work quickly to avoid a disruption of the work flow.

When a non-resident departs, he or she leaves a void of experience and expertise. The cycle can restart with another expatriate, or the position may be filled by a native who is currently abroad and wishes to return home.

The Repatriation Cycle

Repatriation can be just as great a problem as expatriation. When an individual returns to his or her birth country to work after having worked elsewhere, it requires a paradigm shift by both the host organization and the returnee. The human resource department should be sensitive to the mindset of the returnee. Sometimes a resident returning home may have even greater adjustment issues than when he or she left. All too often, the human resource department feels that, because the individual is returning home, Scotty could really just "beam him down" and the person should be able to "hit the ground running." This may not always be the case.

Human resource practitioners should be cognizant of the challenges of at least three different classifications of repatriates, as should managers (see Figure 3). The first category is "college graduate." The characteristics of these individuals are that they have been recruited immediately after completing between four and eight years of university or some professional studies. They most likely have been studying abroad on a student visa and may have visited their native country four to eight times during their studies overseas. These persons would be regarded as completing the exploration stage of their career development. They may be between the ages of twenty-eight and thirty-six. They may also be more flexible in readjusting to home.

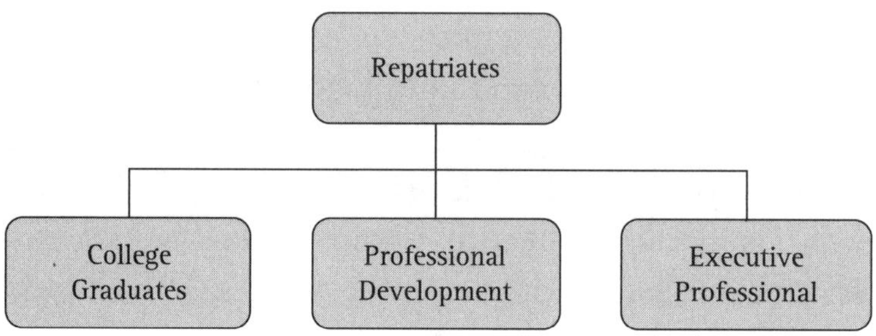

Figure 3. Types of Repatriates

The second category of repatriates is the "professional development" candidate. These individuals have been outside of their native land for more than eight years to obtain certification or accreditation in a specific profession. Invariably, these individuals are older than the former group, ranging in age from thirty-six to forty-six. These individuals are more likely to have a family. Their needs would be different and in a way more demanding for the HR department. When an individual has been away from his or her native land for more than ten years, that person literally and figuratively brings some additional baggage to the workplace. The manager will have to work with the person to ensure the baggage is addressed and productivity remains consistent.

The third category of repatriation is the "executive professional." These individuals typically have been away from their native land for twenty or more years, with an extensive amount of traveling and working in a number of different countries. They are commonly between the ages of forty-seven and sixty. Sometimes these individuals may have only returned home periodically for brief visits. They would be familiar with their native culture, but many things would have changed during their absence. These changes and challenges are a unique human resource problem. The human resource needs and benefit packages of these repatriates will be significantly different from those of the former two groups. Their human resource needs must be handled very gingerly.

Figure 4 illustrates the steps of the Repatriation Cycle that can ensure successful repatriation, regardless of the category. Human resource professionals and managers should recognize the advantages of hiring a resident to return home to work. The first benefit is that the resident understands the culture and the people. Another benefit is that the returnee will have an excellent command of the language. Additionally, the new employee will be able to serve as a positive role model

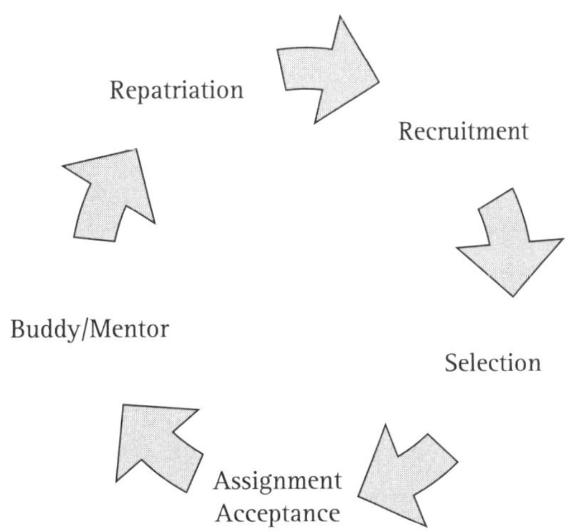

Figure 4. The Repatriation Cycle

for many members of the workforce. This is true in many cases because the resident workers look at their returning compatriot with either pride or envy. They usually accept the returnee's success abroad with admiration and have a desire to follow or emulate his or her professional achievements. Last, there may also be several cost savings with bringing in a returning resident.

The list below shows several of the human resource concerns of an individual repatriating. One of the greatest concerns of professionals returning home, especially from a developed country to a developing country, is whether the move will augment their professional growth. It is important for the organization to highlight the advantages of returning home after having qualified oneself. An attraction for returning home could be the opportunity for promotion to a top executive position.

HR Concerns of the Repatriate

- Professional growth
- Safety
- Benefits
- Personal adjustment
- Spousal adjustment
- Family
- Living conditions
- Benefits
- Retirement benefits
- Language

Issues Impacting the Success of Expatriation

Generational Expectations

People involved in the selection of potential expatriates must be aware of generational differences, which can affect the decision-making process.

Recruitment of potential expatriates is not as easy as it was fifteen or twenty years ago. Then, many professionals, Baby Boomers in particular, felt that foreign work experience was essential to move up the corporate ladder. They were willing to work three to seven years overseas (Armour, 2005). Their expectation was that, after completing a stint abroad, they would have acquired a better understanding of managing in a global environment. Many boomers would have undertaken and completed the assignments with little or no regard for their family and cultural adjustment to the new environment.

The values and expectations of members of Generation X are different. These individuals do not define themselves with their jobs. They seek a balance between their work and their personal lives. Many of them do not wish to leave their countries, provinces, or states just to work. They wish to be close to their homes, friends, and familiar environments. Although they are talented, they value their personal time. They are a difficult group to recruit for an overseas assignment. Their reluctance is also compounded by their inclination to change jobs frequently, specifically for an increase of salary or benefits (Armour, 2005).

Cultural Awareness

Today, cultural awareness may be the most important issue for the successful placement of expatriates. If employees who have been selected for an international assignment are ignorant about the culture of their receiving country, they will inevitably encounter a multitude of problems. At least three skills or abilities are necessary for any expatriate to have a successful tenure abroad: (1) a confident appreciation of his or her own culture, (2) adequate communication skills for the new country, and (3) an understanding of the host culture.

An American who works in Canada, the Caribbean, Australia, or the United Kingdom should be cognizant of the various cultural differences. All too often, however, human resource practitioners believe that if an individual speaks the same language there is little or no need for the person to receive any orientation to the new country. This is a myth. Language is only one aspect of culture.

HR practitioners and management should be cognizant of Hofstede's cultural dimensions (Hofstede & Hofstede, 2005). A checklist should be developed that compares the cultural dimensions of the host country with those of the expatriate's country. Hofstede's model identifies four areas: Power Distance, Individualism/Collectivism, Uncertainty Avoidance, and Long-Term/Short-Term Orientation.

Power distance is the way in which individuals relate to hierarchal power. *Individualism/collectivism* is the manner in which members of a host community prefer to work. Some prefer to work individually, while some prefer working in groups. Hofstede's study highlights the need to be aware of whether a culture prefers a structured or unstructured situation. He refers to this dimension as "*uncertainty avoidance*." Cultures that have a great tolerance of an unpredictable future are considered high on this scale. The fourth dimension, *long-term/short-term orientation*, measures how a culture balances immediate benefits with future rewards.

Strategies for Successful Repatriation

The failure rate of placing expatriates into another country varies from 25 to 45 percent during the first six months, according to Mello (2006). The cost for failure can be greatly reduced by using several proactive strategies, listed below.

Strategies for Success

- Familiarization visit
- Permit application
- Cross-cultural training
- Language training
- Sponsor or buddy
- Monitoring and evaluation
- Resource manual

Human resources should begin by providing a visit to the overseas worksite. The candidate should have an opportunity to meet as many of his or her potential colleagues and managers as possible. The HR department should also provide an opportunity for candidates to visit their future communities, including schools, hospitals, churches, mosques, or synagogues. Visiting realtors would also be essential.

The next step should be for HR to obtain a work permit. Every attempt should be made to overcome bureaucratic hurdles. It's important to obtain documents in advance and also to make duplicate copies. A relationship within the immigration department will be an asset.

The next requirement is designing and conducting cross-cultural training that includes information about the country, its geography, people, and culture. Another component should be a proper language proficiency program supervised and supported for at least six months. Managers must reinforce the learning during this time.

Another strategy is to introduce the expatriate into the professional community and the local community at large. This process should be sponsored by the person's manager and can be enhanced by assigning a sponsor or buddy to the individual. The HR department should be responsible for monitoring and evaluating the entire program in concert with the manager for the first six months, as many expatriate assignments fail within the first three months (Mello, 2006).

Finally, HR managers should provide a resource manual (either in a binder or bound) specifically for expatriates, including the following items:

- Cultural do's and don'ts
- Business attire
- Cultural practices
- Language
- Colloquialisms
- Non-verbal gestures
- Currency exchange
- Driving regulations
- Time, from a cultural perspective
- Country websites with relevant information

Conclusion

Globalization is here to stay. Just as the world continues to turn, people continue to move. Today an employee might leave his or her native land and works overseas for five, ten, or even twenty years. These people must learn to adjust to a new culture and its people. At the other end of the spectrum, expatriates return home after being away for fifteen or twenty years. These individuals will also have to adjust.

Human resource managers and line managers, as appropriate, should be proactive and prepare for all types of new employees in several ways. High on the list are safety on the job and within the community. Ideally, a "buddy" should be assigned to work closely with new employees during the first six months. Guidance in obtaining living accommodations is essential. Once many of his or her personal needs have been addressed, it is possible for the expatriate to apply his or her technical expertise to the job at hand.

References

Armour, S. (2005, November 6). Generation Y: They've arrived at work with a new attitude. *USA Today*. Available: www.usatoday.com/money/workplace/2005-11-06-gen-y_x.htm

DeCenzo, D.A., & Robbins, S.P. (1996) *Human resource management*. Hoboken, NJ: John Wiley & Sons.

Hofstede, G., & Hofstede, G.J. (2005). *Cultures and organizations: Software of the mind.* New York: McGraw-Hill.

Mello, J.A. (2006). *Strategic human resource management* (2nd ed.). Westford, MA: Thomson South-Western.

Noe, R.A., Hollenbeck, J.R., Gerhart, B., & Wright, P.M. (2006). *Human resource management: Gaining a competitive advantage* (5th ed.). New York: McGraw-Hill.

Lincoln H. Marshall, Ph.D., *has been involved in various aspects of the human development industry as an educator, practitioner, and consultant for the past twenty-five years. He is currently the executive director of the Culinary and Hospitality Management Institute at the College of the Bahamas.*

He has conducted training programs in Aruba, Barbados, The Bahamas, The British Virgin Islands, France, Jamaica, Madagascar, Nicaragua, St. Lucia, and Turks & Caicos Island. He has lectured at the university level in Nassau and Freeport, Bahamas; Strasbourg, France; Montego Bay and Kingston, Jamaica; and Panama City, Panama.

Outside of academe, he served as the director of training and development at both Carnival's Crystal Palace Resort and Casino in Nassau, Bahamas, and the Lucayan Beach Resort and Casino in Freeport, Grand Bahama. He also worked as a training consultant in France with Holiday Inn Management. He worked at the Bahamas Hotel Training College serving as the chief training officer and acting executive director.

Contributors

Dr. George Alexakis
Assistant Professor
Florida Gulf Coast University
Resort & Hospitality Management
10501 FGCU Boulevard
Fort Myers, FL 33965
(954) 732-0776
email: alexakis@nova.edu

F. Barry Barnes, Ph.D.
Professor of Management
Huizenga School
Nova Southeastern University
3301 College Avenue
Davie, FL 33314
(954) 262-5113
fax: (954) 262-3964
email: barry@huizenga.nova.edu

Elaine Biech
President
ebb associates inc
Box 8249
Norfolk VA 23503
(757) 588-3939
fax: (757) 480-1311
email: ebboffice@aol.com

Shirley Copeland, Ed.D.
Learning Resource Group, LLC
2361 Lonicera Way
Charlottesville, VA 22911-9044
(434) 975-1834
fax: (434) 975-1834
email: sfcopeland@aol.com

Marilyn J. Corrigan
(952) 942-7737
email: marilyn.corrigan@comcast.net

John E. DiBenedetto, D.B.A.
email: john.dibenedetto@gpi.com or johndibenedetto@aol.com

Maggie W. Dunn, D.B.A.
1317 SW 23rd Street
Fort Lauderdale, FL 33315-2338
(954) 764-4390
email: maggie@hrleadershipsolutions.com

Noam Ebner
Tachlit Mediation and Negotiation Training
Winkler-Ebner Law Offices
36 Keren Hayesod Street
Jerusalem, Israel
+972-523-786996
fax +972-2-5610569
email: noam@tachlit.net

Yael Efron
Tachlit Mediation and Negotiation Training
Ficus 3/3 Street
Modi'in, Israel
+972-523-557898
email: noam@tachlit.net

Ronald C. Fetzer, Ph.D.
7985 Preble County Line Road
Germantown, OH 45327
(937) 787-9190
fax: (937) 787-9180
email: ron-fetzer@worldnet.att.net

Sean T. Foley
Department of Management (B6300)
McCombs School of Business
The University of Texas at Austin
Austin, TX 78712
email: Sean.Foley@mba08.mccombs.utexas.edu

Bevan Gray-Rogel
Graylan Consulting, LLC
4107 Saltwater Boulevard
Tampa FL 33615
(813) 881-0020
fax: (813) 881-0024

Arthur L. Jue, DM, CCD
P.O. Box 610986
San Jose, CA 95161-0986
(408) 227-9098
email: ajue@sbcglobal.net

Paul Kearns
+44 117 9146984
email: info@paulkearns.co.uk

Kristie J. Loescher
Department of Management (B6300)
McCombs School of Business
The University of Texas at Austin
Austin, TX 78712
email: kristie.loescher@mccombs.utexas.edu

Lincoln H. Marshall
(242) 326-5388
email: lincoln.marshall@gmail.com
or lincolnmarshall@cob.edu.bs

Alejandro Palacios
466 Silver Palm Way
Weston, FL 33327
(954) 326-6513
email: alejovirtual@msn.com

Melissa A. Parris, Ph.D.
Lecturer in Management
Bowater School of Management and Marketing
Faculty of Business and Law
Deakin University
221 Burwood Highway
Burwood VIC 3125
Australia
+ 61 3 9244 6726
fax: + 61 3 9251 7083
email: melissa.parris@deakin.edu.au

Catherine (Kitty) Preziosi
Corporate Catalyst
Preziosi Partners, Inc.
9441 Hollyhock Court
Davie, FL 33328
(954) 915-0102
fax: (954) 915-9912
email: kittyprez@aol.com

Anthony Teke Quickel
Intern
Federal Judicial Center
One Columbus Circle, NE
Washington, DC 20002
(202) 502-4106 or (202) 502-4088
email: aquickel@fjc.gov

Dr. Linda M. Raudenbush
HRD/OD Specialist and Leadership Coach
U.S. Department of Agriculture, NASS
Washington, DC 20250
(202) 720-6016
email: linda_raudenbush@nass.usda.gov

Yael Schy
Principal
Dramatic Strides® Consulting
(510) 339-2404
email: yael@dramaticstrides.com
URL: www.dramaticstrides.com

Michael Eric Siegel, Ph.D.
Senior Education Specialist
Federal Judicial Center
One Columbus Circle, NE
Washington, DC 20002
(202) 502-4107 or 202-502-4088
email: mesiegel@fjc.gov

Dr. Michaeline Skiba
Marketing and Management Department
School of Business Administration
Monmouth University
400 Cedar Avenue
West Long Branch, NJ 07764-1898
(732) 263-5862
fax: (732) 263-5128
email: mskiba@monmouth.edu

Steve Sugar
The Game Group
10320 Kettledrum Court
Ellicott City, MD 21042
(410) 418-4930
email: stevesugar@verizon.net
URL: www.thegamegroup.com

Sandra Torres
200 Sycamore Avenue
Folsom, PA 19033
(215) 590-2339
email: storres@comcast.net

Margaret H. Vickers
Director of Research
School of Management, College of Business
University of Western Sydney
Locked Bag 1797
Penrith South DC NSW 1797
Australia
+ 61 2 9685 9227
fax: + 61 2 9685 9593
email: m.vickers@uws.edu.au

Peter Vultaggio
CEO and Co-Founder
The LUMI Company, LLC
(623) 572-0136
email: peterv@thelumicompany.com

About the Editor

Robert C. Preziosi, D.B.A., is professor of management with the H. Wayne Huizenga School of Business and Entrepreneurship at Nova Southeastern University. He has been teaching, training, and educating managers for nearly thirty years. He is the chair of the HRM master's degree program and teaches a capstone course to graduate students. He was recently honored with the inclusion of his autobiography in the book *North American Adult Educators* as one of fifty quintessential adult educators for the 21st century.

Pfeiffer Publications Guide

This guide is designed to familiarize you with the various types of Pfeiffer publications. The formats section describes the various types of products that we publish; the methodologies section describes the many different ways that content might be provided within a product. We also provide a list of the topic areas in which we publish.

FORMATS

In addition to its extensive book-publishing program, Pfeiffer offers content in an array of formats, from fieldbooks for the practitioner to complete, ready-to-use training packages that support group learning.

FIELDBOOK Designed to provide information and guidance to practitioners in the midst of action. Most fieldbooks are companions to another, sometimes earlier, work, from which its ideas are derived; the fieldbook makes practical what was theoretical in the original text. Fieldbooks can certainly be read from cover to cover. More likely, though, you'll find yourself bouncing around following a particular theme, or dipping in as the mood, and the situation, dictate.

HANDBOOK A contributed volume of work on a single topic, comprising an eclectic mix of ideas, case studies, and best practices sourced by practitioners and experts in the field.

An editor or team of editors usually is appointed to seek out contributors and to evaluate content for relevance to the topic. Think of a handbook not as a ready-to-eat meal, but as a cookbook of ingredients that enables you to create the most fitting experience for the occasion.

RESOURCE Materials designed to support group learning. They come in many forms: a complete, ready-to-use exercise (such as a game); a comprehensive resource on one topic (such as conflict management) containing a variety of methods and approaches; or a collection of like-minded activities (such as icebreakers) on multiple subjects and situations.

TRAINING PACKAGE An entire, ready-to-use learning program that focuses on a particular topic or skill. All packages comprise a guide for the facilitator/trainer and a workbook for the participants. Some packages are supported with additional media—such as video—or learning aids, instruments, or other devices to help participants understand concepts or practice and develop skills.

- *Facilitator/trainer's guide* Contains an introduction to the program, advice on how to organize and facilitate the learning event, and step-by-step instructor notes. The guide also contains copies of presentation materials—handouts, presentations, and overhead designs, for example—used in the program.
- *Participant's workbook* Contains exercises and reading materials that support the learning goal and serves as a valuable reference and support guide for participants in the weeks and months that follow the learning event. Typically, each participant will require his or her own workbook.

ELECTRONIC CD-ROMs and web-based products transform static Pfeiffer content into dynamic, interactive experiences. Designed to take advantage of the searchability, automation, and ease-of-use that technology provides, our e-products bring convenience and immediate accessibility to your workspace.

METHODOLOGIES

CASE STUDY A presentation, in narrative form, of an actual event that has occurred inside an organization. Case studies are not prescriptive, nor are they used to prove a point; they are designed to develop critical analysis and decision-making skills. A case study has a specific time frame, specifies a sequence of events, is narrative in structure, and contains a plot structure—an issue (what should be/have been done?). Use case studies when the goal is to enable participants to apply previously learned theories to the circumstances in the case, decide what is pertinent, identify the real issues, decide what should have been done, and develop a plan of action.

ENERGIZER A short activity that develops readiness for the next session or learning event. Energizers are most commonly used after a break or lunch to stimulate or refocus the group. Many involve some form of physical activity, so they are a useful way to counter post-lunch lethargy. Other uses include transitioning from one topic to another, where "mental" distancing is important.

EXPERIENTIAL LEARNING ACTIVITY (ELA) A facilitator-led intervention that moves participants through the learning cycle from experience to application (also known as a Structured Experience). ELAs are carefully thought-out designs in which there is a definite learning purpose and intended outcome. Each step—everything that participants do during the activity—facilitates the accomplishment of the stated goal. Each ELA includes complete instructions for facilitating the intervention and a clear statement of goals, suggested group size and timing, materials required, an explanation of the process, and, where appropriate, possible variations to the activity. (For more detail on Experiential Learning Activities, see the Introduction to the *Reference Guide to Handbooks and Annuals*, 1999 edition, Pfeiffer, San Francisco.)

GAME A group activity that has the purpose of fostering team spirit and togetherness in addition to the achievement of a pre-stated goal. Usually contrived—undertaking a desert expedition, for example—this type of learning method offers an engaging means for participants to demonstrate and practice business and interpersonal skills. Games are effective for team building and personal development mainly because the goal is subordinate to the process—the means through which participants reach decisions, collaborate, communicate, and generate trust and understanding. Games often engage teams in "friendly" competition.

ICEBREAKER A (usually) short activity designed to help participants overcome initial anxiety in a training session and/or to acquaint the participants with one another. An icebreaker can be a fun activity or can be tied to specific topics or training goals. While a useful tool in itself, the icebreaker comes into its own in situations where tension or resistance exists within a group.

INSTRUMENT A device used to assess, appraise, evaluate, describe, classify, and summarize various aspects of human behavior. The term used to describe an instrument depends primarily on its format and purpose. These terms include survey, questionnaire, inventory, diagnostic survey, and poll. Some uses of instruments include providing instrumental feedback to group members, studying here-and-now processes or functioning within a group, manipulating group composition, and evaluating outcomes of training and other interventions.

Instruments are popular in the training and HR field because, in general, more growth can occur if an individual is provided with a method for focusing specifically on his or her own behavior. Instruments also are used to obtain information that will serve as a basis for change and to assist in workforce planning efforts.

Paper-and-pencil tests still dominate the instrument landscape with a typical package comprising a facilitator's guide, which offers advice on administering the instrument and interpreting the collected data, and an initial set of instruments. Additional instruments are available separately. Pfeiffer, though, is investing heavily in e-instruments. Electronic instrumentation provides effortless distribution and, for larger groups particularly, offers advantages over paper-and-pencil tests in the time it takes to analyze data and provide feedback.

LECTURETTE A short talk that provides an explanation of a principle, model, or process that is pertinent to the participants' current learning needs. A lecturette is intended to establish a common language bond between the trainer and the participants by providing a mutual frame of reference. Use a lecturette as an introduction to a group activity or event, as an interjection during an event, or as a handout.

MODEL A graphic depiction of a system or process and the relationship among its elements. Models provide a frame of reference and something more tangible, and more easily remembered, than a verbal explanation. They also give participants something to "go on," enabling them to track their own progress as they experience the dynamics, processes, and relationships being depicted in the model.

ROLE PLAY A technique in which people assume a role in a situation/scenario: a customer service rep in an angry-customer exchange, for example. The way in which the role is approached is then discussed and feedback is offered. The role play is often repeated using a different approach and/or incorporating changes made based on feedback received. In other words, role playing is a spontaneous interaction involving realistic behavior under artificial (and safe) conditions.

SIMULATION A methodology for understanding the interrelationships among components of a system or process. Simulations differ from games in that they test or use a model that depicts or mirrors some aspect of reality in form, if not necessarily in content. Learning occurs by studying the effects of change on one or more factors of the model. Simulations are commonly used to test hypotheses about what happens in a system—often referred to as "what if?" analysis—or to examine best-case/worst-case scenarios.

THEORY A presentation of an idea from a conjectural perspective. Theories are useful because they encourage us to examine behavior and phenomena through a different lens.

TOPICS

The twin goals of providing effective and practical solutions for workforce training and organization development and meeting the educational needs of training and human resource professionals shape Pfeiffer's publishing program. Core topics include the following:

- Leadership & Management
- Communication & Presentation
- Coaching & Mentoring
- Training & Development
- e-Learning
- Teams & Collaboration
- OD & Strategic Planning
- Human Resources
- Consulting